ANIMAL WRITING

Crosscurrents

Exploring the development of European thought through engagements with the arts, humanities, social sciences and sciences

Series Editor
Christopher Watkin, Monash University

Editorial Advisory Board
Andrew Benjamin
Martin Crowley
Simon Critchley
Frederiek Depoortere
Oliver Feltham
Patrick ffrench
Christopher Fynsk
Kevin Hart
Emma Wilson

Titles available in the series

Difficult Atheism: Post-Theological Thinking in Alain Badiou, Jean-Luc Nancy and Quentin Meillassoux
Christopher Watkin

Politics of the Gift: Exchanges in Poststructuralism
Gerald Moore

Unfinished Worlds: Hermeneutics, Aesthetics and Gadamer
Nicholas Davey

The Figure of This World: Agamben and the Question of Political Ontology
Mathew Abbott

The Becoming of the Body: Contemporary Women's Writing in French
Amaleena Damlé

Philosophy, Animality and the Life Sciences
Wahida Khandker

The Event Universe: The Revisionary Metaphysics of Alfred North Whitehead
Leemon B. McHenry

Sublime Art: Towards an Aesthetics of the Future
Stephen Zepke

Mallarmé and the Politics of Literature: Sartre, Kristeva, Badiou, Rancière
Robert Boncardo

Animal Writing: Storytelling, Selfhood and the Limits of Empathy
Danielle Sands

Forthcoming Titles

Visual Art and Projects of the Self
Katrina Mitcheson

Music, Philosophy and Gender in Nancy, Lacoue-Labarthe, Badiou
Sarah Hickmott

The Desert in Modern Literature and Philosophy: Wasteland Aesthetics
Aidan Tynan

Visit the Crosscurrents website at www.edinburghuniversitypress.com/series/CROSS

ANIMAL WRITING

*Storytelling, Selfhood and
the Limits of Empathy*

Danielle Sands

EDINBURGH
University Press

Edinburgh University Press is one of the leading university presses in the UK. We publish academic books and journals in our selected subject areas across the humanities and social sciences, combining cutting-edge scholarship with high editorial and production values to produce academic works of lasting importance. For more information visit our website: edinburghuniversitypress.com

Edinburgh University Press Ltd
The Tun – Holyrood Road
12(2f) Jackson's Entry
Edinburgh EH8 8PJ

First published in hardback by Edinburgh University Press 2019

Typeset in 10.5/13 Sabon by
Servis Filmsetting Ltd, Stockport, Cheshire,
and printed and bound by CPI Group (UK) Ltd,
Croydon, CR0 4YY

A CIP record for this book is available from the British Library

ISBN 978 1 4744 3903 9 (hardback)
ISBN 978 1 4744 3904 6 (paperback)
ISBN 978 1 4744 3905 3 (webready PDF)
ISBN 978 1 4744 3906 0 (epub)

Contents

Acknowledgements   vi
Preface   vii
Series Editor's Preface   ix

Introduction: Ten Statements about Empathy and Animal Studies   1

1. Fragile Bodies, Cross-species Empathy and Suspended Allegories: 'It hurt, it was painful – that's all there is to say'   35
2. Anthropomorphism and the 'Ends of Man' in the Anthropocene: 'My chimp nature'   66
3. Telling Nonhuman Stories: 'The secret contours of objects'   96
4. The Sexual Politics of Nature Writing and Lepidoptery: 'The siren song of entomology'   126
5. Insect Ethics and Aesthetics: 'Their blood does not stain our hands'   154

Conclusion   180

Bibliography   184
Index   201

Acknowledgements

Beginning as an illicit distraction from another project, this book has been a pleasure to write from start to finish. Its completion is down to the intellectual support and inspiration offered by my wonderful students and colleagues at Royal Holloway and beyond, and to the unwavering love, faith and enthusiasm of my family and friends. Particular thanks are due to Carol Hughes, Christopher Watkin, Kirsty Woods and my anonymous readers at Edinburgh University Press, to Nick James for indexing and to Zosia Edwards for her help in preparing the manuscript. Earlier versions of Chapters 1 and 2 were published elsewhere; thanks to Taylor and Francis for permission to reproduce this material here. This book would not exist without my much-missed nonhuman companions E, G, H, LBC, and N. Boundless love and gratitude to my human, AA.

Preface

This book takes its inspiration from Sianne Ngai, whose *Ugly Feelings*, itself a beast*less* 'bestiary of affects', traded desire, a trope rendered politically inert by its 'semantic multiplicity, slippage and flow', for negative affects in the pursuit of more '*critical* productivity'.[1] The provocative unfashionableness of Ngai's appeal to critique in the era of its purported 'redundancy' inspires this book's critical approach to the affective leanings of animal studies.[2] Contemporary animal studies, inspired by an ever-increasing list of remarkably similar 'turns' – materialist, bodily, vitalist, posthumanist, affective – largely adopts an affective monotone: empathy.

While not unaffected by the potency of empathy and its use as a pivot to direct animal studies beyond discourses of rights, and alert to the timely challenges to critique raised by Isabelle Stengers and others,[3] this book contends that the retention of some form of critical methodology leads neither to a 'corrosive skepticism'[4] nor to an inescapable anthropocentrism. Accordingly, it aspires to a critical distancing from the sometimes claustrophobic proximity of empathy, endeavouring to establish sufficient distance to enable the assessment of its ontological, ethical and aesthetic underpinnings without succumbing to the age-old trap of philosophical approaches to animals, which 'prioritised a disembodied and affectless reason'.[5] In this methodological approach, it is indebted to Jacques Derrida, whose deconstruction, often uncomfortably and sometimes frustratingly, is characterised by a kind of 'double

---

[1] Sianne Ngai, *Ugly Feelings* (Cambridge, MA: Harvard University Press, 2005), pp. 7, 344, 3.

[2] Isabelle Stengers makes this claim in *In Catastrophic Times: Revisiting the Coming Barbarism*, trans. Andrew Goffey (London: Open Humanities Press, 2015), p. 11.

[3] See, for example, Bruno Latour's ground-breaking essay, 'Why Has Critique Run Out of Steam? From Matters of Fact to Matters of Concern', *Critical Inquiry*, 30.2 (2004), 225–48.

[4] Donna Haraway, 'In the Beginning was the Word: The Genesis of Biological Theory', *Signs*, 6.3 (1981), 469–81 (p. 478).

[5] Kari Weil, 'Empathy', in *The Edinburgh Companion to Animal Studies*, ed. Ron Broglio, Undine Sellbach and Lynn Turner (Edinburgh: Edinburgh University Press, 2018), pp. 126–39 (p. 129).

strategy'[6] or 'double reading'.[7] As the pervasive mood of contemporary animal studies, empathy provides the starting-, but not the end-point for this book, which will range across the affective spectrum, landing finally on disgust, not incidentally the 'absolute other' of the Kantian aesthetic system.[8] Reading fiction and philosophy alongside each other, it proposes a movement, rather than a solution, a thinking of and with animals that negotiates through and aside from empathy.

[6] Robert Bernasconi, 'The Trace of Levinas in Derrida', in *Derrida and Différance*, ed. David Wood and Robert Bernasconi (Evanston: Northwestern University Press, 1988), pp. 13–29 (p. 16).
[7] John Llewelyn, 'Thresholds', in *Derrida and Différance*, ed. David Wood and Robert Bernasconi (Evanston: Northwestern University Press, 1988), pp. 51–62 (p. 61).
[8] Jacques Derrida, 'Economimesis', trans. R. Klein, *Diacritics*, 11.2 (1981), 2–25 (p. 21).

Series Editor's Preface

Two or more currents flowing into or through each other create a turbulent crosscurrent, more powerful than its contributory flows and irreducible to them. Time and again, modern European thought creates and exploits crosscurrents in thinking, remaking itself as it flows through, across and against discourses as diverse as mathematics and film, sociology and biology, theology, literature and politics. The work of Gilles Deleuze, Jacques Derrida, Slavoj Žižek, Alain Badiou, Bernard Stiegler and Jean-Luc Nancy, among others, participates in this fundamental remaking. In each case disciplines and discursive formations are engaged, not with the aim of performing a pre-determined mode of analysis yielding a 'philosophy of x', but through encounters in which thought itself can be transformed. Furthermore, these fundamental transformations do not merely seek to account for singular events in different sites of discursive or artistic production but rather to engage human existence and society as such, and as a whole. The cross-disciplinarity of this thought is therefore neither a fashion nor a prosthesis; it is simply part of what 'thought' means in this tradition.

Crosscurrents begins from the twin convictions that this remaking is integral to the legacy and potency of European thought, and that the future of thought in this tradition must defend and develop this legacy in the teeth of an academy that separates and controls the currents that flow within and through it. With this in view, the series provides an exceptional site for bold, original and opinion-changing monographs that actively engage European thought in this fundamentally cross-disciplinary manner, riding existing crosscurrents and creating new ones. Each book in the series explores the different ways in which European thought develops through its engagement with disciplines across the arts, humanities, social sciences and sciences, recognising that the community of scholars working with this thought is itself spread across diverse faculties. The object of the series is therefore nothing less than to examine and carry forward the unique legacy of European thought as an inherently and irreducibly cross-disciplinary enterprise.

Christopher Watkin
Cambridge
February 2011

For my parents, Catherine and Peter Sands,
from whom I learned to be attentive to the natural world and its
inhabitants

Introduction: Ten Statements about Empathy and Animal Studies

1 WE LIVE IN AN AGE OF EMPATHY

'Empathy is the grand theme of our time', contends Frans de Waal, predicting, rather too optimistically in 2009, 'a new epoch that stresses co-operation and social responsibility', and tracing the physiological origins of empathy to experiences shared by humans and nonhumans alike.[1] Irrespective of the accuracy of de Waal's political forecast, empathy continues to pervade scholarship in and beyond the humanities. For Kari Weil, 'empathy is in', its reach stretching from economics to cognitive science, from literary theory to ethology.[2] While the term itself is a recent one, and its current usage diverse and disputed, we can trace the contemporary belief that some sense of ethical attunement can be derived from an understanding of other humans' thoughts and feelings to two key eighteenth-century texts: David Hume's *A Treatise of Human Nature* (1739) and Adam Smith's *The Theory of Moral Sentiments* (1759),[3] the latter insisting in its famous opening lines that there are principles in human nature that safeguard humans' 'interest in the welfare of others'.[4] The term itself was coined in 1909 by Edward Titchener, a translation of the German *Einfühlung*, literally 'in-feeling' or 'feeling-into', a concept articulated and explored by Robert Vischer and Theodor Lipps.[5]

More recent engagement with empathy has seen a jockeying for position among different discourses and has generated innumerable different definitions, with emphases lying variously on the affective, cognitive or bodily.[6] Identifying several different mental processes or states which, individually or in combination, fall under the empathy umbrella, Amy Coplan lists:

(A) Feeling what someone else feels (B) Caring about someone else (C) Being emotionally affected by someone else's emotions and experiences, though not necessarily experiencing the same emotions (D) Imagining oneself in another's situation (E) Imagining being another in that other's situation (F) Making inferences about another's mental states (G) Some combination of the processes described in (A)–(F).[7]

Coplan's inventory reveals that empathy is used as a descriptor for both cognitive and emotional identification; accordingly, empathy raises questions that cut across the sciences, social sciences and humanities. These include: What role does cognition play in empathy? How do the sensory, emotional and cognitive components of empathy interrelate? Is empathy comparable with 'emotional contagion'?[8] Is it imitative? How do we ascertain if our empathy is accurate? Does empathy have a moral value and should its cultivation be encouraged? Does the concept of empathy presuppose a certain model of subjectivity that requires a clear differentiation between self and other? Perceiving 'experiential understanding' as central to our understanding of empathy, Coplan herself settles on a tripartite definition: 'only empathy that combines affective matching, other-oriented perspective-taking, and self–other differentiation provides experiential understanding', she insists.[9]

Discussions of empathy raise, rather than resolve, complex questions regarding the relationship between human cognition, emotion and imagination. While in her discussion of literary empathy, Suzanne Keen describes empathy as 'a vicarious, spontaneous sharing of affect', psychologists' and cognitive scientists' definitions suggest that the affective dimension of empathy already presupposes cognitive engagement.[10] For Nancy Eisenberg, for example, empathy is 'an affective response that stems from the apprehension or comprehension of another's emotional state or condition, and that is identical or very similar to what the other person is feeling or would be expected to feel'.[11] Thus, 'it is evident that any sophisticated empathizing requires more advanced cognitive capacities'.[12] The long-held distinction between cognitive empathy ('awareness of another person's internal states') and affective empathy ('the vicarious affective response to another person'),[13] while significant for specific disciplinary approaches, may well prove to be of limited use, not least because our sense of the moral value of empathy assumes a connection between the two. 'Both processes are crucial for our emotional understanding of others', Alexa Weik von Mossner contends, and for Elisa Aaltola, their separation can have 'devastatingly dangerous consequences'.[14]

Complex manifestations of empathy evidently combine cognitive and affective processes. Scientific attention to the specificity of these processes has lent deeper understanding to the differences and similarities between human and nonhuman primates. The discovery of mirror neurons by neuroscientists in the 1980s and 1990s exposed automatic imitation as a rudimentary mechanism among both, and generated deeper understanding of both human infant development[15] and of non-human primates.[16] 'Our brains', Antonio Gallese writes, 'and those of other primates, have developed a basic functional mechanism, embodied simulation, which gives us an experiential insight of other minds.'[17] While mirror neuron enthusiasts have made bold claims, including, as Derek Matravers comments, 'that simulation is what grounds interpersonal understanding', we must interrogate the assumptions underpinning these claims and beware both of posing scientific solutions to philosophical questions and of substituting scientific conceptions of subjectivity for philosophical ones.[18]

It is nonetheless true that science can assist in the framing of philosophical questions and in considering the role and development of the self in different empathetic modes. The distinction between automatic '*emotional contagion* (which involves the spontaneous transfer of emotion)', evident for example in macaque monkeys, and '*imaginative perspective-taking* (which involves perspective-swapping or role-taking)', visible so far only in chimpanzees and humans, appears to reflect a discrepancy between animals that do not have a distinct sense of self and those that do.[19] The former does not require that the empathiser distinguish her feelings from those of the empathised; rather, as Kristin Andrews and Lori Gruen note, 'an awareness of this distinction in agency may not yet have developed and perhaps never will'.[20] As such, unlike imaginative perspective-taking, emotional contagion is best understood as complete identification or immersion. In contrast, as imaginative perspective-taking, 'empathy must involve a clear differentiation between the sphere of the self as opposed to the sphere of the other'.[21] It is, therefore, a kind of doubling, which 'involves a participatory enactment of the situation of the sufferer, but is always combined with the awareness that one is not oneself the sufferer'.[22]

While the distinction between sympathy and empathy is a recent one, it has proven invaluable to critics assessing the moral value of the latter. Whereas empathy requires an imaginative engagement which presupposes both a clear distinction and an affective or creative porosity between subjects, sympathy does not possess the same dynamism. Rather, it means 'having concern for another's well-being',[23] or experiencing 'a particular kind of emotion'.[24] It does not demand what Neil Roughley and Thomas Schramme call 'an affect transfer mechanism',[25] but entails an additional level of detachment; it is 'not so much a matter of feeling someone's pain as of feeling bad or regretful *about* the pain someone is feeling'.[26] It is even possible, as Derek Matravers suggests, 'to feel sympathy towards someone who is not themselves feeling an emotion'.[27]

Although the difference between empathy and sympathy is largely undisputed, their respective ethical merits are not. For Martin L. Hoffman, empathy is 'the bedrock of morality, the glue of society, and an important factor in changing laws and society in a prosocial and projustice direction'.[28] Dan Batson has endeavoured to empirically prove the ethical value of empathy via his 'empathy-altruism hypothesis' in which 'empathetic concern refers to other-oriented emotion elicited by and congruent with the perceived welfare of a person in need'.[29] Others are more sceptical; for Julinna C. Oxley, empathy 'is not intrinsically moral and does not always lead to moral thought or action'.[30] Such concerns will be further explored later. For Daryl Koehn, the superiority of empathy over sympathy is proved by the latter's deficiencies; sympathy 'cannot be relied upon to provide any real insight into [others'] life experiences', she asserts.[31] Peter Goldie inverts this perspective entirely; empathy does not necessitate sympathy or altruism, he argues; rather, 'you can imagine the other's suffering, yet simply disregard it, or you might empathize with a person who has committed a terrible crime, yet feel no sympathy for you think he thoroughly deserves his punishment'.[32] Irrespective of their ethical virtues, the entanglement between the two is clear; empathy, Batson contends, 'helps to power and sustain sympathy'.[33]

2 THE AGE OF EMPATHY IS LINKED TO THE AFFECTIVE TURN

From Lipps to phenomenologists such as Edmund Husserl and Edith Stein, and to contemporary analytic philosophers, cognitive empathy provides a tool for addressing the problem of other minds. Characterising this position and objecting to the recent prioritisation of the affective over the cognitive, Karsten Stueber writes: 'Empathy as understood within the original philosophical context is best seen as a form of *inner or mental imitation for the purpose of gaining knowledge of other minds.*'[34] While this approach continues in contemporary analytic philosophy, it is marginalised in other disciplines as it presupposes a distinction between mind and body which has been problematised both in and beyond philosophy. In other disciplines, the shift in focus from cognitive to affective empathy (or to some combination of the two) reflects a broader interest in affect. As such, insofar as '*The Age of Empathy*'[35] addresses affective, rather than cognitive empathy, it is clearly allied with the 'Episteme of the Affect'.[36]

The latter *episteme* is at once determined by a rejection of earlier paradigms – deconstruction, with its perceived preoccupation with language, and 'psychoanalysis, and psychoanalytic concepts of fantasy and desire'[37] – and the adoption of new source material. For theories of affect, the two central sources are generally understood to be Gilles Deleuze's lectures on Spinoza in 1978, in which he recuperates the concept of *affectus*,[38] and the work of Silvan Tomkins, popularised by Eve Kosofsky Sedgwick and Adam Frank in 1995, with their publication of *Shame and Its Sisters: A Silvan Tomkins Reader*. As attested to by affect theorists such as Lisa Blackman and Teresa Brennan, with the latter insisting that 'all affects [. . .] are material physiological things' and contending that the 'transmission of affect' demands increased attentiveness to the complex, multi-directional interaction between the biological and the social, the turn to affect can be fruitfully read within a larger theoretical re-engagement with the body and materiality.[39]

While Brian Massumi, for example, resists the conflation of affect and emotion, contending that 'emotion is a very partial expression of affect',[40] it is important to retain the tension within the concept of affect between its interruptive force, both material and conceptual, and the inevitable domestication of this force through its expression in pre-existing conceptual (and emotional) forms. Pieter Vermeulen acknowledges this interruptive force; for him, affect names the *'formal operations that aim to undo emotional codification'*.[41] The understanding of affect as interruptive can be traced from Spinoza to Deleuze and is frequently articulated through a Deleuzian vocabulary of intensities, assemblages and becoming. According to Melissa Gregg and Gregory J. Seigworth, affect is

> integral to a body's perpetual *becoming* (always becoming otherwise, however subtly, than what it already is), pulled beyond its seeming surface-boundedness by way of its relation to, indeed its composition through, the forces of encounter. With affect, a body is as much outside itself as in itself – webbed in its relations – until ultimately such firm distinctions cease to matter.[42]

Going beyond the mutuality and vulnerability of affect – that affecting means 'at the same time opening yourself up to being affected in turn'[43] – Gregg and Seigworth suggest that affect necessitates a relational ontology in which subjects and bodies are understood as products, rather than generators, of relations. Other thinkers vary in their emphases. Some, such as Tonya K. Davidson, Ondine Park and Rob Shields, writing in the collection *Ecologies of Affect*, move from the individual to the collective, with affect serving as 'the emotional "glue" that drive[s] bodies to assemble into collectives' and being therefore inextricably connected to *'ecology'*.[44] Vermeulen similarly notes that 'affect dissolves the self-contained interiority of the individual and opens it to new connections and combinations'.[45] The slippage between affect and emotion is again significant. Resisting one pole of scholarship that insists that emotions dwell in the individual, and another that claims that emotions are purely social, Sara Ahmed insists that the distinction between the individual and social is both constructed and malleable; emotions, she writes, 'work to shape the "surfaces" of individual and collective bodies', and in so doing, influence the orientation and 'reorientation' of all bodies.[46] While there are explicit similarities between these positions, the turn to affect, as Eugenie Brinkema notes, has 'always been plural', and differences of inflection result in notably diverse outcomes.[47] Affect theory, therefore, covers a range of perspectives from the unchallenging celebration of individual emotional experience to the interrogation of a biopolitics which precedes and determines the construction of bodies, and to non-anthropocentric ontologies which aspire to radical engagement with, for example, the nonorganic and the technological.[48]

3   AFFECT PROMISES MORE THAN IT DELIVERS

For Brinkema, affect theory is disingenuous and disappointing. She argues:

> the return to affect on the part of critics [. . .] is, in most cases, a naïve move that leaves intact the very ideological, aesthetic and theoretical problems it claimed to confront. Thus, even some of the most radical theory coming out of the humanities today begins with the premise that affects and feelings are the forgotten underside of the linguistic turn. Indeed in some cases the affection for affect has itself been subsumed by a more powerful yearning for a standing before or outside of that very moment in theory that demanded the deep attention required for interminable difficult reading.[49]

The denial that we are inheritors of deconstruction is now widespread in the humanities, voiced by thinkers as diverse as Slavoj Žižek, Rosi Braidotti, Alain Badiou, Quentin Meillassoux and Donna Haraway. For new materialists, affect theorists and posthumanists, the articulation of deconstruction's alleged redundancy is particularly important and urgent. Rosi Braidotti, for example, insists that the 'posthuman subject' is not 'post-structuralist, because it does not function within the linguistic turn or other forms of deconstruction'.[50] The rejection of deconstruction (often accompanied by a denial of the problems that it purports to address) facilitates a swift passage through (or rather around) taxing problems. For Braidotti, the conflation of deconstruction with the linguistic turn permits a dismissal of the former as anthropocentric navel-gazing, evading discussion of the ways in which deconstruction requires us to pause before endorsing materiality, affect or posthumanism. For Žižek, the disavowal of deconstruction enables the pursuit of an overtly political philosophy unencumbered by 'the unstable and unlocatable border between law and justice, between the political and the ultrapolitical'.[51] While the shift away from deconstruction simplifies the relationship between the philosophical and the political, it does so, in Brinkema's terms, at the expense of 'the deep attention required for interminable difficult reading'. While new materialisms and posthumanisms often frame themselves as post-theoretical, in the sense of being informed but not limited by theory, Pieter Vermeulen contends that many position affect as 'a biological bedrock' which is 'blissfully untainted by signification, intention, and mediation' and thus reinstate a 'strict separation between affect and consciousness' which gives affect unmediated access to materiality and therefore immunity to critique.[52] Their post-theoretical stance, therefore, is no such thing.

Recent dismissals of deconstruction have a familiar flavour. Defending poststructuralism against the connected charges that either it cannot offer an account of emotion, or that its account of emotion directly conflicts with its deconstruction of the subject, in 2001 Rei Terada contended both that poststructuralism is pervaded by emotion and that it successfully demonstrates that emotion is fundamentally 'nonsubjective'.[53] Terada's temporally transferable insight is that deconstruction's critics routinely pathologise deconstruction, contending that it is trapped by its own non-problems, in order to neutralise the genuine issues that it raises. The task for deconstruction's defenders is to reinstate these problems *as* problems; in Terada's case, she reminds us that the 'difficulty of representing emotion, in other words, is the difficulty of knowing what it is, not just for poststructuralist theory but for any theory'.[54]

Brinkema contends that affect theory promises much and delivers little. The historical turn to affect, where affect is allied with materiality and the body, marks the moment where Derridean thinking is superseded by Deleuze, with the 'polemical effect of Deleuze's theory of affect', Terada noting, being to produce a schism within poststructuralism along the lines of 'positions on emotive experience'.[55] For Brinkema, Deleuze's employment of Spinoza's notion of *affectus* is ultimately unsatisfactory; while the lineage from Spinoza, Bergson and Whitehead to Deleuze incites a rethinking of bodies as 'assemblages of human and non-human processes'[56] in which the boundaries between bodies are exposed as porous and rich with forces, intensities and affects,[57] Brinkema argues that 'Deleuze loses the subject only to hold tight to the body'.[58] This is magnified by many of Deleuze's inheritors, whose focus on the body often returns to individual visceral experience and emotion, and in so doing, Brinkema contends, retains 'a notion of classical interiority'.[59] Rather than repudiating affect entirely, however, we can recover its potential for radicalism. This, Brinkema argues, like Vermeulen who also advocates a return to form, can only be generated by attention to 'its specificities'.[60] In its reading of the domesticated affects of animal studies, this book will keep in mind the possibility of a more interruptive kind of affect which is 'non-intentional' and 'indifferent'.[61]

4 ANIMAL STUDIES HAS TRADED RIGHTS FOR RELATIONS

The empathetic mood that pervades contemporary animal studies is a recent development.[62] Early texts that asserted the ethical status of animals, notably Peter Singer's *Animal Liberation* (1975) and Tom Regan's *The Case for Animal Rights* (1983), emerged from the rights-tradition and remained within it. Singer popularised the term specie-sism and proposed that the ability of a nonhuman animal to experience suffering, and thus its interest in avoiding it, should be safeguarded in law as a right. The recent shift, identified by Anat Pick as one from *'rights to lives'*, signifies a thoroughgoing change in thinking about animals, ostensibly away from anthropocentrism and to a broader, less subject-centric conception of ethical value.[63] It looks to advance a different approach to animals, primarily informed by continental rather than analytic philosophy, without entirely dismissing the gains of rights-based approaches. It understands relationality in ontological, ethical and political terms.

The limitations of rights-based approaches have been effectively articulated in other political contexts. For the political theorist Hannah Arendt, the naturalisation of human rights is misleading and danger-ous; rights, as we understand them, depend upon the 'right to have rights'.[64] They are meaningless unless they are recognised by function-ing political communities. Simone Weil also reminds us that human rights can be traced to Roman property law and in it, the perception of human slaves as property:

> The notion of rights is linked with the notion of sharing out, of exchange, of measured quantity. It has a commercial flavour, essentially evocative of legal claims and arguments. Rights are always asserted in a tone of contention; and when this tone is adopted, it must rely upon force in the background, or else it will be laughed at.[65]

For Weil and others, justice cannot be reduced to the juridical. As Cora Diamond, following Weil, argues, 'when genuine issues of justice and injustice are framed in terms of rights, they are thereby distorted and trivialised'.[66] Other problems arise with rights-discourse within the context of animal studies. Rights presuppose an individual human subject who is discrete, autonomous and rational. As Deborah Slicer writes, this 'atomistic bundle of interests' is the sole unit 'that the justice tradition recognizes as the basis for moral considerableness'.[67] This approach might lead to the inclusion of the great apes and other intelligent or sentient mammals within the ethical sphere, but, in continuing to assess mammals anthropocentrically, would inevitably omit those insufficiently rational, at least by human standards. Such a model of subjectivity has been effectively dismissed by animal studies; as Donna Haraway writes in *Staying with the Trouble*, 'bounded individualism in its many flavors in science, politics, and philosophy has finally become unavailable to think with, truly no longer thinkable, technically or any other way'.[68]

We can also read the abstract argumentation favoured by rights-based approaches as reinforcing a 'deflection' from embodiment that has long characterised, and thus limited, philosophical thought.[69] Such an approach, visible in a Cartesianism which dismissed animals as machines, both renders animal suffering invisible (because inconceivable) and distances humans from their own embodied experience, 'of what it is', Cora Diamond stresses, 'to be a living animal'.[70] Despite appeals to a broader set of criteria (or even an entire conceptual overhaul), rights-based thinkers have continued to insist on the ongoing value of abstraction and rationality for making ethical judgments; as Tom Regan sternly insists:

> Since all who work on behalf of the interests of animals are more than a little familiar with the tired charges of being "irrational," "sentimental," "emotional," or worse, we can give the lie to these accusations only by making a concerted effort not to indulge our emotions or sentiments.[71]

The intransigence of Regan, who, even writing in 2001, simply could not conceive of 'a theory of animal rights based on appeals to emotion', marks the opening of a gulf:[72] on one side, a rights-discourse whose gains for nonhuman animals cannot be overstated, and on the other, an unexpected alliance between a 'continental' thought aligned with the body and affect and an ethological discourse, epitomised by Marc Bekoff and Frans de Waal, increasingly keen to affirm the value of emotional and anthropomorphic approaches to nonhuman life.[73] It is striking that animal studies is now overwhelmingly characterised by the latter.

5 ANIMAL STUDIES IS UNDERPINNED BY RELATIONALITY

Contemporary animal studies is the site of numerous correctives. That philosophy's historical misrepresentation of 'the animal' is tied to a fetishisation of reason accompanied by a denigration of the body was ably demonstrated by Jacques Derrida in *The Animal That Therefore I Am*, a text promising a deconstructive inscription 'in the name of another history, another concept of history, and of the history *of* the human as well as that of reason'.[74] Animal studies has looked to address these deficiencies and others, including the neglect of 'sensing, [. . .] desire, passion, sexuality, and relations of dependency'.[75] Theorisations of the shift from 'bounded individualism' to 'relations of dependency' draw upon a variety of discourses including Actor Network Theory (Latour), new materialisms and posthumanism (Braidotti, Barad, Bennett, Grosz, Haraway), the affective turn and its focus on embodiment (Gruen, Alaimo), deconstructive readings of precarity and vulnerability (Derrida, Butler, Wolfe) and feminist care ethics (Tronto, Gilligan). Emerging in the 1980s and 1990s, the latter began from 'the fact of human interdependence', cautioning against the danger of perceiving it 'a weakness to be unable to live a totally self-sufficient life devoid of emotional attachments'.[76] While not all of these thinkers endorse a relational ontology, entanglement has become the primary mode for thinking subjectivity and agency within animal studies. This is epitomised by Braidotti's account of the critical posthumanist subject, who exists 'within an eco-philosophy of multiple belongings, as a relational subject that works across differences and is also internally differentiated but still grounded and accountable'.[77]

The widespread objectification of animal life, predicated on the pervasiveness of a subject/object binary in which only the former possesses agency, has historically licensed the abuse of animal life. Such a binary, Bruno Latour argues, is 'less interesting than the complete chain along which competences and actions are distributed'.[78] Through his Actor Network Theory, a key influence on new materialisms and posthumanisms, Latour argued that the subject/object opposition is a secondary consequence of distributed agency rather than a primary ontological descriptor. Advancing the term 'actant' to signify the distribution of agency across human and nonhuman networks, Latour frames humans as complex material systems rather than ensouled subjects. He argues that the simultaneous denial of human embeddedness within networks (with humans *as* networks) and reliance on such networks constitutes the conflicting logic of modernity, and has sustained the conceptual and material hierarchy underpinning anthropogenic environmental destruction.[79] Like Latour, reaching for a more distributive agency, Jane Bennett's vital materialism foresees the political implications of a flattened ontology in which the opposition between human agency and 'passive, mechanistic' matter is displaced by the claim that all matter possesses 'thing-power' and that agency is spread across a range 'of ontological types'.[80] Bennett rejects the classical, theologically informed notion of the subject and its ethical responsibilities; by her account, the 'mingling' between humanity and nonhumanity can no longer be ignored.[81] The political shift is notable; one is no longer individually responsible for one's actions, but responsible for the consequences of the 'assemblages' with which one finds oneself implicated.[82]

Now presupposed by animal studies, the distribution of agency across species (and beyond) and the emergence of dynamic subjects from cross-species networks has precipitated a fast-moving vocabulary. Donna Haraway insists upon the co-constitution of interacting beings, Alexis Shotwell describes corporeal 'inter-absorption' as 'the way things actually are', and Stacy Alaimo coins the phrase 'trans-corporeality' to describe cross-species material entanglements.[83] Haraway's work in particular has been crucial in exploring the ontological and ethical implications of cross-species entanglement. As early as 'A Cyborg Manifesto', a text whose engagement with animals is chiefly implicit, Haraway insists upon the figure of the cyborg as an intervention in human–animal relations as it exposes the originary hybridity of the human (denied in the very functioning of the human/animal distinction) through its constitution via technological prostheses. It is no accident, Haraway notes, that 'the cyborg appears in myth precisely where the boundary between human and animal is transgressed'.[84] Accordingly, the sovereign human individual is a myth; 'no species', she writes, 'not even our own arrogant one pretending to be good individuals in so-called modern Western scripts, acts alone; assemblages of organic species and of abiotic actors make history'.[85] We must begin not from the individual, but from entanglement, as biological, social and historical co-constitution means that 'beings do not pre-exist their relatings'.[86] Similarly, Elisa Aaltola argues for the replacement of 'the atomistic model' by 'intersubjectivity, the idea that we constantly evolve in relation to others, are impacted by and open to those others and due to this dynamic, also capable of understanding them'.[87]

6 ANIMAL STUDIES CHALLENGES THE DISTINCTION BETWEEN ONTOLOGY AND ETHICS

Critiquing abstract rights-based methodologies on the grounds that 'moral theories might alienate us from possible solutions to moral problems', Lori Gruen proposes an approach which accepts, rather than denies, our proximity and relatedness to nonhuman animals.[88] This she terms 'entangled empathy' and explains:

> Entangled empathy: a type of caring perception focused on attending to another's experience of wellbeing. An experiential process involving a blend of emotion and cognition in which we recognize we are in relationships with others and are called upon to be responsive and responsible in these relationships, by attending to another's needs, and interests, desires, vulnerabilities, hopes and sensitivities.[89]

For Gruen, empathy, an ethical attitude, is the appropriate response to the ontological condition of entanglement. Gruen's notion of empathy corresponds with Coplan's definition, which presupposes some degree of 'self–other differentiation', rather than total enmeshment. Gruen's position addresses the ways in which the insights of an 'ethics of care' originating in 1990s and 2000s feminism, and re-emerging in recent work such as that of Michael Slote, can be fruitfully recuperated for animal studies.[90] Such an ethics is ripe for adaptation. For Joan C. Tronto, writing in the 1990s, care already implies 'engagement', movement beyond the self, and a call 'to some type of action'.[91] She observes that 'it is not restricted to human interaction with others', but might include, for example, 'caring [. . .] for the environment'.[92] Gruen's gesture towards this scholarship is strengthened and extended by Maria Puig de la Bellacasa in her 2017 book *Matters of Care: Speculative Ethics in More Than Human Worlds*. Drawing deeply on the feminist care tradition, Bellacasa pitches her position as a counter to normative moral theories, contending that a care position mobilises holistic, yet relational, selves rather than being exclusively cognitively grounded. Care is, therefore, 'about thick, impure involvement' and 'a hands-on ongoing process of re-creation'.[93] Such a position requires a comprehensive revaluation of ethical standards, with 'respect for and attentiveness to possible difference' replacing 'formal consistency' as the 'hallmark of ethical maturity'.[94] Whereas for Gruen and others such as Alexis Shotwell, who advances an 'ethics of entanglement', the ethical remains clearly distinguishable from the ontological, Bellacasa positions relationality or interdependency on the mutable borderline between the two.[95]

'Interdependency', Bellacasa maintains, 'is not a contract, nor a moral ideal – it is a *condition*. Care is therefore concomitant to the continuation of life for many living beings in more than human entanglements – not forced upon them by a moral order, and not necessarily a rewarding obligation.'[96] Bellacasa's primary assumption here is an ontological one, that relationality is 'all there is', and that consequently, 'nonsymmetrical, multilateral, asubjective, obligations [. . .] are distributed across more than human materialities and existences'.[97] Obligation is here ambiguous: Bellacasa exploits its double functioning as, on the one hand, a survival necessity, and on the other, ethical responsibility. This facilitates her next move, which is to present ontological dependency as an ethical model; there is further slippage here, from what is natural to what is good. A similar unexplained slippage occurs in Haraway's recent work on cross-species kinship; 'all earthlings are kin in the deepest sense', she asserts, before inferring that this obliges us to 'make kin, not babies!'[98]

The problem with such claims is not that they politicise ontology. Indeed, a great strength of the work of Haraway, Barad and others is the exposure of the political stakes of existing ontologies, particularly those whose interests lie in the differentiation of humans from other animals. Rather, the problem with such claims is that they depoliticise their own ontologies. Bellacasa disavows the political stakes of her own position; fulfilling Brinkema and Vermeulen's critiques of affect theory, she argues that her ontology strips back the veils of prior ontologies to expose 'all there is'. Alert to the consequences of the feminist care ethics of the 1980s and 1990s, Daryl Koehn is cautious, reminding us that 'the care ethic thus tends to undermine any sense of female power and freedom at the same time as it celebrates the fulfillment and strength allegedly achieved through caring'.[99]

In challenging Bellacasa's claims, I do not assume that all ontologies are equally valid or equally fruitful: clearly, recent scientific advancements have rendered previously imperceptible connections visible and certain ontologies prove more responsive to these discoveries than others. However, this puts us in no position to declare that we have now discovered and understand the nature of reality *in itself*, and that our preferred ontology is non-ideological. Advocating a similarly relational ontology to that of Bellacasa, Jane Bennett admits a strategic pragmatism. 'Why advocate the vitality of matter?' she asks, 'because my hunch is that the image of dead or thoroughly instrumentalized matter feeds human hubris and our earth-destroying fantasies of conquest and consumption'.[100] Similarly, when asked to adjudicate between ontologies, Joanna Zylinska observes that 'the distinction between process and entity is therefore a heuristic, a conceptual device that helps us grasp the world and respond to it, while at the same time moving in it and being moved by it'.[101] The operative value of an ontology is determined by a range of factors. It is, therefore, important to highlight the complex relations between ontology, ethics and politics. This accounts for Karen Barad's appeal to an '*ethico-onto-epistem-ology* – an appreciation of the intertwining of ethics, knowing and being' on the grounds that 'the becoming of the world is a deeply ethical matter'.[102] We must be cautious when evaluating ontological frameworks in terms of veracity; more useful are pragmatic evaluations of their functionality. In his defence of an Object-Oriented Philosophy, for example, Graham Harman argues that 'the primacy of relations over things is no longer a liberating idea (since it reduces things to their pragmatic impact on humans and on each other)'.[103] A similar position is espoused by Claire Colebrook, who asks:

> What if all the current counter-Cartesian, post-Cartesian or anti-Cartesian figures of living systems (along with a living order that is one interconnected and complex mesh) were a way of avoiding the extent to which man is a theoretical animal, a myopically and malevolently self-enclosed machine whose world he will always view as present for his own edification?[104]

Sceptical of claims regarding the objective veracity of any single ontology and alert to the complexity of relations between ontology, ethics and politics, this book will assess ontological claims strategically and pragmatically.

7 ANIMAL STUDIES EXPOSES CROSS-SPECIES VULNERABILITY TO INCITE CROSS-SPECIES EMPATHY

The perceived distinction between humans and other animals is underpinned by the historical framing of Man as *zoon logon echon*, a rational animal whose cognitive capacities both supplement and correct his animal nature. Retaining the focus on reason, rights-based approaches to nonhuman animal life have identified similarities between human and nonhuman cognition, often tracing the evolutionary origins of cognition to provide a counter to the association of rationality with an immaterial soul. More consonant with broader movements in contemporary animal studies is the shift in focus from cognition to sentience, signalled by Derrida's 1997 rearticulation of Jeremy Bentham's 1823 question 'Can they suffer?'[105] Rather than framing his call to sentience as an appeal to pity, which would reinforce the power imbalance presupposed by the human/animal distinction, or proposing an objective assessment of each species' sentience, Derrida advocates an affective awareness of the shared experience of exposure, vulnerability and 'non-power' that defines all mortal, embodied beings.[106] The affective experience of shared embodiment provides a visceral rebuttal to the assumption that 'power over the animal is [. . .] the essence of the human'.[107] Such an admission offers the possibility of grounding an alternative politics in embodied vulnerability and empathy, rather than human sovereignty:

> Being able to suffer is no longer a power; it is a possibility without power, a possibility of the impossible. Mortality resides there, as the most radical means of thinking the finitude that we share with animals, the mortality that belongs to the very finitude of life, to the experience of compassion [. . .][108]

While the apparently arbitrary reinscription of the human/animal distinction by biopolitical technologies – which render us 'all always already (potential) "animals" before the law' – often has devastating effects, in its mobility this distinction is exposed as 'a discursive resource, not a zoological designation'.[109] Without endorsing the abuses of biopolitical thinking, or following Giorgio Agamben in a 'condemnation and disavowal of embodied life as something constitutively deficient', we can use biopolitics to see the ways in which acknowledgement of the animal vulnerability of the human deflates the exceptionalist fantasies of Cartesian Man, and, as Cary Wolfe suggests, enables us to articulate 'the disjunctive and uneven quality of our own political moment'.[110] Derrida's appeal for the replacement of a politics of power by one that exposes shared vulnerability demands the ongoing deconstruction of the oppositions that shore up anthropocentric hegemony.

Inevitably, given current animal studies' engagement with embodiment and relationality, Derrida's focus on embodied vulnerability both reflects and informs recent work. Proceeding from a new materialist rather than a deconstructive position, Stacy Alaimo echoes Derrida's stress on cross-species vulnerability and his aspiration towards a postsovereign politics established not from the figure of Man as *zoon logon echon*, but through awareness of humans as affecting and affected bodies. We should 'occupy exposure as insurgent vulnerability', Alaimo contends.[111] Similarly, Myra J. Hird calls for 'an environmental ethics of vulnerability in which humans are vulnerable to living and nonliving earth processes. [. . .] This vulnerability, in turn, calls for a *heightened*, not diminished, assumption of responsibility.'[112] On these grounds, we should aspire to an empathy which is grounded in embodied, affective experience; 'at its most basic level', James Mensch observes, 'empathy is bodily. Another person hurts his hand and we reach for our own.

We see someone cut himself and we wince. In each case, we take on the other's embodiment.'[113]

Of recent interventions, that of Anat Pick in *Creaturely Poetics* is among the most persuasive. Informed by the work of Simone Weil and Emmanuel Levinas on vulnerability and alterity respectively, Pick outlines an ethics of vulnerability – where vulnerability is irreducible to sentience – which incorporates human and nonhuman life. Given their shared inspiration in the work of Weil, it is unsurprising that there are parallels between Diamond and Pick, with the former reminding us of the stakes of our physical vulnerability:

> The awareness we each have of being a living body, being 'alive to the world,' carries with it exposure to the bodily sense of vulnerability to death, sheer animal vulnerability, the vulnerability we share with them. This vulnerability is capable of panicking us.[114]

Like Diamond, for whom 'moral thought gets no grip' on our experience of the fragility entailed by embodiment,[115] Pick insists that we resist the desire to defuse vulnerability by codifying it or responding with a moral prescription, instead retaining its affective power.[116] 'Vulnerability as an object of attention does not yield a moral "reading"', she argues. 'I am interested instead in the ramifications (for thought and also for action) of being oriented toward vulnerability as a universal mode of exposure.'[117] One limitation of Pick's position is her tendency, like Bellacasa, to reach for an essentialist ontology to secure the ethical strength of her claims; unable to rely on the force of her position despite its contingency (ultimately, the best for which we can hope), Pick insists that 'exposure [. . .] is the properly universal condition that underlies the ordinariness of all life'.[118] There is also a danger that Pick's universalising move, in combination with her resistance to moral prescriptivism, devalues the ethical charge of her account: if exposure is both the condition of life and generates an ethical claim, to whom do we owe what? How should we discriminate between moral claims? This reflects a problem that characterises 'entangled ethics': how do we translate the demands created by interdependency into a political and juridical context that remains dominated by 'bounded individualism'?

8 A RELATIONAL ONTOLOGY IS NOT SUFFICIENT

While these questions remain largely unaddressed, and often unacknowledged, within animal studies, a key issue – that of accounting for an interdependency that entails vulnerability without ceding calls for 'bodily integrity and self-determination' – is fruitfully raised by Judith Butler in the context of human precarity.[119] For Butler, interdependency is a problem that, she admits, 'I confess to not knowing how to theorize'.[120] By her account, the ontological is always already political. While interdependency names 'a common human vulnerability, one that emerges with life itself', 'life' is, for Butler, always already social life.[121] As such, she argues,

> each of us is constituted politically in part by virtue of the social vulnerability of our bodies [. . .] Loss and vulnerability seem to follow from our being socially constituted bodies, attached to others, at risk of losing those attachments, exposed to others, at risk of violence by virtue of that exposure.[122]

Here, while the emphasis is on the social rather than biological, like Haraway and others, Butler's account of the constitution of subjectivity is grounded in relationality.

Alert to criticisms of her 'overly hasty association of agency with personhood',[123] Butler undertakes a distinct shift to recognise the 'precarity of any and all living beings' without endorsing 'radical substitutability' across species.[124] Stressing that ethical obligation is not reducible to, but should never be separated from, the politico-juridical, that ontology cannot be thought 'outside the operations of power', Butler aims to articulate what it might mean for beings to be 'bound to one another in precariousness' in a mode that 'precedes contracts', and how best we might respond juridically to that 'binding' without appropriating or domesticating it.[125] Her methodological solution is unmistakably deconstructive; rather than jettisoning the figure of the independent human entirely (a position exemplified by Braidotti's posthumanist subject), she proceeds using two apparently conflicting ontologies. Alert to the fact that 'it is important to claim that our bodies are in some sense *our own* and that we are entitled to claim rights of autonomy over our bodies',[126] she sustains some connection with 'bounded individualism', while continuing to assert the primacy of the 'dependency, contiguity and unrivalled proximity that now defines each population, which exposes each to the fear of destruction [. . .]'.[127] It is important to note, however, that, contra Bellacasa and Haraway, she politicises rather than naturalises relationality, alert to the political dangers of asserting that relations are 'all there is'.

The editors of a recent volume locating itself in 'multispecies studies' made the following claim for their discipline:

> Refusing the tired opposition between three incommensurable demands – social justice in a humanist vein, ethics focused on the well-being of

individual entities (usually nonhuman animals but to a lesser extent plants, fungi, stones, and others), and an environmental ethics concerned primarily with the health of ecosystems and species – work in multispecies studies has embraced relational ethical approaches to grapple with diverse competing claims.[128]

The problem with this solution is that rather than evenly adjudicating between differing demands, or deconstructing the oppositions between them, by adopting relationality as its mode it already favours relational entities over individual ones. It proposes an easy solution where only a difficult one, Brinkema's 'deep attention', will have any chance of success. Similarly, Haraway proceeds from the physical and biological proximity of humans and nonhumans, 'the extraordinary tentacular closeness of processes of semiosis and fleshliness', to a suspicion, 'at the level of both affect and cognitive apparatus [. . .] of the division between the human and everybody else'.[129] Accordingly, she proposes an ethics and politics grounded in proximity or cross-species kinship, from which the figure of the human is largely absent. On the contrary, Butler argues for a selective, strategic retention of the human. To disavow the term is to let its power continue unchecked. Rather we should perceive the human as 'a differential of power that we must learn to read, to assess culturally and politically, and to oppose in its differential operations', as well as 'to assert it precisely where it cannot be asserted, and to do this in the name of opposing the differential of power by which it operates'.[130] History, which reveals both the oppressive and liberatory power of the figure of the human, should direct us in the dilemmas we face here. 'How does one object to human suffering', Butler asks, 'without perpetuating a form of anthropocentrism that has so readily been used for destructive purposes?'[131] One solution is to continue the ongoing process of remaking and redefining the human, rather than letting it be defined by sovereignty and exceptionalism; in itself, the human is not a figure of self-identity or sameness. Rather, as Butler highlights, 'where there is the human, there is the inhuman'.[132] This book will pursue the ethical implications of this claim.

The ethical limitations of relationality are also exposed by a philosophy of empathy. We have already seen that empathy entails a kind of double perspective and that the 'intersubjectivity in empathy is most easily captured by positing a strong mental divide between oneself and another'.[133] This structural necessity is also an ethical one; blurring the identities of empathiser and empathised makes it impossible to discern how to proceed ethically. This marks the difference between emotional contagion, where there is 'little or no self–other differentiation [. . .] and no imaginative component', and therefore little ethical potential, and imaginative perspective-taking empathy.[134] In proceeding from 'the otherness of the other',[135] imaginative perspective-taking empathy respects 'the boundaries of the other' and 'the singularity of the other's experience'.[136] We do not need to understand the individual as the only ethical unit, or as pitted against relationality, to think of it as an essential ethical term. Rather, as Dan Zahavi contends, instead of 'impeding a satisfactory account of intersubjectivity, an emphasis on the inherent and essential individuation of experiential life must be seen as a prerequisite for getting the relation and difference between self and other right'.[137]

9 THE MORAL VALUE OF EMPATHY IS DISPUTED

In the provocatively titled *Against Empathy*, Paul Bloom assembles criticisms of empathy from different disciplines to present the case that, 'on the whole', empathy is 'a poor moral guide' which is not equivalent to compassion or fairness.[138] It was already clear from Coplan's sexpartite definition that empathy is an imprecise tool whose ambiguity hampers lucid understanding, assessment and use. Bloom's criticism runs deeper: the shared features across the variant definitions all harbour the same limitations, annulling the value of empathy as a moral aid. Bloom argues that empathy is, by its definition, narrowly focused. It depends on proximity and interaction with an individual or small number of individuals. As a consequence, it 'does poorly in a world where there are many people in need, and where the effects of one's actions are diffuse, often delayed, and difficult to compute'.[139] Not only is it narrow in its focus and therefore its impact, Bloom argues that empathy is subject to irrational biases and preferences. It facilitates a kind of parochialism that fosters existing relationships and limits the production of new ones.[140] In cross-species interactions, this could easily become species-parochialism, where empathy is reserved for nonhuman animals that exhibit qualities perceived as human. In a more focused challenge, Jesse Prinz looks to demonstrate the dispensability of empathy for morality. He argues that empathy is poor at motivating changes; it leads to preferential treatment, is too selective, and is subject to biases; it can be manipulated; and it is subject to salience and proximity effects.[141] Unlike Bloom, however, he proposes the cautious retention of empathy, suggesting ways to develop its resistance to bias and to boost its political and ethical force. Similar positions are expressed by Koehn, who frames empathy as 'morally neutral', and Matravers, who argues in favour of 'quarantining our moral thinking from the biases of empathy'.[142]

That empathy replicates existing prejudices and biases might prove a significant problem for animal studies, particularly in a context where rights-based approaches have long insisted on the necessity of hierarchising nonhuman animals to ascertain their value. An empathy dependent on projection or simulation might lose its way across species, inadvertently reinforcing an anthropomorphic anthropocentrism. As Elisa Aaltola identifies, there is a striking gap between the potential gains and losses of cross-species empathy; 'we are left, then', she concludes, 'at a junction between empathy as the pathway towards recognizing the morally significant individuality of pigs and pikes and empathy as a nullification of any such recognition'.[143] Although premised on relationality, Gruen's 'entangled empathy' presupposes individual subjects who might respond emotionally and cognitively to each other. It is explicitly limited by sentience: while it is relatively easy to empathise with mammals and nonhuman animals with which we share characteristics, can we empathise with 'non-individuals, such as forests, art and the oceans?'[144] Can we conceive of vulnerability without sentience? Kari Weil reiterates this problem, noting that:

> This difficulty of empathising across difference may be one reason for the disproportionate attention given to apes or to animals we live with like dogs and cats within animal studies; those we find most like us, or whom we most wish to be like.[145]

Gruen concedes that empathy favours certain species over others but does not clarify whether this has any bearing on ethical value, preferring to endorse a diverse toolkit for responding to different beings; 'empathy does not appear to be the appropriate ethical response to the non-sentient world', she notes.[146]

The limitations of empathy are acutely problematic in the context of a growing environmental crisis in which the significance of non-sentient, and even inanimate, forces is ever-increasing. Such an era calls for new alliances and modes of attentiveness, particularly to the composite relationships between large-scale environmental forces and 'the minute and the barely felt'.[147] At the end of the empathy spectrum is the insect; often generating an 'immense sense of estrangement',[148] it is hard to imagine responding empathetically to insects.[149] However, as Stephen Loo and Undine Sellbach assert, we disregard insects at our peril. Rather, they argue:

> we can no longer afford to think about ethics in separation from insects, and the big and small edges of sentience they evoke. Insects are reminders that we are ecologically entangled in ways we often only dimly perceive and are impacting the environment and other species in damaging ways we frequently ignore.[150]

Two main consequences follow Loo and Sellbach's claim: first, that if empathy is to be of any use at all, we must reconfigure it imaginatively in ways that resist its potential parochialism. Here, Pick's 'creaturely ethics', which does not depend on personhood but on 'the recognition of the materiality and vulnerability of all living bodies', might be useful.[151] Secondly, empathy is only part of the diverse, developing toolkit that we need to respond meaningfully to the changing world we inhabit. While it is clear that 'moral considerability cannot be reduced to individual subjects', it is important to remember that 'the subject (and thus empathy) can still hold principal relevance and support the appreciation of non-individual things'.[152] Indeed, rather than dismissing the subject on philosophical or ethical grounds, we must continue to grapple with both the problems and the solutions it presents.

10 FOR CROSS-SPECIES STORYTELLING, WE MUST UNDERSTAND HOW TEXT WORKS

While ethological advancements have subdued most appeals to human exceptionalism (such as those premised on cognition, language, tool-use or sentience), the truism that the human is unique as 'a storytelling animal' persists.[153] This is often combined with the assumption that storytelling is a fundamental component in world-making, and that those who are incapable of constructing worlds are destined to passively inhabit those imagined and realised by others. Note, most famously, Martin Heidegger's contention that 'the stone is worldless. Similarly, plants and animals have no world; they belong, rather, to the hidden throng of an environment into which they have been put.'[154] In its multi-dimensional assault on anthropocentrism, however, animal studies has turned to narrative; 'storying', Haraway contends, 'cannot any longer be put into the box of human exceptionalism'.[155] By this, we should read at least the following: that closer observation will reveal nonhuman animals to be active participants in, and creators of, stories; and that stories are ideal spaces for imaginative cross-species connections. For J. M. Coetzee's character Elizabeth Costello in *The Lives of Animals*, 'there are no bounds to the sympathetic imagination'.[156] In other words, as Costello expands: 'If I can think my way into the existence of a being who has never existed, then I can think my way into the existence of a bat or a chimpanzee or an oyster, any being with whom I share the substrate of life.'[157] Costello's is an extreme example of an empathy – not always for the human – often ascribed to literature. As Suzanne Keen states:

In its strongest form, aesthetics' empathy describes a projective fusing with an object – which may be another person or an animal, but may also be a fictional character made of words, or even, in some accounts, inanimate things such as landscapes, artworks, or geological features.[158]

Rejecting Heidegger's position in favour of Jakob von Uexküll's identification of *Umwelten* or 'animal worlds' which characterise different animals' phenomenal experience,[159] David Herman argues that narrative 'affords a bridge between the human and the nonhuman'.[160] 'By modeling the richness and complexity of "what it is like" for non-human others', he continues, 'stories can underscore what is at stake in the trivialization – or outright destruction – of their experiences.'[161] Can reading fiction, Keen asks, prove sufficiently powerful to enable us to 'transmute empathetic guilt into prosocial action'?[162] That stories have a role to play in a re-narrativising of the world, 'a *reworlding*' in which humans are not the only active agents, has become a commonplace.[163] If the human perception of itself as steward and storyteller has precipitated serious environmental damage, then, as Van Dooren et al. contend: 'Only-human stories will not serve anyone in a period shaped by escalating and mutually reinforcing processes of biosocial destruction – from mass extinction to climate change, from globalization to terrorism.'[164] Myra Hird similarly foresees cross-species 'world-making' as the inevitable consequence of acknowledging the networked relations within which we all participate.[165] At these points, these ideas are highly abstracted and leave many questions unanswered. How would a cross-species storytelling avoid the tendency towards appropriation and monologue? Is it possible to bring forth the 'powerful infidel heteroglossia' of which Haraway speaks?[166]

While cross-species storytelling is an admirable goal to pursue, it remains nascent and undertheorised. It cannot be fulfilled by simplistic reiterations of multi-species relationality. As we follow its potential, we should also be alert to the disruptive, inhuman potential of existing forms of writing. Often mistakenly subsumed under the aegis of the 'linguistic turn', deconstructive accounts of 'textuality' and 'writing' expose that which defies or disrupts language, where language is understood as embodying closure and systematicity; as Derrida explains: 'The critique of logocentrism is above else the search for the "other" and "the other of language".'[167] 'Text' therefore is not synonymous with language, but haunts or contaminates language (and other similarly constrained systems). As Claire Colebrook observes, text is 'an "untamed genesis", an anarchic dispersal, a *mal d'archive* or an evil that works against logic, works against "gathering", and against any notion of life as *oikos*'.[168] It is, as Derrida reminds us in *Limited Inc.*, 'limited neither to the graphic, nor to the book, nor even to discourse, and even less to the semantic, representational, symbolic, ideal, or ideological sphere'.[169] That text describes a force which is irreducible to, and uncontrollable by, the human is recognised by Brinkema in her appeal to 'sensitivity to textuality'.[170] Such a sensitivity makes visible the ways in which human attempts at mastery and projection are destined to fail. Literature, as 'the institution which allows one to *say everything*', is an event through which the human both projects itself and encounters the limits of its own powers.[171] This book presupposes that literature offers a privileged space in which these questions – and the emergence of the textual – are played out. It endorses Pick's claim that literature reflects 'the incomplete becoming – the struggle of the human to assume and to inhabit a definite form' and 'to come to terms with and give shape to an entirely accidental embodiment'.[172] It follows Brinkema and Vermeulen in suggesting that this is how we should understand the role of affect in literature; not, as Vermeulen describes, 'a fatefully pre-linguistic and pre-conscious substance, but an effect of the inability of literary works to fully contain the intensities they irresistibly unleash'. Textual affect is, as Vermeulen notes via Colebrook, 'a placeholder for unreadability'.[173] In this sense, we must resist the domestication of affect in the form of cross-species emotions and experience, and think again about the interruptive potential of the alliance between affect, text and theory, where theory is not an instance of human mastery, but, as Colebrook writes, 'an acceptance of a distinction between a strong sense of the inhuman (that which exists beyond, beyond all givenness and imaging, and beyond all relations) and an unfounded imperative that we must therefore give ourselves a law'.[174]

OUTLINE

This book consists of five chapters. Chapter 1 examines nonhuman animal suffering and the generation of empathy in Yann Martel's allegorical novels *Life of Pi* and *Beatrice and Virgil*. Informed by Haraway's assertion that nonhuman animals 'are not an alibi for other themes', it compares *Beatrice and Virgil*, a novel censured for the parallels it draws between the Holocaust and nonhuman animal suffering, to Art Spiegelman's graphic novel *Maus*.[175] It considers our responsibilities to real and figurative animals and the tools through which we assess and compare suffering, asking whether we should cultivate cross-species empathy as a means to develop cross-species ethics, or whether empathy is limiting in its aims and reach. Assessing Martel's depiction of nonhuman animals' suffering and vulnerability, it turns to the work of Derrida, Wolfe, Alaimo, Pick and others, as well as considering the implications of Elaine Scarry's scholarship on the relationship between pain, language and subjectivity for nonhuman animals. Focusing, too, on Martel's interrogation of the complexities of the storytelling impulse and the possibilities of a cross-species storytelling, it argues that Martel adopts an ironic or deconstructive approach to storytelling, shuttling between critique (stories tend towards the reactionary reiteration of the familiar) and affirmation (stories promise imaginative innovation which enables '*reworlding*').[176] It closes by proposing an inhuman ethics, drawing on Martel's enactment of deconstructive storytelling and Derrida's account of ethics beginning from 'the monstrously other [. . .] the unrecognizable'.[177]

Chapter 2 considers the relationship between the story of the 'anthropos' and twentieth- and twenty-first-century representations of nonhuman primates. Examining Haraway's critique of primatological practices and narratives, it explores the ways in which an account of human identity generated in response to nonhuman primates substitutes for an 'anthropos' which is always in flight, or now, as Claire Colebrook and Tom Cohen argue, only constructed retroactively in response to apocalyptic (and ultimately, redemptive) Anthropocene narratives. Accordingly, the chapter traces the impact of the Anthropocene on our conception of the human, identifying a tension between the tendency to employ the Anthropocene narrative as a tool to reunify the human subject and reinforce species identity in service of a common cause, and the understanding that humanity is splintered according to different degrees of responsibility for environmental destruction; in other words, that the universalism of the universal human was always fictitious. In response to Haraway's appeal for a less anthropocentric storytelling with 'many tellers and hearers'[178] and Colebrook's contention that the figure of Man is 'an effect of a failure to read',[179] this chapter examines Karen Joy Fowler's fictional account of primate relations, *We Are All Completely Beside Ourselves*, interrogating the relationship between the 'anthropos' and anthropomorphism within part of a broader discussion of the value of literary, scientific and philosophical anthropomorphisms. Focusing on Fowler's ambivalence towards anthropomorphism, it considers the relationship between anthropomorphism and empathy. Drawing on Tom Tyler's distinction between types of anthropomorphism, this chapter interrogates his contention that anthropomorphism necessarily depends on the mistaken designation of specific attributes as uniquely human. Rather, it argues that anthropomorphism can be a useful, if clumsy, tool to explore interspecies difference, provided that we reject the assumption that either term – the human or its nonhuman associate –

has a fixed essence. Similarly, arguing that both anthropomorphism and empathy are inescapable components of cross-species relations, it contends that we should welcome anthropomorphic empathy in its capacity to stimulate new ethical and political responses to nonhuman life from affective responses to cross-species similarity, while acknowledging its lingering anthropocentrism and generating new kinds of response to nonhuman life. The final part of the chapter combines the notion of a 'chimped-up' writing with Haraway's account of cross-species storytelling to ask whether different modes of primatological reading and writing might generate alternatives to the figure of Man which are better able to acknowledge and fulfil our ethical responsibilities to nonhuman life by generating a shift from a 'politics of representation' to a 'politics of articulation'.[180]

Chapter 3 puts the novels of Jim Crace, distinguished, one commentator notes, by an 'occultish grammar of objects – beetles, stones, cracks in wood', in conversation with Graham Harman's brand of Speculative Realism, Object-Oriented Philosophy. Beginning with a discussion of the development of OOP in contradistinction to Bruno Latour's Actor Network Theory, it assesses the claims made by Harman for the superiority of OOP over contemporary relational ontologies, such as that espoused by Bennett. Turning to Crace, the chapter argues that Crace's fiction enacts a sustained movement away from anthropocentrism, demonstrating the collaborative nature of storytelling and absenting the human from a variety of different landscapes. In their examination of the 'allure' of objects, it argues that these novels espouse a position closer to Harman than Bennett. Finally, the chapter addresses Harman's presentation of aesthetics as first philosophy, asking whether this claim might illuminate the interruptive nature of affect.

Chapter 4 interrogates the desire for order and mastery inherent in natural history, focusing on entomological collecting and the changing figure of the collector. Beginning with Walter Benjamin's claim that 'ownership is the most intimate relationship that one can have to objects', this chapter considers the ethical and aesthetic implications of collecting insects.[181] Arguing that the discourse of insect collecting is one of objectification and domination, and that entomological classification and practices continue to reflect concerns about sex and gender which were present in its eighteenth- and nineteenth-century instantiations, it aligns the objectification of women with that of insects. Interrogating the notion of aesthetic disinterestedness as licence for such objectification, it asks whether aesthetic disinterestedness permits an empathetic disengagement which, at its worst, leads to a sociopathic lack of ethical awareness. The chapter has three parts, focusing on John Fowles's *The*

Collector, insects in contemporary nature writing and, finally, the most famous lepidopterist of all, Vladimir Nabokov. The concluding section examines the relationship between ethics and aesthetics, appealing for the joint necessity of cross-species empathetic engagement and a distancing that is alert to its own subjective positioning.

In contrast to Chapter 4, which focuses on captured and pinned lepidoptera, Chapter 5 tracks the flying and scurrying of disparate unpinned insects, emphasising both their instrumental and intrinsic value and the necessity of supplementing empathetic with non-empathetic approaches when thinking and writing with them. It will examine three figures of the insect: the first, the insect as *other* other in Damien Hirst's work, exposes the limitations of empathetic responses to nonhuman life. The second, the queer insect, draws on Elizabeth Grosz's reading of Darwin, Roger Caillois's interpretation of mimicry and Lee Edelman's work in queer theory to argue that the insect provides a figure of the inhuman that counters logics of heteronormative futurity. The final figure, that of the disgusting insect, is generated through Braidotti's reading of Clarice Lispector's novel *The Passion of G.H.* and Derrida's reading of Kant's third critique, and advances disgust as a useful tool – one that defies figuration – in the development of an inhuman ethics. The book concludes by outlining a methodology for such an ethics.

NOTES

1. Frans de Waal, *The Age of Empathy: Nature's Lessons for a Kinder Society* (London: Souvenir Press, 2010 [2009]), p. ix. His prediction here refers specifically to American politics.
2. Kari Weil, 'Empathy', in *The Edinburgh Companion to Animal Studies*, ed. Ron Broglio, Undine Sellbach and Lynn Turner (Edinburgh: Edinburgh University Press, 2018), p. 126.
3. Amy Coplan and Peter Goldie, 'Introduction', in *Empathy: Philosophical and Psychological Perspectives*, ed. Amy Coplan and Peter Goldie (Oxford: Oxford University Press, 2011), pp. ix–xlvii (p. ix).
4. Adam Smith, *The Theory of Moral Sentiments*, http://www.earlymoderntexts.com/assets/pdfs/smith1759.pdf (accessed 19 February 2019), p. 1.
5. Suzanne Keen, *Empathy and the Novel* (Oxford: Oxford University Press, 2007), p. 39.
6. Nancy Eisenberg provides an excellent summary of these. See Nancy Eisenberg, 'Empathy and Sympathy', in *Handbook of Emotions*, ed. Michael Lewis and Jeannette M. Haviland Jones (New York: The Guildford Press, 2nd edn, 2000), pp. 677–91.

7. Amy Coplan, 'Understanding Empathy: Its Features and Effects', in *Empathy: Philosophical and Psychological Perspectives*, ed. Amy Coplan and Peter Goldie (Oxford: Oxford University Press, 2011), pp. 3–18 (p. 4).

8. Eisenberg, 'Empathy and Sympathy', p. 677.

9. Coplan, 'Understanding Empathy', p. 17.

10. Keen, *Empathy and the Novel*, p. 4.

11. Eisenberg, 'Empathy and Sympathy', p. 677.

12. Heide L. Maibom, 'Introduction: (Almost) Everything You Ever Wanted to Know about Empathy', in *Empathy and Morality*, ed. Heidi L. Maibom (New York: Oxford University Press, 2014), pp. 1–40 (p. 2).

13. Martin L. Hoffman, *Empathy and Moral Development: Implications for Caring and Justice* (Cambridge: Cambridge University Press, 2000), p. 29. See also Alexa Weik von Mossner, *Affective Ecologies: Empathy, Emotion, and Environmental Narrative* (Columbus: Ohio State University Press, 2017), p. 80.

14. Weik von Mossner, *Affective Ecologies*, p. 80; Elisa Aaltola, *Varieties of Empathy: Moral Psychology and Animal Ethics* (New York: Rowman and Littlefield, 2018), para 10.64.

15. See, for example, Vittorio Gallese's claim that 'at the very beginning of our lifetime, we almost immediately interact with others by *reproducing* some of their behaviours'. Vittorio Gallese, 'Embodied Simulation: From Mirror Neuron Systems to Interpersonal Relations', in *Empathy and Fairness: Novartis Foundation Symposium 278* (Chichester: Wiley, 2007), pp. 3–19 (p. 3).

16. 'These neurons discharge not only when the monkey executes goal-related hand actions like grasping objects, but also when observing other individuals (monkeys or humans) executing similar actions.' Gallese, 'Embodied Simulation', p. 5.

17. Gallese, 'Embodied Simulation', pp. 10–11.

18. Derek Matravers, *Empathy* (Cambridge: Polity, 2017), p. 52.

19. Julinna C. Oxley, *The Moral Dimensions of Empathy: Limits and Applications in Ethical Theory and Practice* (New York: Palgrave Macmillan, 2011), p. 16.

20. Kristin Andrews and Lori Gruen, 'Empathy in Other Apes', in *Empathy and Morality*, ed. Heidi L. Maibom (New York: Oxford University Press, 2014), pp. 193–209 (p. 195).

21. Aaltola, *Varieties of Empathy*, para. 14.141.

22. Martha Nussbaum, *Upheavals of Thought: The Intelligence of Emotions* (Cambridge: Cambridge University Press, 2001), p. 327.

23. Amy Coplan, 'Empathetic Engagement with Narrative Fictions', *The Journal of Aesthetics and Art Criticism*, 62.2 (2004), 141–52 (p. 145).

24. Neil Roughley and Thomas Schramme, 'Forms of Fellow Feeling: Empathy, Sympathy, Concern and Moral Agency', in *Forms of Fellow Feeling: Empathy, Sympathy, Concern and Moral Agency*, ed. Neil

Roughley and Thomas Schramme (Cambridge: Cambridge University Press, 2018), pp. 3–55 (p. 18).

25. Roughley and Schramme, 'Forms of Fellow Feeling', p. 18.
26. Michael Slote, 'Empathy as an Instinct', in *Forms of Fellow Feeling: Empathy, Sympathy, Concern and Moral Agency*, ed. Neil Roughley and Thomas Schramme (Cambridge: Cambridge University Press, 2018), pp. 133–64 (p. 133).
27. Matravers, *Empathy*, p. 23.
28. Martin L. Hoffman, 'Empathy, Justice, and Social Change', in *Empathy and Morality*, ed. Heidi L. Maibom (New York: Oxford University Press, 2014), pp. 71–96 (p. 96).
29. Dan Batson, 'Empathy, Altruism and Helping: Conceptual Distinctions, Empirical Relations', in *Forms of Fellow Feeling: Empathy, Sympathy, Concern and Moral Agency*, ed. Neil Roughley and Thomas Schramme (Cambridge: Cambridge University Press, 2018), pp. 59–77 (p. 59).
30. Oxley, *Moral Dimensions of Empathy*, p. 4.
31. Daryl Koehn, *Rethinking Feminist Ethics: Care, Trust and Empathy* (London: Routledge, 1998), p. 57.
32. Peter Goldie, cited in Coplan, 'Empathetic Engagement', p. 145.
33. Slote, 'Empathy as Instinct', p. 133.
34. Karsten Stueber, cited in Matravers, *Empathy*, p. 18.
35. de Waal, *Age of Empathy*, p. ix.
36. Eugenie Brinkema, *The Forms of the Affects* (Durham, NC: Duke University Press, 2015), p. xi.
37. Lisa Blackman, *Immaterial Bodies: Affect, Embodiment, Mediation* (London: Sage, 2012), p. 86. See also Patricia Ticineto Clough, 'Introduction', in *The Affective Turn: Theorizing the Social*, ed. Patricia Ticineto Clough with Jean Halley (Durham, NC: Duke University Press, 2007), pp. 1–33 (p. 2).
38. For a discussion of this, see Tonya K. Davidson, Ondine Part and Rob Shields, 'Introduction', in *Ecologies of Affect: Placing Nostalgia, Desire and Hope*, ed. Tonya K. Davidson, Ondine Part and Rob Shields (Waterloo, ON: Wilfrid Laurier University Press, 2011), pp. 1–15.
39. Teresa Brennan, *The Transmission of Affect* (Ithaca, NY: Cornell University Press, 2004), p. 6.
40. Brian Massumi, *Politics of Affect* (Cambridge: Polity, 2015), p. 5.
41. Pieter Vermeulen, *Contemporary Literature and the End of the Novel: Creature, Affect, Form* (Basingstoke: Palgrave Macmillan, 2015), p. 11.
42. Melissa Gregg and Gregory J. Seigworth, 'An Inventory of Shimmers', in *The Affect Theory Reader*, ed. Melissa Gregg and Gregory J. Seigworth (Durham, NC: Duke University Press, 2010), pp. 1–28 (p. 3).
43. Massumi, *Politics of Affect*, p. 4.
44. Davidson, Park and Shields, 'Introduction', p. 6.

45. Vermeulen, *Contemporary Literature*, p. 8.
46. Sara Ahmed, *The Cultural Politics of Emotion* (Edinburgh: Edinburgh University Press, 2014), pp. 1, 8.
47. Brinkema, *Forms of the Affects*, p. xii.
48. On the latter, see Clough, 'Introduction', p. 2.
49. Brinkema, *Forms of the Affects*, p. xiv.
50. Rosi Braidotti, *The Posthuman* (Cambridge: Polity, 2013), p. 188.
51. Jacques Derrida, *Rogues: Two Essays on Reason*, trans. Pascale-Anne Brault and Michael Naas (Stanford: Stanford University Press, 2005), p. 39.
52. Vermeulen, *Contemporary Literature*, pp. 8–9.
53. Rei Terada, *Feeling in Theory: Emotion after the 'Death of the Subject'* (Cambridge, MA: Harvard University Press, 2001), p. 3.
54. Terada, *Feeling in Theory*, p. 41.
55. Terada, *Feeling in Theory*, p. 111.
56. Blackman, *Immaterial Bodies*, p. 1.
57. See, for example, Gregg and Seigworth, 'An Inventory of Shimmers', p. 1: '[affect] is found in those intensities that pass body to body [. . .], in those resonances that circulate about, between, and sometimes stick to bodies and worlds, *and* in the very passages or variations between these intensities and resonances themselves'.
58. Brinkema, *Forms of the Affects*, p. 24.
59. Brinkema, *Forms of the Affects*, p. 32.
60. Vermeulen, *Contemporary Literature*, p. 14; Brinkema, *Forms of the Affects*, p. xv.
61. Brinkema, *Forms of the Affects*, p. 33.
62. For a comprehensive summary of, and insightful reflection on, contemporary animal studies and its philosophical underpinnings, see Derek Ryan, *Animal Theory: A Critical Introduction* (Edinburgh: Edinburgh University Press, 2015).
63. Anat Pick, *Creaturely Poetics: Animality and Vulnerability in Literature and Film* (New York: Columbia University Press, 2011), p. 11.
64. Hannah Arendt, *Origins of Totalitarianism* (New York: Meridian, 1958), p. 297.
65. Simone Weil, 'Human Responsibility', in *Simone Weil: An Anthology*, ed. Siân Miles (London: Penguin, 2005), pp. 69–98 (p. 81).
66. Cora Diamond, 'Injustice and Animals', in *Slow Cures and Bad Philosophers: Essays on Wittgenstein, Medicine and Bioethics*, ed. Carl Elliott (Durham, NC: Duke University Press, 2001), p. 120.
67. Deborah Slicer, cited in Cary Wolfe, *Animal Rites: American Culture, the Discourse of Species, and Posthumanist Theory* (Chicago: University of Chicago Press, 2003), p. 36.
68. Donna Haraway, *Staying with the Trouble: Making Kin in the Chthulucene* (Durham, NC: Duke University Press, 2016), p. 5.
69. Cora Diamond, 'The Difficulty of Reality and the Difficulty of

Philosophy', *Partial Answers: Journal of Literature and the History of Ideas*, 1.2 (2003), 1–26 (p. 13).

70. Diamond, 'Difficulty of Reality', p. 8.

71. Regan, cited in Cathryn Bailey, 'On the Backs of Animals: The Valorization of Reason in Contemporary Animal Ethics', *Ethics and the Environment*, 10.1 (2005), 1–17 (pp. 1–2).

72. Tom Regan, *Defending Animal Rights* (Urbana: University of Illinois Press, 2001), p. 63.

73. See, for example, Marc Bekoff, *Minding Animals: Awareness, Emotions and Heart* (Oxford: Oxford University Press, 2002), and Frans de Waal, *Chimpanzee Politics: Power and Sex Amongst Apes* (Baltimore: Johns Hopkins University Press, 2007).

74. Jacques Derrida, *The Animal That Therefore I Am*, trans. David Wills (Ashland, OH: Fordham University Press, 2008), pp. 7, 105.

75. Judith Butler, *Senses of the Subject* (New York: Fordham University Press, 2015), p. 15.

76. Koehn, *Rethinking Feminist Ethics*, p. 5.

77. Braidotti, *The Posthuman*, p. 49.

78. Bruno Latour, 'Where Are the Missing Masses? The Sociology of a Few Mundane Artifacts', in *Shaping Technology – Building Society*, ed. Wiebe Bijker and John Law (Cambridge, MA: MIT Press, 1992), pp. 151–80 (p. 165).

79. Bruno Latour, *We Have Never Been Modern*, trans. Catherine Porter (London: Harvester Wheatsheaf, 1993).

80. Jane Bennett, *Vibrant Matter: A Political Ecology of Things* (Durham, NC: Duke University Press, 2010), pp. xiii, 10, 9.

81. Bennett, *Vibrant Matter*, p. 31.

82. Bennett, *Vibrant Matter*, p. 37.

83. Alexis Shotwell, *Against Purity: Living Ethically in Compromised Times* (Minneapolis: University of Minnesota Press, 2016), p. 85; Stacy Alaimo, *Exposed: Environmental Politics and Pleasures in Posthuman Times* (Minneapolis: University of Minnesota Press, 2016), p. 112.

84. Donna Haraway, *Manifestly Haraway* (Minneapolis: University of Minnesota Press, 2016), p. 11.

85. Donna Haraway, 'Anthropocene, Capitalocene, Plantationocene, Chthulucene: Making Kin', *Environmental Humanities*, 6 (2015), 159–65 (p. 159).

86. Donna Haraway, *The Companion Species Manifesto: Dogs, People and Significant Otherness* (Chicago: Prickly Paradigm Press, 2003), p. 6.

87. Aaltola, *Varieties of Empathy*, para. 15.7.

88. Lori Gruen, *Entangled Empathy: An Alternative Ethic for our Relationships with Animals* (New York: Lantern Books, 2015), p. 14.

89. Gruen, *Entangled Empathy*, p. 3.

90. Gruen, *Entangled Empathy*, p. 29.

91. Joan C. Tronto, *Moral Boundaries: A Political Argument for an Ethic of Care* (London: Routledge, 1993), p. 102.

92. Tronto, *Moral Boundaries*, p. 103.

93. Maria Puig de la Bellacasa, *Matters of Care: Speculative Ethics in More Than Human Worlds* (Minneapolis: University of Minnesota Press, 2017), p. 6.

94. Koehn, *Rethinking Feminist Ethics*, p. 7.

95. Shotwell, *Against Purity*, p. 121.

96. Bellacasa, *Matters of Care*, p. 70.

97. Bellacasa, *Matters of Care*, pp. 78, 221.

98. Haraway, 'Anthropocene', p. 162.

99. Koehn, *Rethinking Feminist Ethics*, p. 48.

100. Bennett, *Vibrant Matter*, p. ix.

101. Joanna Zylinska, *Minimal Ethics for the Anthropocene* (London: Open Humanities Press, 2014), p. 42.

102. Karen Barad, *Meeting the Universe Halfway: Quantum Physics and the Entanglement of Matter and Meaning* (Durham, NC: Duke University Press, 2007), p. 185.

103. Graham Harman, 'Art Without Relations', http://artreview.com/features/september_2014_graham_harman_relations/ (accessed 14 July 2016).

104. Claire Colebrook, 'Not Symbiosis, Not Now: Why Anthropogenic Change is Not Really Human', *Oxford Literary Review*, 34.2 (2012), 185–209 (p. 193).

105. Bentham, cited in Derrida, *The Animal That Therefore I Am*, p. 27.

106. Derrida, *The Animal That Therefore I Am*, p. 28.

107. Derrida, *The Animal That Therefore I Am*, p. 93.

108. Derrida, *The Animal That Therefore I Am*, p. 28.

109. Cary Wolfe, *Before the Law: Humans and Other Animals in a Biopolitical Frame* (Chicago: University of Chicago Press, 2013), p. 10.

110. Wolfe, *Before the Law*, pp. 30, 104.

111. Alaimo, *Exposed*, p. 5.

112. Myra J. Hird, 'Waste, Landfills, and an Environmental Ethic of Vulnerability', *Ethics and the Environment*, 18.1 (2013), 105–24 (p. 107).

113. James Mensch, 'Empathy and Rationality', in *The Politics of Empathy: New Interdisciplinary Perspectives on an Ancient Phenomenon*, ed. Barbara Weber, Eva Marsal and Takara Dobashi (Berlin: Lit, 2011), pp. 17–24 (p. 21).

114. Diamond, 'Difficulty of Reality', p. 22.

115. Diamond, 'Difficulty of Reality', p. 15.

116. Weil's influence on Pick is evident here. See Weil: 'Human thought is unable to acknowledge the reality of affliction.' Cited in Diamond, 'Difficulty of Reality', p. 23.

117. Pick, *Creaturely Poetics*, p. 5.

118. Pick, *Creaturely Poetics*, p. 188.

119. Judith Butler, *Precarious Life: The Powers of Mourning and Violence* (London: Verso, 2004), p. 25.

120. Butler, *Precarious Life*, p. xiii.

121. Butler, *Precarious Life*, p. 31.

122. Butler, *Precarious Life*, p. 20.

123. Wolfe, *Before the Law*, p. 20.

124. Judith Butler, *Frames of War: When is Life Grievable?* (London: Verso, 2016), p. xvi.

125. Butler, *Frames of War*, pp. 1, xxv.

126. Butler, *Precarious Life*, p. 25. On this point, see also Brian Massumi's concession that 'there needs to be an ecology of practices that does have room for pursuing or defending rights based on an identification with a certain categorized social group, that asserts and defends a self-interest but doesn't just do that'. Massumi, *Politics of Affect*, p. 42.

127. Butler, *Frames of War*, p. xxvi.

128. Thom van Dooren, Ursula Munster, Eben Kirksey, Deborah Bird Rose, Matthew Chrulew and Anna Tsing, 'Multispecies Studies: Cultivating Arts of Attentiveness', *Environmental Humanities*, 8.1 (2016), 1–23 (p. 15).

129. Haraway, *Manifestly Haraway*, p. 268.

130. Butler, *Frames of War*, p. 76.

131. Butler, *Frames of War*, p. 76.

132. Butler, *Frames of War*, p. 76.

133. Joshua May, 'Empathy and Intersubjectivity', in *The Routledge Handbook of Philosophy of Empathy*, ed. Heidi L. Maibom (London: Routledge, 2017), para 26.48.

134. Coplan, 'Empathetic Engagement', p. 145.

135. Lou Agosta, *Empathy in the Context of Philosophy* (New York: Palgrave Macmillan, 2010), p. 75.

136. Coplan, 'Empathetic Engagement', p. 144.

137. Dan Zahavi, *Self and Other: Exploring Subjectivity, Empathy and Shame* (Oxford: Oxford University Press, 2014), p. 189.

138. Paul Bloom, *Against Empathy: The Case for Rational Compassion* (London: Vintage, 2007), p. 2.

139. Bloom, *Against Empathy*, p. 31.

140. Bloom, *Against Empathy*, p. 9.

141. Jesse J. Prinz, 'Is Empathy Necessary for Morality?', in *Empathy: Philosophical and Psychological Perspectives*, ed. Amy Coplan and Peter Goldie (Oxford: Oxford University Press, 2011), pp. 211–29 (pp. 226–7).

142. Koehn, *Rethinking Feminist Ethics*, p. 58; Matravers, *Empathy*, p. 120.

143. Aaltola, *Varieties of Empathy*, para. 8.18.

144. Aaltola, *Varieties of Empathy*, para. 15.13.

145. Weil, 'Empathy', p. 128.

146. Gruen, *Entangled Empathy*, p. 68.

147. Stephen Loo and Undine Sellbach, 'Insect Affects', *Angelaki*, 20.3 (2015), 79–88 (p. 86).

148. Rosi Braidotti, *Metamorphoses: Towards a Materialist Theory of Becoming* (Cambridge: Polity, 2002), p. 149.

149. Prinz, 'Is Empathy Necessary for Morality?', p. 212.

150. Loo and Sellbach, 'Insect Affects', p. 80.

151. Pick, *Creaturely Poetics*, p. 193.

152. Aaltola, *Varieties of Empathy*, para. 15.14.

153. Jonathan Gottschall, *The Storytelling Animal: How Stories Make Us Human* (Wilmington, MA: Mariner Books, 2013).

154. Martin Heidegger, 'The Origin of the Work of Art', in *Off the Beaten Track*, ed. and trans. Julian Young and Kenneth Haynes (Cambridge: Cambridge University Press, 2002), p. 23.

155. Haraway, *Staying with the Trouble*, p. 39.

156. J. M. Coetzee, *The Lives of Animals*, The Tanner Lectures on Human Values, Princeton University, 15 and 16 October 1997, https://tan nerlectures.utah.edu/_documents/a-to-z/c/Coetzee99.pdf (accessed 18 February 2019), p. 133.

157. Coetzee, *The Lives of Animals*, p. 133.

158. Keen, *Empathy and the Novel*, p. 28.

159. Jakob von Uexküll, *A Foray into the Worlds of Animals and Humans*, trans. Joseph D. O'Neil (Minneapolis: University of Minnesota Press, 2010 [1934]), p. 199.

160. David Herman, 'Storyworld/Umwelt: Nonhuman Experiences in Graphic Narratives', *SubStance*, 40.1 (2011), 156–81 (p. 159).

161. Herman, 'Storyworld/Umwelt', p. 159.

162. Keen, *Empathy and the Novel*, p. 18.

163. Haraway, *Manifestly Haraway*, p. 215.

164. Van Dooren et al., 'Multispecies Studies', pp. 2–3.

165. Hird, 'Waste', p. 109.

166. Haraway, cited in Joseph Schneider, *Donna Haraway: Live Theory* (London: Continuum, 2005), p. 75.

167. Jacques Derrida, 'Deconstruction and the Other', in *States of Mind: Dialogues with Contemporary Thinkers on the European Mind*, ed. Richard Kearney (Manchester: Manchester University Press, 1995), p. 173.

168. Colebrook, 'Not Symbiosis', p. 196.

169. Jacques Derrida, *Limited Inc.*, trans. Samuel Weber and Jeffrey Mehlman, ed. Gerald Graff (Evanston: Northwestern University Press, 1988), p. 148.

170. Brinkema, *Forms of the Affects*, p. 37.

171. Jacques Derrida, '"This Strange Institution Called Literature": An Interview with Jacques Derrida', trans. and ed. Rachel Bowlby, in *Acts of Literature*, ed. Derek Attridge (London: Routledge, 1992), p. 36.

172. Pick, *Creaturely Poetics*, p. 83.

173. Vermeulen, *Contemporary Literature*, p. 9, citing Claire Colebrook, 'The Calculus of Individual Worth', in Tom Cohen, Claire Colebrook and J. Hillis Miller, *Theory and the Disappearing Future: On De Man, on Benjamin* (London: Routledge, 2012), p. 144.
174. Claire Colebrook, *Death of the PostHuman: Essays on Extinction, Vol. 1* (London: Open Humanities Press, 2014), p. 31.
175. Haraway, *The Companion Species Manifesto*, p. 5.
176. Haraway, *Manifestly Haraway*, p. 215.
177. Jacques Derrida, *The Beast and the Sovereign: Volume I*, trans. Geoffrey Bennington (Chicago: University of Chicago Press, 2009), p. 108.
178. Donna Haraway, *Primate Visions: Gender, Race and Nature in the World of Modern Science* (London: Verso, 1989), p. 8.
179. Colebrook 'What is the Anthropo-Political?', p. 93.
180. While Cohen and Colebrook use the term 'Anthropos' specifically to refer to the subject that is generated by, or at least perceived in light of, the Anthropocene, I shall be using the terms Man and Anthropos interchangeably to illustrate that this Anthropocene subject does not break with, but reinforces, the 'metaphysical heritage' of the figure of Man.
181. Walter Benjamin, *Illuminations*, trans. Harry Zohn, ed. Hannah Arendt (New York: Schocken Books, 1969), p. 67.

1. Fragile Bodies, Cross-species Empathy and Suspended Allegories: 'It hurt, it was painful – that's all there is to say'

A fascination with the power and possibilities of storytelling pervades Yann Martel's fiction, from the early story 'The Facts behind the Helsinki Roccamatios', a paean to 'the transformative wizardry of the imagination',[1] through his best-selling novel *Life of Pi*, which promises 'a story that will make you believe in God',[2] and its less critic-friendly and altogether more sceptical successor, *Beatrice and Virgil*. For Martel, storytelling is a fitting response to the bleakest and most destructive circumstances; in the face of imminent death, Paul, in 'The Facts behind the Helsinki Roccamatios', commits to a storytelling pact designed to 'embrace the world' and 'destroy void'.[3] In *Beatrice and Virgil*, unceremoniously dismissed by critic Sarah Churchwell as 'by turns pretentious, humourless, tedious, and obvious', Martel is ruthlessly interrogative of the storytelling impulse, exposing it as a confused amalgam of desires to witness, master and celebrate.[4]

The possibility that storytelling and empathy might be inexorably connected is addressed by Suzanne Keen in *Empathy and the Novel*. We perceive empathetic abilities as a gauge of psychological health and storytelling as key to the construction of human communities; empathy, like reading, is 'a complex imaginative process involving both cognition and emotion'.[5] There is a long debate as to whether the imaginative and empathetic engagement required by reading literature might make us better, or even worse, people,[6] with a shift in our perception of the moral value of fiction occurring, Keen contends, with the translation of *Einfühlung* in the early twentieth century.[7] Can fiction teach us to be empathetic? Can reading help us to convert empathetic impulses into 'prosocial action'?[8] As Keen notes: 'The same drive to affiliate with others for comfort and safety that expresses itself in empathy and sympathy may also play a role in our species' enthusiasm for narrative.'[9]

In positing a connection between empathy and storytelling, however, we tend to assume that these empathetic feelings are generated and shared among humans, with nonhuman animals reduced to tropes. The 'use of animal-signs for charting the experience of the world' is, John Berger contends, 'universal', with the metaphorical nature of the human–animal relationship resulting in the high likelihood that 'the first metaphor was animal'.[10] Humans think figuratively and animals, ubiquitous and 'ambiguous', are perfect tools for figurative thought, for the human across history to track itself and its environment.[11] Animal characters and anthropomorphised figures are part of 'a perceptual strategy by which we attempt to glean the greatest meaning from the world around us'.[12] For Jacques Derrida, the human is not just a 'storytelling animal', but an 'autobiographical animal' who fabulates in order to construct a self-identity that is not pre-given.[13] The figure of the 'animal' appears as a negative reflection – lacking sentience, rationality, or divinity – or serves as 'the abyssal limit of the human [. . .] the bordercrossing from which vantage man dares to announce himself to himself'.[14] As guarantor of the plenitude of human self-image, the 'animal' is denied self-image or *ipseity*, its inability to recognise or refer to itself, or to leave a linguistic trace, taken for granted. It is thus assumed that human stewardship entails ventriloquising nonhuman muteness by naming, classifying and dominating the 'animal'. For Derrida, the human autobiography is underpinned by the systematic subjugation – literal and figurative – of the 'animal'.

That there might be other modes of storytelling is suggested by Derrida's vision of a '*zootobiography*' which would acknowledge and examine animal abilities to construct traces, to self-relate, to communicate and to tell stories.[15] Derrida's 'zootobiography' would entail a radical break with the 'post-Cartesian genealogy' of philosophical misrepresentations of animal life.[16] It would contain cognitive and affective dimensions. The former would require the supersession of the 'general singular' term 'animal' – which licenses the erasure of nonhuman animal difference and overlooks the 'unsubstitutable singularity'[17] of each individual creature – by an alternative conceptual schema instantiated in the figure of the 'animot'. 'Animot' gestures towards its homonym *animaux*, ensuring 'the plural' is 'heard in the singular' and acknowledging the existence of a 'multiplicity of heterogeneous structures and limits';[18] it foregrounds the power of the word, highlighting the force of naming and classifying, and questioning the propriety of (self-)naming as an immovable limit between human and animal; and it exposes the contingency of human value systems. The latter, the affective component, would compel an encounter between embodied beings and entertain the previously disavowed possibility of animal gaze, address and response; 'the animal looks at us', Derrida recounts, 'and we are naked before it. Thinking perhaps begins there.'[19] This interaction, underpinned by active engagement on both sides, would open a new kind of vulnerability, the capacity to affect and be affected by the other: a generative 'passivity'.[20]

This chapter will focus on Yann Martel's allegorical novels *Life of Pi* and *Beatrice and Virgil* to assess the possibility of articulating the kind of cross-species vulnerability identified by Derrida, Wolfe, Pick and others, and its connection to cross-species empathy, where empathy is understood as imaginative perspective-taking: '*using our imaginations as a tool so as to adopt a different perspective in order to grasp how things appear (or feel) from there*'.[21] Both acknowledging and, ultimately, resisting the temptation to reinstate the human as master-storyteller, Martel adopts an ironic or deconstructive approach to storytelling, shuttling between critique (stories tend towards the reactionary reiteration of the familiar) and affirmation (stories promise imaginative innovation which enables '*reworlding*').[22] The chapter will close by proposing an inhuman ethics, grounded in deconstructive storytelling.

WRITING ANIMAL SUFFERING I: *LIFE OF PI* AND LITERARY EMPATHY

In his reading of Martel's Booker Prize-winning novel *Life of Pi*, Arne De Boever invokes the language of the controversial political theorist Carl Schmitt to describe protagonist Pi Patel's situation. Shipwrecked on a journey from India to Canada with his family, Pi offers two accounts of his improbable survival. In the first, he is surrounded by dangerous zoo animals, including a Bengal tiger, with which he learns to live harmoniously; in the second, a bleaker tale of brutality and cannibalism, he has human company. Trapped in the lifeboat, De Boever writes, Pi inhabits 'a situation in which a human being is stripped of all legal and political protections, and is confronting her or his life-world from scratch, outside the usual guarantees of rights or regulations'. In Schmitt's phrase, Pi occupies 'the state of exception'.[23] Schmitt invokes the 'exception' to explain sovereignty; for him, the 'sovereign is he who decides on the exception', where the usual rule of law is suspended.[24] In his identification of 'bare life' (through the figure of the *homo sacer* in Roman law), Italian philosopher Giorgio Agamben outlines a condition that is synonymous neither with *zoē* (natural life) nor *bios* (politicised life) – as distinguished by Aristotle – but is the politicisation of natural life by means of its exclusion; bare life is that which 'cannot be sacrificed and yet may be killed'.[25] For Agamben, there is a structural parallel between the sovereign and the *homo sacer*; while the sovereign is, 'at the same time, outside and inside the juridical order', the *homo sacer* is figured in law through 'an inclusive exclusion'.[26] In De Boever's reading, Pi quickly transforms the 'state of exception' into a 'state of government' over the one remaining animal – the others having died or been eaten – a Bengal tiger named Richard Parker.[27] Like Robinson Crusoe, De Boever argues, Pi becomes a model of anthropocentric sovereignty. By his account, Pi's narrative is an example of human superiority and his relationship with Richard Parker one of 'enlightened despotism'.[28]

De Boever's perception of Pi's survival as the triumph of human sovereignty is shared by other critics. James Wood welcomes 'the familiar pleasures of a survivor story', whereas Florence Stratton, more critically, finds 'a very conventional [. . .] story of male courage, endurance, and survival'.[29] Philip Armstrong distrusts the outward appearance of the novel as 'an allegory of biodiversity' as a dupe on the grounds that Pi, speaking, Armstrong presumes, for Martel, frames criticism of zoos as misguided, underpinned by a tendency to misunderstand the nature of freedom.[30] Armstrong concludes that 'Martel is less concerned with the fate of animals than with advancing a particular view of the human condition, which is – despite the novel's glossy postmodern style – fundamentally that of humanist modernity.'[31] However, we should be cautious about taking such readings at face value, given that anthropocentrism is so deeply rooted in our reading practices that 'readers have to struggle against the desire to put the human at the center of our interpretations of this novel'.[32] Rather than identifying an imbalance between the roles of Pi and Parker, we might read them as similarly beleaguered, 'two emaciated mammals, parched and starving' (*LP*, 239), employing their different abilities to maximise their chances of survival. In diminishing the gap between the pair and emphasising their shared vulnerability, Martel employs what Keen calls '*authorial strategic empathizing*', redirecting anthropocentric empathetic impulses to cross-species affliction.[33]

Whereas De Boever perceives a reinstatement of the *zoon logon echon* in Pi's behaviour, attentiveness to the animals' embodiment and their 'shared need' undermines the tendency to interpret their relationship in terms of domination and control.[34] Accordingly, Martel's description of Pi and Parker exposes, in Cora Diamond's words, 'the bodily sense of vulnerability to death, [the] sheer animal vulnerability' that we share with nonhuman animals.[35] Disrupting our anthropocentric expectations, Martel 'foreground[s] the tiger's subjectivity, and we witness the breakdown of power positions and speciesist hierarchies that place humans above other animals'.[36] Even Pi's training of Richard Parker is ambiguous; Pi, too, is trained to respond to Parker's needs and to interpret his signal. Both are implicated in an exchange of resources: Pi trades his ability to source food and water for Parker with the emotional support the tiger provides. In this instance of cross-species entanglement, as Wood observes, 'Pi becomes something of an animal' and 'the tiger becomes something of a person', not just figuratively, but literally.[37] In this process, 'Richard Parker's agency butts up against any predetermined expectations of human superiority readers may have.'[38] Derrida's account of the 'Cartesian genealogy' of philosophical misrepresentation of animal life details the way in which these misrepresentations proceed from Descartes' claim that animals react mechanistically, and thus the distinction between humans and other animals is that between the abilities to react (instinctive) and to respond (agential).[39] Martel's responsiveness to the minutiae of Parker's behaviour challenges the assumption that his behaviour is purely reflexive.

Parker's agency and independence emerges most starkly in the final interaction between the two, when Parker leaves the boat and disappears into the jungle, apparently unmoved by Pi's desire for a sentimental denouement to their relationship. McFarland reads this as Martel's measured resistance to 'the final and anthropomorphic moment', a resistance which leaves Parker's 'tigerness' and Pi's 'humanness' uncompromised.[40] We can also read it as resistance to a practice of storytelling which employs and de-natures nonhuman agents in service of a story in which the human always prevails. In his instinct towards freedom above all else, Parker destabilises the endorsement of zoos that provoked Armstrong. Not only do Pi and Parker respond with similar frustration to the shared experience of captivity, but we learn that Pi, figuring as 'bare life', was himself herded on to the boat, not as a human, but 'to be the next goat' (*LP*, 99), to serve as a meal to distract the tiger from the other human survivors. Similar too, in Pi's alternative human account, is the brutal amputation of the sailor's leg for '*fishing bait*' (*LP*, 306). Martel's subtle exposure of the biopolitical processes that determine the value of a life show Agamben's 'anthropological machine', by which lives are valued and classified, in action.[41] Here the class of 'bare life' does not accord any species advantages; this is instantiated by Agamben in the figure of the refugee, 'a limit concept that radically calls into question the fundamental categories of the nation-state, from the birth-nation to the man-citizen link', ultimately de-naturalising the concept of human rights.[42] That the logic upon which humanist subjectivity is grounded remains sacrificial, where the sacrificed is the animal or the human deemed animal, is effectively argued by Derrida, who interrogates the 'noncriminal putting to death', both literal and figurative, of the non-subject.[43] In this context of '*carno-phallogocentrism*', he argues, subjectivity is formed in contradistinction to the killable, with the non-subject's suffering and death rendered imperceptible.[44] The edict 'Thou shalt not kill'[45] is already premised on a speciesism that presupposes, in Wolfe's terms, 'that the full transcendence of the "human" requires the sacrifice of the "animal" and the animalistic'.[46]

Richard Parker is not the only animal to whose needs and capacities Martel makes us attentive. Rather, like Pi, we become witnesses 'to the highly mannered, manifold expressions of life that grace our planet' (*LP*, 15). Here we can see the beginnings of a Derridean 'zootobiography', with each living organism Pi encounters described in draughtsman's detail *in-itself*, not in accordance with its instrumental value. The intruding rat, for example, 'completed the turn of his head with a slow turn of his body, moving his forepaws sideways along the side bench', before dropping to the floor 'with ponderous ease' (*LP*, 152) and is carefully observed from 'its outstretched claws and erect tail, its tiny elongated scrotum and pinpoint anus' (*LP*, 153). Again, we are invited to notice the shared experience of pain; 'the relationship between vulnerability, existence, and beauty cuts across the confines of the human', while emerging through species' and individual difference.[47] The first dorado Pi kills is depicted as 'a magnificent-looking fish, large, fleshy and sleek, with a bulging forehead that speaks of a forceful personality, a very long dorsal fin as proud as a cock's comb' (*LP*, 184), a creature rich with 'unsubstitutable singularity'.[48] Its death-throes are kaleidoscopic: 'Blue, green, red, gold and violet flickered and shimmered neon-like on its surface as it struggled' (*LP*, 185). The narrative's unbroken gaze on Pi at these moments, whose dorado-killing is akin to 'beating a rainbow to death' (*LP*, 185), invites recognition of the ethical dilemmas generated by entanglement. Scholars differ on how we should respond to these: in her critique of Temple Grandin, famous for using insights from her autistic experience to improve slaughterhouse conditions for meat animals, Anat Pick advances an abolitionist approach which aims to eliminate animal suffering.[49] Conversely, assuming that instrumentalisation is inescapable, Donna Haraway argues that to behave ethically is 'to recognize copresence in relations of use and therefore to remember that no balance sheet of benefit and cost will suffice'.[50] For Haraway, 'staying with the trouble' requires acknowledging that entanglement has costs, rather than imagining that human behaviour can avoid causing harm. It means continuing to look in an era of 'unprecedented looking away',[51] and accepting responsibility for the consequences of one's affective engagements, 'to reckon with', as Stacy Alaimo contends, 'the particular entanglements of vulnerability and complicity' that emerge from human behaviours.[52] Similarly, Alexis Shotwell perceives recognition of complicity as essential for action; 'purism is a de-collectivizing, de-mobilizing, paradoxical politics of despair. This world deserves better', she insists.[53]

At its most affecting moments, the novel reminds us that while we might be able to recognise 'the materiality and vulnerability' of all living beings without, as Pick suggests, 'any preliminary criteria of subjectivity and personhood', empathy functions most effectively across narrow species gaps, reinforcing existing alliances.[54] Accordingly, employing a strategy that Alexa Weik von Mossner calls the *'insider perspective'* of strategic empathising, Martel invites us to empathise with the mammalian victims on the lifeboat.[55] These include the orangutan Orange Juice, shamelessly anthropomorphised by Pi: 'to the end she reminded me of us: her eyes expressed fear in such a humanlike way, as did her strained whimpers' (*LP*, 131); her innocent suffering renders her 'like a simian Christ on the cross' (*LP*, 132). Even more affecting is the decline of the mortally wounded zebra, whose prey-animal instinct to minimise its expression of pain is defied by the sheer visibility of its injury. Pi records:

> The zebra was still alive. I couldn't believe it. It had a two-foot-wide hole in its body, a fistula like a freshly erupted volcano spewed half-eaten organs glistening in the light or giving off a dull, dry shine, yet, in its strictly essential parts, it continued to pump with life, if weakly. Movement was confined to a tremor in the rear leg and an occasional blinking of the eyes. I was horrified. I had no idea a living being could sustain so much injury and go on living. (*LP*, 128)

The suffering of the zebra in the first account is mirrored by the suffering of the sailor in the second, of which Pi observes, in a self-conscious echo of the zebra's death: 'I couldn't believe a human being could survive so much pain, so much butchery' (*LP*, 305). Remarkable here is the way that the similarities between the accounts highlight the similarities between human and animal suffering – a shared finitude, in Derrida's vernacular – without diminishing the specificity of the zebra's suffering. In *Life of Pi*, the latter is more memorable than the former, with the zebra exhibiting a quiet courage that evades the human characters. With this attentiveness to animal life and suffering, and challenge to human practices of stewardship, the novel explicitly defies the claim that Martel is uninterested in the 'fate of animals'.

Fiction is, Martel states in his introductory Author's Note, 'the selective transforming of reality [. . .] the twisting of it to bring out its essence' (*LP*, x). This stewarding of reality, of facts, resembles human stewardship of the natural world, which tends to have at least twin aims: to protect and separate human beings, and to limit animal suffering. In *Life of Pi*, a novel that presents two conflicting accounts of the same events, the metaphorical violence of storytelling and the irreducibility of truth to veracity are foregrounded. De Boever is right to suggest that *Life of Pi* generates an allegorical bridge between Pi's two survival narratives by providing cross-species parallels between the narratives' characters. Reading the first story through this link reframes the animal figures as allegorical tools; Pi's nonhuman lifeboat companions enable him to express his own complicity in the brutal violence of the second account. 'The tiger', De Boever writes, 'may have been a means for Pi to separate himself from the animal-like, inhuman dimensions of his life.'[56] James Mensch makes a similar case, viewing Parker as a representation of 'the acts that he [Pi] cannot own'. Mensch continues: 'The assertion that he is a human being conceals from him the truth that his humanity includes the animality of the tiger.'[57] There are clear psychological gains for Pi in projecting the awful events of the second survival story, including his own apparently *inhuman* behaviour, on to an external nonhuman figure.

Accepting the allegorical reading of the first account has drawbacks, however. For De Boever, the allegory – in which the therapeutic service of the first narrative is premised on an absolute difference between humans and animals – is beneficial in that it 'dismantles the tense state of exception'.[58] Yet, as Wolfe argues, moving beyond the anthropocentrism of Schmitt and Agamben, the 'state of exception' demonstrates the fragility of the human/animal distinction, reminding us that we 'are all always already (potential) "animals" before the law'.[59] Like Agamben himself, De Boever is indifferent to the implications of Agamben's work on biopolitics and the 'state of exception' for nonhuman life. Pursuing a different angle, Florence Stratton also roots her reading in allegory. She claims that *Life of Pi* is about aesthetic practice and frames Parker as representative of 'the incantatory or transcendent power of art: the imaginative truths or realities that great art encompasses'.[60] For Stratton, despite Martel's keen attention to the specificity of Parker as a living being, Parker is merely 'an aesthetic object' denoting both the power of art and 'Pi's fate or destiny'.[61] The effect of the singularly allegorical reading, in short, is to render Martel's attentiveness to nonhuman life irrelevant, a classic example of 'careful application of conventional realist techniques' and essential to the construction of Martel's magical realist edifice.[62]

It is clear, therefore, that while *Life of Pi* provokes allegorical readings, it resists the complete collapse of the first narrative into an allegory
of the second. This is made explicit in the final words of the novel, lifted
directly from Mr Okamoto's report, which return us to the first story
to the exclusion of the second: '*Very few castaways can claim to have
survived so long at sea as Mr. Patel, and none in the company of an
adult Bengal tiger*' (*LP*, 319). De Boever frames Martel's 'indecisive-
ness' between allegorical and non-allegorical readings as an 'aesthetic
decision' which prevents the novel from sedimenting around a fixed
meaning.[63] Wood, too, engages with the aesthetic implications of this
decision; *Life of Pi* is, he notes, 'proud to be a delegate for magic realism'
and explicitly defends 'the inevitability of the magical in storytelling'.[64]
Reducing the first account to allegory would undermine this magical
element. While this is true, there is more at stake in the magical than
aesthetic enjoyment; it represents the contingency of singularly rational
(human) explanations of the world. This position is voiced by Pi as he
dismissively responds to his interrogators' request that he reveal the
'straight facts' (*LP*, 302). 'The world isn't just the way it is', he insists. 'It
is how we understand it, no? And in understanding something, we bring
something to it, no? Doesn't that make life a story?' (*LP*, 302). Echoing
Haraway, Pi both endorses the value of embodied experience and examines the arbitrariness of the distinction between fiction and non-fiction.

In upholding the gap between the allegorical and non-allegorical
readings, *Life of Pi* also resists the claim, made by Armstrong and
others, that Martel endorses modern humanism. Stratton, for example,
tracks the ways in which the novel 'is organized around a philosophical
debate about the modern world's privileging of reason over imagination, science over religion, materialism over idealism, fact over fiction
or story'.[65] She concludes that the deconstructive project of *Life of Pi* is
'to replace the Enlightenment belief in the power of reason to liberate
humanity with a belief in the transforming power of story', and identifies a clear critique of modern humanism via an association between
secular materialism and cannibalism – the all-consuming rationality
of modernity.[66] It is no accident that Martel endorses an explicitly
democratic and decentred process of storytelling which accounts for all
living beings. Mensch finds it significant that Pi's name is an irrational
number which 'expresses the inability to find a common measure [. . .]
This suggests that there is the same irrationality in man: there is no
common measure – no ratio linking him either to his animality or to
his divinity. He is in his being made up of incommensurables.'[67] While
Pi resists the erroneous application of reason, he insists that it retains
importance: 'Reason is excellent for getting food, clothing and shelter.

Reason is the very best tool kit. Nothing beats reason for keeping tigers
away. But be excessively reasonable and you risk throwing out the
universe with the bathwater' (*LP*, 298). Martel is certainly not naive
enough to reject the gains of rational modernity; rather, he both rejects
the reduction of human life to modernity and, like Derrida, the assessment of nonhuman life in terms of its perceived rational competence. In
our approach to reason, we must first acknowledge that the opposition
between reason and emotion is a flawed one, that they are interconnected and codependent; in the case of empathy, this means both that
'empathy requires rationality' and that 'empathy allows the other to
call us into question in our positing of the world'.[68] We must then use
this knowledge to review the foundations of ethics as we understand
them; this means challenging the traditional opposition between moral
rationalism and sentimentalism and acknowledging, as Michael Slote
writes, that 'reason has a significant and substantial place within the
ethics of care'.[69] For the novel, this entails a double reading that recognises both the 'rational', allegorical interpretation – in which Parker
represents the inhuman element of Pi – and the reasons why the novel
resists this closed reading.

WRITING ANIMAL SUFFERING II: UNREPRESENTING PAIN IN *BEATRICE AND VIRGIL*

The successor to *Life of Pi*, Martel's 2010 novel *Beatrice and Virgil* is
also preoccupied with the implications of humans being 'story animals'
who are inclined to generate and absorb narrative and to frame events
in ways that add depth and interest or promote understanding.[70] The
protagonist Henry is a successful novelist in a crisis: his third book, a
flip-book about the Holocaust, is dismissed by his editor as 'a complete,
unpublishable failure' (*BV*, 17). As readers we track Henry's story as
he jettisons writing, determined instead to 'write a beautiful life story'
(*BV*, 24) with his newborn son. Events conspire against this peaceful
plan: he is solicited for writing aid by a sinister taxidermist who is
finally exposed as a Nazi sympathiser. Fleeing the taxidermist's burning
shop in fear for his life, Henry finally puts pen to paper, triggering the
reader's realisation that s/he is reading the fictional telling of the novel's
genesis.

Beatrice and Virgil inflamed numerous critics, who were infuri-
ated by its reflexive, preening style and horrified by its treatment of
the Holocaust. Writing in the *New York Times*, Michiko Kakutani
described the novel as 'misconceived and offensive':

Meant as a kind of 'Animal Farm'-like parable, this book reads as an allegory about the Holocaust in which the tragic fate of the title characters – a donkey named Beatrice and a monkey named Virgil, who are stuffed animals in a taxidermy shop – is seen 'through the tragic fate of Jews.' [. . .] [It is] a botched and at times cringe-making fable – a far cry, indeed, from what say, Art Spiegelman achieved in "Maus," his 1986 graphic novel, which in depicting Jews as mice and the Nazis as cats did not diminish the event, but instead goaded the reader into looking at the Holocaust anew.[71]

Kakutani's appraisal is rather unclear; is the novel, as she suggests, a text that approaches and interprets animal suffering and extermination through the Holocaust, or is it the opposite, 'a kind of philosophical meditation on the Holocaust', in which animals are employed as a defamiliarising tool? *Maus*, a marker of Martel's failure for Kakutani, is, in contrast, a marker of Martel's success for the critic Laura Peterson, who identifies parallel strategies in Spiegelman and Martel and outlines 'a more positive reading' of *Beatrice and Virgil* in which 'Martel present[s] readers with horrific subject matter through story animals'.[72] Peterson's dogged insistence – like that of Martel in interviews following the uproar at the novel's publication – on a tidy and redemptive resolution of the text's allegory shuts down the most interesting questions. Both critics reduce Martel's novel to a dull and derivative version of *Maus*. In contrast, I shall argue that the novel's resistance to allegory contributes to a cross-species ethics informed by an awareness of 'carno-phallogocentrism' – the parallel between sacrificing the animal and sacrificing the human *as* animal.

As the taxidermist in *Beatrice and Virgil* observes, 'reality escapes us. It's beyond description, even a simple pear' (*BV*, 115). In an extended dialogue, Martel's animal protagonists – the donkey Beatrice and the howler monkey Virgil, two of the taxidermist's subjects and characters in his play – slowly try to discern what constitutes the 'pearness' of a pear. This is clearly an attempt to re-establish a relationship with words and things after an event, or events, which have exposed the opacity of that relationship. From Henry's Holocaust flip-book to Beatrice and Virgil's references to 'Aukitz' (*BV*, 184), *Beatrice and Virgil* targets the problem of responding meaningfully to the Holocaust through art and thought, given that the Holocaust evacuates our very structures of meaning-construction and questions the possibility of accurate representation. As the Auschwitz survivor Elie Wiesel writes:

Now, one generation after the event, one can still say – or one can already say – that what is called the literature of the Holocaust does not exist, cannot exist. It is a contradiction in terms, as is the philosophy, the theology, the psychology of the Holocaust. Auschwitz negates all systems, opposes all doctrines. They cannot but diminish the experience which lies beyond our reach [. . .] A novel about Treblinka is either not a novel or not about Treblinka; a novel about Treblinka is about blasphemy – is blasphemy. For Treblinka means death – absolute death – death of language and of the imagination. Its mystery is doomed to remain intact.[73]

Wiesel gestures towards a double-bind: the necessity of responding to the Holocaust to bear witness to its victims and prevent its repetition, yet without succumbing to the temptation to conceptualise. The latter is prohibited not only because conceptualisation has been rendered impossible – as Theodor Adorno tells us in *Negative Dialectics*: 'Our metaphysical faculty is paralyzed because actual events have shattered the basis on which speculative metaphysical thought could be reconciled with experience' – but also because conceptualisation itself, in its attempt to totalise, systematise and master, is complicit with structures that facilitated the Holocaust.[74] Consistently haunted by this dilemma, and, like Wiesel, unfailingly suspicious of systematicity, Adorno begins to suggest ways in which we might respond to the Holocaust through philosophy and art. For Adorno, however, this is anything but a recuperative or redemptive process. Lawrence L. Langer suggests that 'the Holocaust requires us to *unlearn* something'[75] about Western ideals and the meaning of progress, and Adorno's work advocates and adopts a critical, reflexive mode of thinking and unthinking, the 'thinking against itself' of negative dialectics.[76] This strategy might have the potential to express suffering without assimilating, appropriating or commodifying it, without trading in melancholia for mourning.[77] 'Our feelings resist any claim of the positivity of existence as sanctimonious, as wronging the victims; they balk at squeezing any kind of sense, however bleached, out of the victims' fate', Adorno tells us.[78]

Relating these insights to *Beatrice and Virgil*, we might ask how literature can avoid the potential for 'blasphemy' that Wiesel detects. Implicit in Wiesel's claim is the assumption that novels attempt to impose narrative closure or definitive meaning which defies the incomprehensibility of the Holocaust. A similar supposition accounts for Adorno's rejection of realist modes of art and his preference for the fragmentation and indigestibility of modernist art forms. Of particular interest for him is Samuel Beckett, whose work is clearly, but always implicitly, shadowed by the Holocaust. Of *Endgame*, Beckett's bleak, post-apocalyptic play, Adorno writes: 'Understanding it can mean only understanding its unintelligibility, concretely reconstructing the meaning of the fact that it has no meaning.'[79] From the *Godot*-esque dialogue between Beatrice and Virgil, to Beatrice's reference to 'The Unnameable'

(*BV*, 135), Martel frequently directs a knowing nod towards Beckett, alert to the challenges posed by Beckett's non-representative strategies and, like Beckett, convinced that literature is an appropriate space for philosophical questions.

The tension between the accessibility and familiarity of realist literary modes and the need for different languages and genres to express the horrors of the Holocaust is played out in Holocaust writing and within *Beatrice and Virgil* itself, with the novel's narrator asserting the need for a 'supplementary way of thinking about the Holocaust' (*BV*, 11). Although as Michael Rothberg testifies, 'the realist approach has characterized the dominant scholarly methodology' of Holocaust writing, it is clear that Holocaust literature has pursued more experimental pathways.[80] Following the work of the critic Sue Vice, Robert Eaglestone observes: 'Holocaust fiction is highly intertextual and uses anterior sources much more self-consciously than other genres and in very specific ways',[81] and Laura Peterson identifies 'a meta-Holocaust approach' in Holocaust writing.[82]

One critically lauded example of the 'meta-Holocaust approach', which, like *Beatrice and Virgil*, employs animal figures, is Art Spiegelman's Pulitzer-winning graphic novel *Maus*. Spiegelman constructs a frame narrative in which the protagonist Art's father Vladek reflects upon his experiences between the mid-1930s and the end of the Second World War. *Maus* employs animal figures – mice as Jews, cats as Germans, pigs as Poles etc. – to trace the events of the Holocaust. Spiegelman's animal figures facilitate the presentation of 'a history that would otherwise be intolerable in its horror', and mobilise a critique of the ideological assumptions underpinning the Holocaust.[83] 'By drawing Jews as mice', Eric Berlatsky claims, 'Spiegelman concretizes the ways in which contemporary discourses about Jews might have looked had they been transparently true, ironically revealing their inherent falsehood.'[84] That Spiegelman discovered a critical mode that re-sensitised jaded readers is commendable, yet his strategy of representation is problematic. One particularly arresting image in *Maus* sees Spiegelman at work atop a pile of mouse corpses, the latter representing 'the carnage of the Holocaust and his [Spiegelman's] own guilty role as the maker and destroyer of the characters in his own work'.[85] While the mice are a useful tool to critique the Nazi depiction of Jews as vermin, the notion of vermin goes uncritiqued and the mice themselves become the 'absent referent', with Spiegelman reproducing an accepted but not incontrovertible hierarchy between humans and nonhuman animals. Richard de Angelis explains: 'There is no instance in *Maus* where the animal metaphor is meant to be taken at face value; rather than representing other species, the mouse and cat heads are meant to be transparent, serving as windows into human – not animal – nature.'[86]

Spiegelman's critique of the misrepresentation and exclusion of one group of beings is reliant on another act of exclusion and misrepresentation. We do not have to regard the exclusions as equivalent to see that Spiegelman's critique is thus destabilised, and that by employing animal figures merely as a tool to portray humans, and the trope of large-scale animal death as a symbol of human death, *Maus* overlooks the reality of nonhuman suffering. The distinction between species has only aesthetic significance for Spiegelman; we see clearly how 'animal', 'a word that men have given themselves the right to give', serves only to objectify and homogenise nonhuman animals, obfuscating their suffering.[87] *Maus* perpetuates a sense of human identity that is forged through conceptual and material mastery and violence, and a model of the human as master-storyteller who is free to use and abuse other life forms in service of his stories. It defies Haraway's edict, that nonhuman animals 'are not an alibi for other themes'.[88]

The 'cultural anxiety over species identity' that Pick perceives as pervading Holocaust discourse is magnified by *Maus*, reflecting a highly charged space in which the desire to resist the 'contagious proximity' between human and animal turns into over-zealous policing of 'legitimate from illegitimate Holocaust imagery'.[89] A similar anxiety attends any suggestion of comparison or equivalence between human and nonhuman suffering. Even Haraway is rigid here:

> It is not that the Nazi killings of the Jews and others and mass animal slaughter in the meat industry have no relation; it is that analogy culminating in equation can blunt our alertness to irreducible difference and multiplicity and their demands. Different atrocities deserve their own languages, even if there are no words for what we do.[90]

Haraway's desire that we generate an entirely fresh idiom to bear witness to the singularity of an atrocity is not only impossible but also disavows her faith in the process of storytelling.[91] A story is the hinge between the singular and the general. Stories – and the metaphors, analogies and allegories that they employ – are the blunt but indispensable tools that we adapt to bridge old languages and new ones, to bear witness to the singularity of an event within a universally accessible medium. Human beings conceptualise within a broader associative framework; each new event is understood through its differences from the last. We are historical and spatial beings who cannot think pure singularity; metaphoricity is a tool for comprehending our surroundings. Stories are, therefore, both necessary and necessarily violent. As such, they require our ongoing vigilance.

Haraway's rejection (tempered but not retracted in a recent interview with Wolfe)[92] of any comparison between human and animal suffering through the figure of the Holocaust reflects the tendency to sacralise the Holocaust, regarding comparisons as an affront to its uniqueness. This seems misplaced, not least because of the history of the term; as Boria Sax explains: 'A Holocaust was a Hebrew sacrifice in which the entire animal was given to Yahweh to be consumed by fire [. . .] The usage of the word for the Nazi murders is based on an identification between the Jewish people and the sacrificed animal.'[93] The Holocaust (like all events or concepts of great significance) is already embedded in a network of historical and cultural associations, here explicitly across species. In this light, comparisons are both legitimised and inescapable; 'there is no good reason', Karen Davis asserts, 'to insist that one form of suffering and oppression is so exclusive that it may not be used to raise moral concerns about any other form of oppression'.[94] The criterion of ethical soundness, Davis concludes, is to ensure that the compared term is not 'treated as a mere figure of speech, a mere point of reference. It must not be treated illogically as a lesser matter than that which it is being used to draw attention to.'[95] This too, is where *Beatrice and Virgil* differs from *Maus*; whereas the latter text overlooks the animal suffering which shadows its metaphor, the indeterminacy of the allegory in the former means that we are forced to consider, both cognitively and affectively, human and animal suffering. Martel's allegories are intentionally unclear, incomplete and in conflict; they comment on the limitations of allegory itself, and the violence of trying to achieve allegorical or narrative closure. These allegories are frequently punctured by the specificities of suffering, of 'affliction', in the term Pick adopts from Weil, and thus require us to honestly face 'the Holocaust's systematic demystification of human identity', and 'to think through the insufficiencies of a humanist project of remembrance', both for nonhuman animals and for animalised humans.[96]

Given that, as Claire Jean Kim writes, 'race, species, and other taxonomies of power structure how we see, think, feel, and act', and that 'race has been articulated in part as a *metric of animality*, as a classification system that orders human bodies according to how animal they are – and how human they are not', one would expect a strong existing alliance between animal studies and anti-racist studies.[97] That the proximity between animalisation and racialisation, a 'strict colonialist homology', has instead tended to lead to anxieties about species identity and to the assertion of the inferiority of nonhuman animals is, however, unsurprising, given the differing attitudes of these discourses to the humanist project.[98] As Kalpana Rahita Seshadri notes, 'antiracist work finds its justification within the parameters of humanism, whereas speciesism is nothing if not a radical critique of humanism as unjustified anthropocentrism'.[99] It is only recently, in accounts such as those of Kim and Seshadri, that we have begun to fashion an intersectional approach that does not address one form of oppression by reinforcing another. Rather, we must insist, Kim contends, that the question of the priority of speciesism or racism is necessarily 'irresolvable'.[100]

Martel's perception of the storytelling impulse, as constituted by the contradictory desires to witness and master, is reflected in his approach to the apparatus of storytelling and to the human subject. While the construction of metaphor entails reaching beyond current horizons in search of fresh understanding and new connections, in practice metaphor crystallises novelty, abstraction or ambiguity into known, and inevitably restrictive, forms and frameworks. 'Metaphor', James Geary asserts, 'is a lens that clarifies and distorts. It focuses our attention on a specific set of associated commonplaces, but in so doing also narrows our view.'[101] By highlighting one facet of something to draw a connection to another, every other facet is lost. It is in the context of this tension, and the simultaneously creative and controlling human subject – epitomised by Henry – which it exposes, that *Beatrice and Virgil* both exploits and interrogates metaphor.

That metaphor at best instrumentalises, and at worst forcibly subdues or masters, has ethical implications, and these are compounded in the case of Martel's animal metaphors. This is evident not only in the ongoing allegorical exploration of the relationship between animal suffering and the Holocaust, but, in a more prosaic way, through the novel's animal metaphors – the books that 'hog all the publicity' (*BV*, 3), the 'heavy, black ox' (*BV*, 21) of Henry's Mozart rendition, and the 'cold, muddy toads' (*BV*, 88) of words that fail to capture elusive meaning. As readers, we are invited both to enjoy the satisfyingly visceral nature of these images and to critique their tendency to mislead: in positing the equivalence of the two terms, and endorsing a limited view of the 'hog', 'ox' or 'toads', these metaphors reinforce human stereotypes and the formative assumption of human superiority. When Henry's clarinet playing finally improves, it sheds its metaphorical shackles and takes flight, leaving the reader with only the limitations of the weighty and wingless ox, not the strength and reliability that has been harnessed for human gain over millennia.

Perhaps Henry speaks for the author when he declares that 'craft' not 'sentiment' dictates the prominence 'of animals in his novel' (*BV*, 29), a procedure which encourages readers to suspend their cynicism and think afresh. Yet the assumption that fictional animals can be instrumentalised and objectified without any ethical repercussions jars within the novel's framework. This becomes most visible in Henry's visits to the taxidermist's shop. As a 'story animal', the shop is Henry's natural environment, his fascination and imagination presented as 'animal' impulses, rendering him silenced and 'wide-eyed' (*BV*, 61) as he examines its inhabitants. As readers, we too are fascinated by this 'stage full of stories' (*BV*, 61), the theatrical image stimulating the unsettling realisation that the animals are not actors; 'frozen to the spot' (*BV*, 60), they lack all agency. Henry's role is ambivalent: his solemn animal litany lures the reader into perceiving the text as testimony to each individual loss, yet this is undercut as he is unable to observe anything meaningful, noting banally 'a shared culture of animalness' (*BV*, 63). Listing the animals in this way also recalls Flaubert's story 'The Legend of St Julian the Hospitaller' – cited at length in *Beatrice and Virgil* – in which animals are listed proprietorially, either as destined for slaughter or, from the 'twenty-four greyhounds of Barbary' to the 'seventeen couples of Breton dogs', as part of a crack team assembled to savage other creatures.[102]

Martel highlights the sense of artifice in the taxidermist's shop. The animals are a vehicle to display the taxidermist's 'superlative' skills, yet these skills are utilised to deceive and master. The dead animals 'positively glistened with life' (*BV*, 66) and each is presented in a 'completely natural pose' (*BV*, 67) which suggests 'its own personal situation, its own story' (*BV*, 66). The cold, sinister taxidermist is counterbalanced by jovial Henry, yet the latter's impulses are suspicious: to whom is his 'impulse of pity' directed (*BV*, 70)? And why is he so keen to become 'involved with all these animals' (*BV*, 71)? Our readerly apprehension is fulfilled as we are led to the preparation area in the shop:

> A chain was hanging from the wall with a hook at the end of it. There were animals again, on shelves and on the floor, though far fewer than in the display room, and some were entirely disembodied, just a pile of hide or a mound of feathers, and others were works-in-progress [. . .] At the moment, the taxidermist appeared to be working on a deer head mount. The skin was not yet properly fitted on the fibreglass mannequin head and the mouth was a tongueless, toothless gaping hole revealing the yellow fibreglass jaw of the mannequin. The eyes had that same yellow glow. It looked grotesquely unnatural, a cervine version of Frankenstein. (*BV*, 72–3)

Martel spares nothing in this grisly description, inviting us to view the taxidermist as a reconstructor of appearances, behind which lie devastation and destruction, 'tongueless' subjects who are denied speech. In his simultaneous repulsion and intrigue, Henry is complicit. Martel invites a comparison with the work of writing and re-presenting memory and history, of re-packaging other peoples' lives, perhaps a nod to Adorno's unrelenting indictment of the way in which 'the victims are turned into works of art, tossed out to be gobbled up by the world that did them in'.[103] This passage also serves as a caveat against settling for the clean lines and closure of the story, a lesson that the task of remembering and reinterpreting is endless, that we must keep returning to the horror and disorder behind the gloss of the story, reading round and round the flip-book without resolution. We must continue to acknowledge our complicity, rather than protesting our innocence; 'the search for innocence', Haraway maintains, 'is exterminationist'.[104] It is no accident that Martel confuses Frankenstein with his monster; given historical atrocities, it is the human, not the creature, who should be regarded as 'grotesquely unnatural'.

Animals have a double presence in *Beatrice and Virgil*, through the protagonists themselves and in this hideous backdrop which feels radically disordered, 'all wrong, all inside out' (*BV*, 156). In one way, the novel's allegory presents the animal characters Beatrice and Virgil as a fresh lens through which to view the horrors of the Holocaust, the radical powerlessness of the animals re-sensitising the reader, and reiterating the ways in which the Holocaust challenges the ways we construct meaning. 'Allegory', Jeremy Tambling asserts, 'serves as a way to describe the indescribable, or the monstrous.'[105] By diverging from the surface phenomena of an event such as the Holocaust, strategies such as metaphor and allegory can begin to gesture towards the epistemic shift which it generated. Yet Martel shies away from this allegory, wary of suggesting complete correspondence between the terms and of closing the story or advancing a clear message. Instead he suggests a competing, inverted allegory. Rather than the animals being a lens for viewing the Holocaust, here the Holocaust itself is the image repository; as we learn of Henry, 'It wasn't that he saw the Holocaust in everything. It's that he saw everything in the Holocaust, not only camp victims, but also capitalists and many others, perhaps even clowns' (*BV*, 116). Later, in case we were insufficiently alert to the duality of the allegory, Martel projects this perspective on to the taxidermist:

> Here was irrefutable proof that he was using the Holocaust to speak of the extermination of animal life. Doomed creatures that could not speak for themselves were being given the voice of a most articulate people who had been similarly doomed. He was seeing the tragic fate of animals through the tragic fate of Jews. The Holocaust as allegory. (*BV*, 173)

By attributing it to the taxidermist, Martel partially discredits this perspective. The overall effect, however, is rather more complicated. While it results in a double-ended allegory, whereby the animal characters enable us to see the Holocaust afresh and the Holocaust helps us to reconsider animal suffering, it also generates a critique of the allegorical method itself.

It is tempting to read the taxidermist's death as either punishment or redemption; however, if anything, it represents the impossibility of a definitive allegorical or theological narrative. The taxidermist's fixation on Flaubert's pseudo-biblical account of St Julian is framed by his desperate urge for salvation, and its appeal based on its provision of 'redemption without remorse' (*BV*, 189). However, following Beckett, Martel depicts a post-Holocaust landscape not only divested of the divine, but which renders the notion of divine justice or adjudication absurd. Consequently, the taxidermist's attempt to act *in loco dei*, as master-storyteller fitting events in his play to a biblical narrative, pointing out, for example, 'the expulsion from Eden! The Fall!' (*BV*, 129), is dangerously deluded. Its inevitable conclusion – and thus Martel's indictment of his claims – is the destruction of the 'Noah's Ark' (*BV*, 60) of his shop, destroying the animals he sought to shelter. While readers inevitably perceive the taxidermist as an unhinged aberration, we should avoid reading Martel's critique too narrowly. Rather, here Martel condemns over-zealous expressions – either figurative, in the form of coercive or repressive storytelling, or literal – of an ethic of stewardship. It is the taxidermist's inflated and distorted sense of his own role in managing the natural world, and his concurrent underestimation of nonhuman agency, which underpins his execrable behaviour. The parallel between stewardship and storytelling, which both balance productive or protective impulses with those towards domination, is also developed in *Life of Pi*.

The critique of allegorical method is nowhere stronger than in the searingly visceral description of Beatrice and Virgil's fate at the hands of their torturer towards the end of the novel. For Laura Peterson, this is 'an unexpectedly explicit passage [which] appears unnecessary and arguably undermines the subtleness of the earlier animal-driven messages'.[106] It is no accident that this section poses a problem for Peterson's reading, which, you may recall, interprets Martel's animals as tools through which to view the Holocaust, 'granting a difficult topic a new artistically and ethically satisfying means of expression' and providing a means to 'bring us back to ourselves, back to the horror, in a way that touches us deeply'.[107] For Peterson, the suffering animals in *Beatrice and Virgil* are, like the mouse corpses in *Maus*, utterly transparent, a symbol for human suffering and a vehicle for the construction of allegory. What renders Peterson's reading insufficient here is the specificity of the animals' suffering in *Beatrice and Virgil*. As readers, we inhabit Beatrice's body as her foot is nailed to the floor 'just above the rim of the hoof' (*BV*, 178) and Virgil's too, as his 'soft tail' (*BV*, 184) is severed, launched into the air, and tossed to the ground. 'It is', as Michael Slote writes of empathy, 'as if their pain invades us.'[108] A lucid example of embodied empathy in which we are able to 'directly and affectively perceive mental states as expressing foreign subjectiv- ity',[109] rather than bringing us 'back to ourselves', 'the sheer effort of imagination distances us from our own feelings'.[110]

Torture, an extreme example of violence and suffering that 'aspires to the totality of pain', highlights the ways in which pain defies our capacities for communication and representation.[111] In its generation of an experience where the intellect is entirely eclipsed by bodily experi- ence, where the body is 'emphatically and crushingly *present*', torture defies the intellectual distancing that makes allegory possible.[112] If Martel permits us to escape the specificity of the animals' suffering for a second it is only to recognise 'the radical subjectivity of pain' in both senses: the uniqueness of pain to each individual body and its role in subject-formation.[113] In the same way that it simultaneously erects and critiques allegory, the novel performs a double move here: eliciting 'the measuring and comparing of physical pains' (*BV*, 127) and revealing the violence and inadequacy of comparison. In obstructing articulation, pain exposes a shared animal experience; as Elaine Scarry writes, it generates 'an immediate reversion to a state anterior to language, to the sounds and cries a human being makes before language is learned'.[114] In making visible 'the structure and enormity of what is usually private and incommunicable, contained within the boundaries of the sufferer's body', it breaks down social and subjective boundaries.[115] Pain, here, is both an affect which exposes the construction of subjectivity, and necessitates an empathetic response that simultaneously breaches and restores disintegrating subjective boundaries. Through the 'reflex- ive empathy' – a combination of embodied, cognitive and affective empathy – that we experience for Beatrice and Virgil, we 'come to wit- ness' them 'as concrete creatures with their own experiences, wants and traits and therefore their own realities, equally as valid and valuable as those of our own'.[116]

In their acknowledgement of the other's suffering, Beatrice and Virgil enact cross-species awareness and compassion through empathetic engagement. This speaks to Derrida's proposal that a 'non-power' which emerges from cross-species vulnerability, 'the finitude that we share with animals', might lead first to 'the experience of compassion', and ultimately to a community grounded in compassion rather than sovereignty.[117] Scarry contends that pain is fundamentally world-destroying and language-destroying: 'as the self disintegrates, so that which would express and project the self is robbed of its source and its subject'.[118] Sympathy, therefore, figures as a kind of world-holding or world-sitting for the hurt other. She explains:

> An act of human contact and concern, whether occurring here or in private contexts of sympathy, provides the hurt person with worldly self-extension: in acknowledging and expressing another person's pain, or in articulating one of his nonbodily concerns while he is unable to, one human being who is well and free willingly turns himself into an image of the other's psychic or sentient claims, an image existing in the space outside the sufferer's body, projected out into the world and held there intact by that person's powers until the sufferer himself regains his own powers of self-extension. By holding that world in place, or by giving the pain a place in the world, sympathy lessens the power of sickness and pain counteracts the force with which a person in great pain or sickness can be swallowed alive by the body.[119]

Writing before the expansion of animal studies, Scarry is uninterested in nonhuman animal pain, but her insights are applicable beyond the human. The experience of pain is one of contraction or obfuscation of world; it presupposes a different kind of relational experience without pain. Running counter to Heidegger's distinction of the animal as having 'no world', it is clear that nonhuman animals also have this kind of worldly experience, and that this is actively diminished by their suffering.[120] Contra Spiegelman, who compresses nonhuman worlds into tropes, by resisting the assimilation of animal experience into allegory Martel's novels retain a sympathetic space for the construction, existence and acknowledgement of animal worlds. In so doing, he resists reinstating realism over the figurative – a move which, as Lynn Turner writes, mistakenly 'assumes a firm division between need and desire, the world and language', instead retaining a dynamic space for that which resists the totalisation of allegory.[121]

In her appeal to a 'reworlding', Haraway calls for a decentralised model of storytelling as a dynamic, cross-species community project where stories are 'a complex production with many tellers and hearers, not all of them visible or audible'.[122] Reworlding, therefore, demands the inscription of diverse new stories (both on pages and bodies through the interaction between flesh and text) which entwine different discourses and acknowledge the 'authorship' of nonhuman life, as well as making space within these narratives for existing nonhuman worlds.[123] In her discussion of the criticisms of empathy, Suzanne Keen describes the position of '*failed empathy* critics' who 'lament the inefficiency of shared feelings in provoking action that would lead to positive social or political change'.[124] As we saw earlier, similar issues were raised by

Paul Bloom and Jesse Prinz. Scarry's account of sympathy, a process distinguished from empathy by its experience of identifying with rather than identifying as, challenges the distinction between affect and action that these criticisms raise. Sympathy, an affect, is also an act of place-holding or space-making which is generated by empathy and goes beyond it. While, in Eisenberg's words, 'empathy, and especially sympathy, appear to play a major role in the development of other-oriented values, moral reasoning, and behaviour',[125] empathy, particularly literary empathy, should not be thought of as a moral end in itself. Rather, as Eileen John writes, empathy is 'part of a process in which [we] hope to do a particular kind of justice to the work'.[126]

'THE MONSTROUSLY OTHER': INHUMAN ETHICS WITH AND WITHOUT EMPATHY

In her review, Joy Lo Dico suggests that '*Beatrice and Virgil* is about crushing belief. In the artifice, in the author, in our emotional response to writing, the novel seeks to destroy as much as it creates [. . .] one can no longer indulge in the artifice of fiction.'[127] Lo Dico is right; *Beatrice and Virgil* is not a romantic paean to storytelling. Martel writes in the shadow of Adorno and Beckett, teasing the reader with a little lyricism only to chastise: 'How can there be anything beautiful after what we've lived through? It's incomprehensible. It's an insult' (*BV*, 112). Martel maintains that the desire to recuperate, sanitise or monumentalise transforms one into the taxidermist, oppressively demanding 'a proper interpretation of the event' (*BV*, 93–4) and, deluded to the last, sewing subjects' mouths firmly shut in the mistaken belief that it sustains a relationship with them. The Holocaust is not 'a healable offence'.[128]

The intentional brittleness and imprecision of Martel's allegories serves as a critique of the urge to 'interpret and conclude' (*BV*, 15), offering intersecting, sometimes contradictory stories, instead of a master-narrative. This is not to say that Martel's novels disavow all ethical claims or conclusions. On the contrary, *Beatrice and Virgil* invites the reader to distinguish between watching and witnessing, identifying and collaborating, ethics and aesthetics. Bearing witness is often a central aim of Holocaust writing, yet *Beatrice and Virgil* interrogates witnessing, associating it with the taxidermist's misguided belief in the recuperative value of taxidermy 'once the irreparable had been done' (*BV*, 98). Witnessing is also blurred with passive watching in the case of Beatrice and Virgil, both victims and silent observers of brutality with the 'desire to inspect' (*BV*, 184), and with voyeurism, as the reader, alongside Henry, views the taxidermist at work on a fox, 'the skin and the flayed carcass, like a baby that has been taken out of its red pyjamas' (*BV*, 155). The novel form is not glorified as a monument to human *or* animal suffering; witnessing, its aims and practices must be critiqued and rethought, must not become dogmatic. Readers must be responsible collaborators; the novel, in the form of the unfinished final section, *Games for Gustav*, is literally incomplete.

Projections, inevitably inaccurate and sometimes dangerous, are what Mensch describes as 'the distortions of symbolic substitutes'.[129] Anthropocentric storytelling is complicit with modern humanism as both render the human the measure of all things. In his refusal to allow the collapse of the first survival account into allegory, Martel envisages a kind of storytelling in which the inhuman participants of stories and the inhuman processes of language are permitted to emerge and open difference. As Mensch suggests, 'we have to go beyond the things for which we have common measures'.[130] In Martel's novels, anthropomorphic projections are counterbalanced by an excavation of the human, an introspection through which humans acknowledge the elements within them that do not coincide with orthodox notions of the human as sovereign, rational and exceptional. This entails a twin admission of the destructive nature of the human and of our continuing disavowal of this destructiveness. The power and aggression of Richard Parker serves to expose the violence of the human: while superficially Parker is the terrifying figure, ultimately it is human ruthlessness and brutality – deceptively cloaked in the slight figure of the orphan Pi – which proves the most chilling. As we are warned by Pi's father at the start of the novel, 'the most dangerous animal in a zoo is Man' (*LP*, 29).

Mensch, reading *Life of Pi* through the philosophies of Derrida and Emmanuel Levinas, describes it as 'an account of alterity – the alterity both of animals and God'.[131] Whereas Levinas is interested only in human alterity, Derrida looks to challenge the restriction of ethical responsibility to the human; for him, the animal is 'more radically other' still.[132] As 'the excluded, foreclosed, disavowed, tamed, and sacrificed foundation of [. . .] the symbolic order, the human order, law and justice', for Derrida, the divine and the inhuman are both figures of originary exclusion, linked by 'their being-outside-the-law'.[133] Framing the human as *zoon logon echon*, modernity develops a model of political sovereignty rooted in the 'anthropo-theological', a belief in human exceptionalism grounded in the presupposition of a privileged relationship between humans and God, instantiated in the *imago Dei* in Christian tradition.[134] What happens, however, ask both Derrida and Martel, to the components of human life that have been 'run over by modernity'?[135] For Derrida, they return via the '*unheimlich*, uncanny reciprocal haunting' of the beast and the sovereign, the figure of '*divinanimality*', which disrupts the closed logics of symmetrical specularity that inform the privileging of the 'anthropo-theological'.[136] Accordingly, Derrida proposes a strategic reconfiguration of God outside 'the model of sovereignty',[137] where God, no longer conceived as omnipotent and unchanging, would become, as Richard Kearney says, a 'God – or post God – of radical powerlessness'.[138] Given the inextricable connection between religious and political paradigms, such a God might assist in the exposure of human sovereignty as a 'prosthetic monstrosity'[139] which is performatively generated to conceal the absence of a human essence and bring about a range of alternative 'theo-zoomorphic possibilities'[140] rooted in the political potential of '(not) being-able'.[141] This, again, is rooted in pairing cognitive and affective responses with material, mortal embodiment.

Laura Peterson's discovery of an 'ethically satisfying' conclusion to *Beatrice and Virgil* is misplaced. Martel denies the possibility of ethical satisfaction not only because he is well schooled in the lessons of Adorno, Beckett and Wiesel, but also because his animal characters unsettle the foundations of our ethical framework. These are not animals that 'bring us back to ourselves', where selfhood is premised on the sacrificial logic that supports the 'transcendence of the human', but that summon us to familiarise ourselves with our strangeness, our inhumanity, rather than projecting it outside. They are also animals, in both novels, that – clearly and distinctly – represent themselves, rather than human desires or imaginaries. The first stage in an alternative, less narcissistic storytelling is the adjustment of our metrics of success: in both novels, Martel abandons the role of master-storyteller, disrupting his carefully constructed allegories and opening the texts to a more democratic, responsible form of storytelling where stories are dynamic and *metaplasmic*.[142] Martel's torture scenes expose the violence of storytelling; that stories and beliefs are inscribed on bodies, that flesh, too, is a system of signs.[143] The failures of storytelling and stewarding might be framed as markers of success; Pi's failure 'as a zookeeper' (*LP*, 242) is actually a deliberate abdication of his zoo-keeping responsibilities: when he lets Richard Parker disappear into the jungle, he rejects a domineering model of stewardship in which the human subjugates nonhuman life.

It is easy to identify an ethics of cross-species empathy within Martel's novels. Both contain scenes of highly affective nonhuman animal suffering, which, via a repurposing of biopolitical logic, we can read as exposing the condition of 'bare life' to which all embodied creatures might be reduced. In this light, species difference is nullified: we empathise, we sympathise, we feel pity. As 'story animals' and narrative consumers, we are seduced. Such practices are important, even necessary; at best, emotional responses trigger cognitive reflection on the practices that permit nonhuman animal suffering. However, we must ensure that empathetic engagement begins with imaginative perspective-taking and recognises the 'otherness of the other', while heeding its limitations. Empathy struggles to articulate the complexity of species distance or cross-species relations. It cannot reflect critically on the implications of the 'ultimate fantasy': the escape from all violence.[144] It cannot acknowledge that a cross-species ethics must decide what to kill, rather than not to kill.[145] At worst, it summons a kind of colonial caretaking.

The emotional immediacy of the empathetic response is, however, complemented by these texts' formal aesthetic resistance: in resisting the closure of anthropocentric allegory, they generate space for attentiveness to, and production of, nonhuman worlds and stories. This enforced distancing and opposition to closure also figures as a challenge to the reification of human identity around sovereignty, independence and exceptionalism. Derrida writes of an ethics which begins not from the human, but from 'the monstrously other [...] the unrecognizable'.[146] An ethics grounded only in empathy is limited to the degree of difference that it can think. Ethics, rather, as Derrida frames it, is a yielding to one's non-power, ceding to the unknownness of oneself and others; it requires us to make a space for this difference within ourselves and our communities, and to relinquish an account of the human in which 'power over the animal is the essence of the "I" or the "person," the essence of the human'.[147] It envisages monstrosity, or inhumanity, as difference that cannot be assimilated. We can see this first in the taxidermist and Pi, who, despite their differences, represent the 'inhuman' desires and capacities which we have tried to expel from our notion of the human; and secondly, in the animals in the texts, whose living, sentient experience again defies our classification. Both novels permit the banished inhuman to resurface – in animals, humans, and, in *Life of Pi*, in the form of God. It also figures as a force within writing, its 'animality'.[148] This inhuman cannot be conceptualised or domesticated; it forces the texts to remain open and invites us to refigure the human relationship with its own strangeness and with the needs and desires of nonhuman strangers.

NOTES

1. Yann Martel, *The Facts behind the Helsinki Roccamatios and Other Stories* (Edinburgh: Canongate, 2005), p. 17.

2. Yann Martel, *Life of Pi* (Edinburgh: Canongate, 2009), p. xii. Subsequent references will be given in parentheses in the text.
3. Martel, *The Facts behind the Helsinki Roccamatios*, p. 18.
4. Sarah Churchwell, '*Beatrice and Virgil* by Yann Martel', *The Observer*, 30 May 2010.
5. Coplan, 'Empathetic Engagement', p. 143.
6. For the former, see Martha C. Nussbaum's work on moral imagination in *Love's Knowledge: Essays on Philosophy* (Oxford: Oxford University Press, 1990). For the latter, see Plato's famous critique of the poets in Books II, III and X of *The Republic*: Plato, *The Republic*, trans. Melissa Lane (London: Penguin, 2007).
7. Keen, *Empathy and the Novel*, p. 39.
8. Keen, *Empathy and the Novel*, p. 21.
9. Keen, *Empathy and the Novel*, p. 5.
10. John Berger, *Why Look at Animals?* (London: Penguin, 2009), pp. 17, 16.
11. Berger, *Why Look at Animals?*, p. 17.
12. Stewart Cole, 'Believing in Tigers: Anthropomorphism and Incredulity in Yann Martel's *Life of Pi*', *Studies in Canadian Literature*, 29.2 (2004), 22–36 (p. 30).
13. Derrida, *The Animal That Therefore I Am*, p. 2. There is also a connection between animals and Derrida's individual sense of autobiography: 'animals [. . .] show up each time Derrida's discourse shifts to an autobiographical mode'. Anne Emanuelle Berger and Marta Segarra, 'Thoughtprints', in *Demenageries: Thinking (of) Animals after Derrida*, ed. Anne Emanuelle Berger and Marta Segarra, *Critical Studies*, 35 (2011), 3–22 (p. 4).
14. Derrida, *The Animal That Therefore I Am*, p. 12.
15. Derrida, *The Animal That Therefore I Am*, p. 65.
16. Derrida, *The Animal That Therefore I Am*, p. 88.
17. Derrida, *The Animal That Therefore I Am*, pp. 41, 9.
18. Derrida, *The Animal That Therefore I Am*, pp. 47, 48.
19. Derrida, *The Animal That Therefore I Am*, p. 29.
20. Derrida, *The Animal That Therefore I Am*, p. 27.
21. Matravers, *Empathy*, pp. 1–2.
22. Haraway, *Manifestly Haraway*, p. 215.
23. Arne De Boever, *States of Exception in the Contemporary Novel: Martel, Eugenides, Coetzee, Sebald* (London: Continuum, 2012), p. 16.
24. Carl Schmitt, *Political Theology: Four New Chapters on the Concept of Sovereignty*, trans. Paul Kahn (New York: Columbia University Press, 2011), p. 31.
25. Giorgio Agamben, *Homo Sacer: Sovereign Power and Bare Life*, trans. Daniel Heller-Roazen (Stanford: Stanford University Press, 1998), p. 82.
26. Agamben, *Homo Sacer*, pp. 15, 8.
27. De Boever, *States of Exception*, p. 17.

28. De Boever, *States of Exception*, p. 22.

29. James Wood, 'Credulity', *London Review of Books*, 24.22 (14 November 2002), https://www.lrb.co.uk/v24/n22/james-wood/credulity (accessed 20 March 2019); Florence Stratton, '"Hollow at the Core": Deconstructing Yann Martel's *Life of Pi*', *Studies in Canadian Literature*, 19.2 (2004), 5–21 (p. 17).

30. Philip Armstrong, *What Animals Mean in the Fiction of Modernity* (Abingdon: Routledge, 2008), p. 177.

31. Armstrong, *What Animals Mean*, p. 178.

32. Sarah E. McFarland, 'Animal Studies, Literary Animals, and Yann Martel's *Life of Pi*', in *The Cambridge Companion to Literature and the Environment*, ed. Louise Westling (Cambridge: Cambridge University Press, 2014), p. 157.

33. Keen, *Empathy and the Novel*, p. 82.

34. McFarland, 'Animal Studies', p. 159.

35. Diamond, 'Difficulty of Reality', p. 22.

36. McFarland, 'Animal Studies', p. 156.

37. Wood, 'Credulity'.

38. McFarland, 'Animal Studies', p. 157.

39. Derrida, *The Animal That Therefore I Am*, p. 88.

40. McFarland, 'Animal Studies', p. 159.

41. Giorgio Agamben, *The Open: Man and Animal*, trans. Kevin Attell (Stanford: Stanford University Press, 2004), p. 37.

42. Agamben, *Homo Sacer*, p. 134.

43. Jacques Derrida, '"Eating Well," or the Calculation of the Subject', trans. Peter Connor and Avital Ronell, in *Points... Interviews 1974–1994*, ed. Elisabeth Weber (Stanford: Stanford University Press, 1995), pp. 255–87 (p. 278).

44. Derrida, 'Eating Well', p. 280.

45. Derrida, 'Eating Well', p. 279.

46. Cary Wolfe, *Animal Rites: American Culture, the Discourse of Species, and Posthumanist Theory* (Chicago: University of Chicago Press, 2003), p. 39.

47. Pick, *Creaturely Poetics*, p. 131.

48. Derrida, *The Animal That Therefore I Am*, p. 9.

49. Pick, *Creaturely Poetics*, p. 66.

50. Donna Haraway, *When Species Meet* (Minneapolis: University of Minnesota Press, 2008), p. 76.

51. Haraway, *Staying with the Trouble*, p. 35.

52. Alaimo, *Exposed*, p. 5.

53. Shotwell, *Against Purity*, pp. 8–9.

54. Pick, *Creaturely Poetics*, p. 193.

55. Weik von Mossner, *Affective Ecologies*, p. 83.

56. De Boever, *States of Exception*, p. 25.

57. James Mensch, 'The Intertwining of Incommensurables: Yann Martel's

Life of Pi', in *Phenomenology and the Non-Human Animals: At the Limits of Experience*, ed. Corinne Painter and Christian Lotz (Dordrecht: Springer, 2007), pp. 135–47 (p. 140).

58. De Boever, *States of Exception*, p. 27.
59. Wolfe, *Before the Law*, p. 10.
60. Stratton, 'Hollow at the Core', p. 10.
61. Stratton, 'Hollow at the Core', pp. 10, 11.
62. Wood, 'Credulity'.
63. De Boever, *States of Exception*, p. 34.
64. Wood, 'Credulity'.
65. Stratton, 'Hollow at the Core', p. 6.
66. Stratton, 'Hollow at the Core', pp. 18–19, 14.
67. Mensch, 'Intertwining of Incommensurables', p. 146.
68. Mensch, 'Intertwining of Incommensurables', p. 24.
69. Michael Slote, *The Ethics of Care and Empathy* (London: Routledge, 2007), p. 119.
70. Yann Martel, *Beatrice and Virgil* (Edinburgh: Canongate, 2010), p. 7. Subsequent references will be given in parentheses in the text.
71. Michiko Kakutani, 'From "Life of Pi" Author: Stuffed-Animal Allegory about Holocaust', *The New York Times*, 12 April 2010, https://www.nytimes.com/2010/04/13/books/13book.html (accessed 20 March 2019).
72. Laura Peterson, '"We Are Story Animals": Aesopics in Holocaust Literature by Art Spiegelman and Yann Martel', in *Aesopic Voices: Re-framing Truth through Concealed Ways of Presentation in the 20th and 21st Centuries*, ed. Gert Reifarth and Philip Morrisey (Newcastle-upon-Tyne: Cambridge Scholars, 2011), pp. 174–207 (p. 201)
73. Elie Wiesel, 'Art and Culture after the Holocaust', in *Auschwitz: Beginning of a New Era? Reflections on the Holocaust*, ed. Eva Fleishner (New York: KTAV Publishing, 1977), pp. 403–15 (p. 405).
74. Theodor W. Adorno, *Negative Dialectics*, trans. E. B. Ashton (London: Routledge, 1973), p. 362.
75. Lawrence L. Langer, *Using and Abusing the Holocaust* (Bloomington: Indiana University Press, 2006), p. 117.
76. Adorno, *Negative Dialectics*, p. 365.
77. For a critique of the commodification of the Holocaust, see Norman G. Finkelstein, *The Holocaust Industry: Reflections on the Exploitation of Jewish Suffering* (London: Verso, 2000).
78. Adorno, *Negative Dialectics*, p. 361.
79. Theodor W. Adorno, 'Trying to Understand *Endgame*', in *Notes to Literature Volume I*, ed. Rolf Tiedemann, trans. Shierry Weber Nicholsen (New York: Columbia University Press, 1991), pp. 241–76 (p. 243).
80. Michael Rothberg, *Traumatic Realism* (Minneapolis: University of Minnesota Press, 2000), p. 4.
81. Robert Eaglestone, *The Holocaust and the Postmodern* (Oxford: Oxford

University Press, 2004), p. 107. See, for example, the work of Jenni Adams, who identifies magical realist features in recent post-Holocaust writing: 'Magical realism, I suggest, offers an important strategy in attempts to continue the project of Holocaust representation into the post-testimonial era.' Jenni Adams, *Magic Realism in Holocaust Literature* (Basingstoke: Palgrave Macmillan, 2011), p. 1.

82. Peterson, 'We Are Story Animals', p. 175. For a lucid synopsis of this, see Deborah R. Geis, 'Introduction', in *Considering Maus: Approaches to Art Spiegelman's 'Survivor's Tale'*, ed. Deborah R. Geis (Tuscaloosa, AL: University of Alabama Press, 2003), p. 3: 'horror in its deepest manifestation cannot risk being sanitized and framed as "art". If the Holocaust somehow stands outside the realm of narration, though, one must ask what is to prevent it from becoming mystified or depoliticized. Since to tell the story of the Holocaust is to call forth an area of representation that is ultimately unspeakable or untellable because no form of narrative can hope to portray it, second-generation Holocaust writers have frequently shown the problematics of representation within their work as part of what they also see as an ethical response to the past; they engage in what Jean-Francois Lyotard refers to as the act of making the "*un*representable" into the process of representation.' See also Marianne Hirsch's discussion of the way that the 'post' of 'postmemory' signifies 'more than a temporal delay and more than a location in an aftermath', and causes second-generation post-Holocaust writers to experiment with different literary forms. Marianne Hirsch, *The Generation of Postmemory: Writing and Visual Culture after the Holocaust* (New York: Columbia University Press, 2012), p. 5.

83. David Mikics, 'Underground Comics and Survival Tales: *Maus* in Context', in *Considering Maus: Approaches to Art Spiegelman's 'Survivor's Tale'*, ed. Deborah R. Geis (Tuscaloosa, AL: University of Alabama Press, 2003), pp. 15–25 (p. 20).

84. Eric L. Berlatsky, *The Real, the True and the Told: Postmodern Historical Narrative and the Ethics of Representation* (Columbus: Ohio State University Press, 2011), p. 155.

85. Geis, 'Introduction', p. 2.

86. Richard de Angelis, 'Of Mice and Vermin: Animals as Absent Referent in Art Spiegelman's *Maus*', IJOCA, 7.1 (2005), 230–49 (p. 232).

87. Derrida, *The Animal That Therefore I Am*, p. 32.

88. Haraway, *The Companion Species Manifesto*, p. 5.

89. Pick, *Creaturely Poetics*, pp. 24–5.

90. Haraway, *When Species Meet*, p. 336. Haraway gestures towards a more hesitant position in *Manifestly Haraway*, pp. 230–1.

91. There is a clear parallel with Derrida here, whose work tirelessly insists upon the ethical urgency of writing idiomatically in order to respond to singularity, and yet repeatedly demonstrates that this task is impossible (and infinite). See, for example, his assertion that 'It is necessary in each

situation to create an appropriate mode of exposition, to invent the law of the singular event.' Jacques Derrida, *Learning to Live Finally: An Interview with Jean Birnbaum* (Hoboken, NJ: Melville House Publishing, 2007), p. 31.

92. Haraway, *Manifestly Haraway*, pp. 230–1.

93. Boria Sax, *Animals in the Third Reich: Pets, Scapegoats, and the Holocaust* (London: Continuum, 2000), p. 156.

94. Karen Davis, *The Holocaust and the Henmaid's Tale: A Case for Comparing Atrocities* (New York: Lantern Books, 2005), p. 4.

95. Davis, *The Holocaust and the Henmaid's Tale*, p. 4.

96. Pick, *Creaturely Poetics*, p. 51.

97. Claire Jean Kim, *Dangerous Crossings: Race, Species, and Nature in a Multicultural Age* (Cambridge: Cambridge University Press, 2015), p. 20.

98. Kalpana Rahita Seshadri, *HumAnimal: Race, Law, Language* (Minneapolis: University of Minnesota Press, 2012), p. 7.

99. Seshadri, *HumAnimal*, p. 10.

100. Kim, *Dangerous Crossings*, p. 19.

101. James Geary, *I Is An Other: The Secret Life of Metaphor and How it Shapes the Way we See the World* (New York: Harper Collins, 2011), p. 147.

102. Gustave Flaubert, 'The Legend of Saint-Julian the Hospitaller', *The Literature Network*, http://www.online-literature.com/gustave-flau bert/2122/ (accessed 20 December 2018).

103. Theodor W. Adorno, 'Commitment', in *Notes to Literature Volume II*, ed. Rolf Tiedemann, trans. Shierry Weber Nicholsen (New York: Columbia University Press, 1992), pp. 76–94 (p. 88).

104. Haraway, *Manifestly Haraway*, p. 236.

105. Jeremy Tambling, *Allegory* (London: Routledge, 2010), p. 92.

106. Peterson, 'We Are Story Animals', p. 199.

107. Peterson, 'We Are Story Animals', p. 202.

108. Michael Slote, *The Ethics of Care and Empathy* (London: Routledge, 2007), p. 13.

109. Aaltola, *Varieties of Empathy*, para 12.20.

110. Koehn, *Rethinking Feminist Ethics*, p. 58.

111. Elaine Scarry, *The Body in Pain: The Making and Unmaking of the World* (Oxford: Oxford University Press, 1985), p. 55.

112. Scarry, *The Body in Pain*, p. 49.

113. Scarry, *The Body in Pain*, p. 50.

114. Scarry, *The Body in Pain*, p. 4.

115. Scarry, *The Body in Pain*, p. 27.

116. Aaltola, *Varieties of Empathy*, para. 15.16.

117. Derrida, *The Animal That Therefore I Am*, p. 28.

118. Scarry, *The Body in Pain*, p. 35.

119. Scarry, *The Body in Pain*, p. 50.

120. Heidegger, 'Origin of the Work of Art', p. 23.
121. Lynn Turner, 'The Animal Question in Deconstruction', in *The Animal Question in Deconstruction*, ed. Lynn Turner (Edinburgh: Edinburgh University Press, 2013), pp. 1–8 (p. 4).
122. Haraway, *Primate Visions*, p. 8.
123. Haraway, *Primate Visions*, p. 8.
124. Keen, *Empathy and the Novel*, p. 159.
125. Nancy Eisenberg, 'Empathy-related Responding and Prosocial Behaviour', in *Empathy and Fairness: Novartis Foundation Symposium 278* (Chichester: Wiley, 2007), pp. 71–88 (p. 78).
126. Eileen John, 'Empathy in Literature', in *The Routledge Handbook of Philosophy of Empathy*, ed. Heidi L. Maibom (London: Routledge, 2017), para. 40.26.
127. Joy Lo Dico, '*Beatrice and Virgil*, by Yann Martel', *The Independent*, 30 May 2010, https://www.independent.co.uk/arts-entertainment/books/reviews/beatrice-and-virgil-by-yann-martel-1984399.html (accessed 20 March 2019).
128. Langer, *Using and Abusing the Holocaust*, p. xii.
129. Mensch, 'Intertwining of Incommensurables', p. 146.
130. Mensch, 'Intertwining of Incommensurables', p. 146.
131. Mensch, 'Intertwining of Incommensurables', p. 135.
132. Derrida, *The Animal That Therefore I Am*, p. 107.
133. Derrida, *The Animal That Therefore I Am*, p. 132; Derrida, *Beast: Volume I*, p. 17.
134. Derrida, *Beast: Volume I*, p. 14.
135. Yann Martel, *The High Mountains of Portugal* (Edinburgh: Canongate, 2016), p. 27.
136. Derrida, *Beast: Volume I*, p. 17; Derrida, *The Animal That Therefore I Am*, p. 132.
137. Derrida, *Beast: Volume I*, p. 81.
138. Richard Kearney, *Anatheism: Returning to God after God* (New York: Columbia University Press, 2010), p. 58.
139. Derrida, *Beast: Volume I*, p. 27.
140. Derrida, *The Animal That Therefore I Am*, p. 131.
141. Wolfe, *Before the Law*, p. 78.
142. Haraway, *The Companion Species Manifesto*, p. 100.
143. Human beliefs, Haraway maintains, 'have been written into the body of nature'. Haraway, *Primate Visions*, p. 1.
144. Wolfe in *Manifestly Haraway*, p. 233.
145. See Haraway's contention that 'in order to be *for* some ways of living and dying and not others [. . .] I/we must kill'. *Manifestly Haraway*, p. 236.
146. Derrida *Beast: Volume I*, p. 108.
147. Derrida, *The Animal That Therefore I Am*, p. 93.
148. Derrida, *The Animal That Therefore I Am*, p. 52.

2. *Anthropomorphism and the 'Ends of Man' in the Anthropocene: 'My chimp nature'*

But who, we?

Jacques Derrida[1]

It is a widely held belief that a conceptual destabilisation issues from the identification of the Anthropocene, manifesting itself, as Timothy Clark writes, 'in innumerable possible hairline cracks in the familiar life-world', and that such a destabilisation is experienced as a disintegration of narratives – the record of a known past and a relatively predictable future – which elucidate the human condition.[2] The subject experiencing this disintegration of narratives is, however, only constructed retroactively. As Tom Cohen and Claire Colebrook explain: 'There is no "we", no "anthropos," until, in a final moment of inscribed and marked destruction, a species event appears by way of a specific geological framing.'[3] This retrospective emergence of the Anthropocene subject appears to jeopardise the possibility of exactly the kind of coherent action required to temper the anthropogenic destruction which is now perceptible and quantifiable, if not fully comprehensible.

Initially, it appears that the Anthropocene condition, an unprecedented realisation of human narcissism, is unique in its impact on the dominant narratives of the human. The conceptual model of the Anthropocene – the human as destroyer who may yet redeem itself – appears to supersede and override earlier models, 'erasing the fiction of Cartesian "man"' by virtue of its appeal to both the sensory immediacy and scientific verifiability of its claims.[4] Despite auguring environmental catastrophe, the Anthropocene narrative reassuringly reunifies the human in an intellectual era largely defined by its attentiveness to human difference. This accounts for the tone of much contemporary environmental writing, which sees no contradiction in affirming the existence of a unified human community to be marshalled in service of a common cause; 'this is our moment', Eileen Crist and H. Bruce Rinke write, 'it is the moment to face the root of the terrible trouble we have unleashed for the biosphere and for ourselves'.[5] Yet rather than establishing or reinforcing the species identity of the human, the Anthropocene actually splinters humanity according to differing degrees of responsibility for environmental destruction. Cohen and Colebrook ask: 'Why would "we" want to sully the entirety of humanity by placing it as the author or agent of this late-modern event?'[6] To do so, to accept the 'anthropos' as an unexamined category, is to overlook the relationship between anthropogenic destruction and capitalism, and to revert to a model of the 'universal "human"' whose universalism was always fictitious.[7] Furthermore, rather than reinforcing the identity of the human, the Anthropocene exposes its contingency and precarity; it is with shock, not mastery and understanding, that the human encounters the extent and nature of its impact. Rather, the Anthropocene marks 'severe discontinuities',[8] even a 'total *disconnect*',[9] between humans and the natural world, and accordingly, within the 'human' itself, as it fails to fully comprehend its own legacy.

As a consequence of this apparent disconnect, Cohen and Colebrook pursue the Anthropocene subject, contending that it emerges from a misidentification between the human and its effects, and presupposes an exemplary pre-lapsarian subject. 'The very figure of a humanity oriented towards a history of flourishing, self-realization, universal scope and a proper future', they argue, 'relies upon an accidental and temporary corruption.'[10] Balancing chastisement and redemption in a way that facilitates an impassioned call to arms, the Anthropocene provides an ideal context for the reinvention of the 'human', with the 'anthropos' generated by a process of 'guilt and diagnosis'.[11] Rather than illustrating the unique effect of the Anthropocene on conceptions of human identity, as described by Cohen and Colebrook, this process – consisting of guilt and repentance – feels distinctly theological, reinstating God as the guarantor of human superiority. For this reason, it is no surprise that 'the end of man' that we witness in the Anthropocene has generated an entire industry of recuperative 'new dawns'.[12]

Colebrook's reference to Jacques Derrida's 1972 essay 'The Ends of Man' invites us to locate the invention of the 'anthropos', with all of its 'metaphysical heritage', in a philosophical history whose eschato-teleological conception of the human is no stranger to the apocalypticism of the Anthropocene.[13] The end, or termination, of Man, announced almost routinely in this history, is inseparable from the end (*telos*) of Man. As Colebrook later demonstrates in the context of the Anthropocene, it is only at a point where the – literal or figurative – death of Man is promised that Man's *telos* emerges. Derrida's essay, a 1968 riposte to Heidegger's 'Letter on Humanism' and an exploration of the complex relationship between humanism and anti-humanism in post-war France, focuses on contemporary misreadings of Hegel, Husserl and Heidegger as metaphysical humanists. One reason for such misreadings, Derrida suggests, is because in each the figure of Man is transformed but not eliminated; 'Man' undergoes sublation. In the case of Heidegger, 'the thinking of Being', Derrida writes, 'remains as thinking *of* man'.[14] In all three thinkers, the concept of Man is inscribed in terms of its 'ends'. Derrida states:

> Man is that which is in relation to his end, in the fundamentally equivocal sense of the word. Since always. The transcendental end can appear to itself and be unfolded only on the condition of mortality, of a relation to finitude as the origin of ideality. The name of man has always been inscribed in metaphysics between these two ends. It has meaning only in this eschato-teleological situation.[15]

The 'ends of man' are modified and multiplied in the Anthropocene, informed both by a messiah complex which asserts that only we can correct the damage we have created, and by the contradiction between the power and longevity suggested by our geological influence and the looming possibility of our own extinction. While we are unable to decisively escape the 'metaphysical heritage' of the figure of Man, Derrida suggests that we may not be doomed to repeat it indefinitely. Rather, he advises that we might 'weave and interlace' two strategies of deconstructive resistance, both remaining within and decisively breaking with familiar 'terrain', aiming at the production of 'several texts at once'.[16] Despite its potential to symbolise 'what is outside narrative'[17] or to bring forth a 'radical trembling [. . .] from the *outside*',[18] the Anthropocene, Colebrook demonstrates, has been used to reinstate the 'metaphysical heritage' of the figure of Man, to reinvigorate the most reactionary and anti-theoretical conceptual frameworks.[19]

This chapter will address the relationship between the story of the 'anthropos' and twentieth- and twenty-first-century representations of nonhuman primates. Examining Donna Haraway's critique of primatological practices and narratives, it will explore the ways in which an account of human identity generated in response to nonhuman primates substitutes for an 'anthropos' in flight from its own constitutive deficits. In response to Haraway's appeal for a less anthropocentric storytelling with 'many tellers and hearers'[20] and Colebrook's contention that the figure of Man is 'an effect of a failure to read',[21] it will examine Karen Joy Fowler's fictional account of primate relations, *We Are All Completely Beside Ourselves*. Focusing on Fowler's ambivalence towards anthropomorphism and linking this to the recent resurgence of scientific interest in anthropomorphism, it will develop a parallel between anthropomorphism and empathy. Like empathy, anthropomorphism is an inescapable component of cross-species relations. In its capacity to stimulate new ethical and political responses to nonhuman life from affective responses to cross-species similarity, we should cultivate it. However, noting the ways in which it remains anthropocentric and presupposes a human essence, we should retain a critical distance from it. This chapter will conclude by asking whether different modes of primatological reading and writing might generate alternatives to the figure of Man which are better able to acknowledge and fulfil our ethical responsibilities to nonhuman life.

PRIMATOLOGY AND THE 'METAPHYSICAL HERITAGE' OF MAN

In *Ecology Without Nature*, Timothy Morton tracks the inevitable failure of attempts to locate and ground human identity and the anxieties this failure generates. 'Wherever I look for my self', he explains, 'I only encounter a potentially infinite series of alterities: my body, my arm, my ideas, place of birth, parents, history, society [. . .] the ultimate paradox is that wherever we look for the self, we won't find it.'[22] We have witnessed the transformation of this anxiety in the Anthropocene: the human experiences both guilt and relief at uncovering sufficient tangible evidence of its impact to ground a distinct species identity. While the identification of the Anthropocene marks a particular stage in this process, the unease surrounding anthropogenic environmental destruction characterises a longer period and manifests itself both generally, in cultural perceptions, and in the development of specific disciplines. In *Primate Visions*, for example, Donna Haraway scrutinises the complex entangling of human self-perception and primatological history, recounting the ways in which the story of the 'anthropos' is strengthened by perceptions of other primates. Haraway frames the history of primatology as a cluster of subjective stories of the 'anthropos' whose fictionality is obscured and disavowed by their employment of a scientific methodology which is illegitimately ring-fenced in a kind of scientific 'wilderness preservation'.[23] As we saw in Chapter 1, she suggests that we should supplement such disingenuous storytelling with a decentred storytelling which accounts for nonhuman agency. Her primatological history examines the ways in which we have posited nonhuman primates as 'natural objects that can show people their origin', and as a way for humans – rendered anxious by anthropogenic environmental devastation – to heal their separation from the earth.[24] Prior to the designation Anthropocene, 'apes', Haraway claims, 'modeled a solution to a deep cultural anxiety sharpened by the real possibility in the late twentieth century, of western people's destruction of the earth' by offering the hope of a re-naturalisation of Man.[25] If primatology is, on one hand, propelled by a desire to salvage the human relationship with the natural world, it is also, on the other, driven by a desire to reassert human exceptionalism by distinguishing between nonhuman primate bodies, made available as material and conceptual resources, and human primate bodies, possessing, at least in principle, intrinsic value.

The classification of different life forms has long occupied humans, perceived as an extension to Adam's divinely endorsed naming of the animals in the first book of Genesis. The primatological end of the classificatory process is, of course, the most significant for the delineation of human identity. Primates serve as 'troubling doubles' that reflect a past with which we have lost touch and provide the raw materials through which we can envisage alternative futures.[26] For Haraway, the anthropocentrism of primatology is barely concealed. The lauded primatologist Robert Yerkes assumed that culture was unique to humans and assessed primate mental faculties according to their similarity to human abilities. Mid-twentieth-century primatology looked to ease cultural anxieties by naturalising the prevailing narratives of gender, sexuality, family and social order, coding, classifying and biopoliticising nonhuman primate bodies, their 'naturalness' a political tool. Later, 1970s primatology reflected the gendered language and ideology of the 'space race', reframing evolution as a '"hero-quest" in which early man steps out into an alien environment, braves formidable challenges and emerges the better for his primordial trial by fire', to reveal his inherent superiority to other animals.[27] All of these narratives re-theologise evolutionary history, implying that human development is planned and teleological, and that humans are thus unique. Repurposing the work of Edward Said, Haraway argues that Western primatology is a kind of 'simian Orientalism', which is grounded in 'the construction of the self from the raw material of the other, the appropriation of nature in the production of culture, the ripening of the human from the soil of the animal'.[28] Interest in primates is ultimately interest in humans and in the ways that 'the raw materials' of human and nonhuman bodies might be manipulated in service of narratives of human progress.[29]

Haraway reinforces this position in *When Species Meet*, indicting humanism on the grounds that in its 'entrails' it assumes the existence of a rational human subject whose identity is determined by its superiority over its 'others'.[30] The story of the human which emerges through primatology is a story of violence and exclusion. However, Haraway is motivated by the possibility that the curiosity at the heart of primatology might be channelled into the production of different stories, that it might be possible

> to shift the webs of intertextuality and to facilitate perhaps new possibilities for the meanings of difference, reproduction, and survival for specifically located members of the primate order – on both sides of the bio-political and cultural divide between human and animal.[31]

Primate Visions is a retelling of primatological history in which the outcomes are not already pre-determined by a fixed model of the 'anthropos', and which replaces projection with negotiation between shifting anthropomorphisms and zoomorphisms, between the 'situated knowledges' of embodied life.[32] 'Situated knowledges' offer a negotiation between the disingenuous objectivity of science and relativism. They depend on the notion that nature is both something we discover and something that is 'constituted historically'[33] and that the objective perspective that science promises is a myth that leads, as Kristin Andrews and Lori Gruen remark, 'to a danger of unwitting anthropomorphism in that the ethical norms that are being tested are thought to be the same across species and cultures'.[34] Rather, Haraway argues, 'embodiment is significant prosthesis; objectivity cannot be about fixed vision when what counts as an object is precisely what world history turns out to be about'.[35] One consequence of the notion of 'situated knowledges' is a disruption of the subject/object binary; they require that we see the object as 'an actor and agent', not a harvestable resource.[36]

Haraway's work exposes humanity's inescapable reliance on prostheses, the figure of Man as necessarily self-*insufficient*. Her notion of the cyborg, first advanced in 'The Cyborg Manifesto', challenges the distinction between free, rational human beings and the 'animal-machine', the Cartesian notion that animal behaviour is mechanistically determined.[37] Haraway's cyborg undermines the separation 'between automaton and autonomy' which underpins the notion of the human as an autonomous agent.[38] Haraway argues that 'we can learn from our fusions with animals and machines how not to be Man, the embodiment of Western logos'.[39] Haraway's vision is decidedly non-utopian; the cyborg's association with hybridity, difference and contamination guards against a transhumanist future which would aspire to a technological reinscription of Man. Rather, contrary to expectations, Haraway's cyborg reiterates the limitations and vulnerabilities generated by cross-species embodment; we should set aside the philosophical fantasies of disembodied reason (which presuppose perfect representation, translation and communication, 'the central dogma of phallogocentrism') in order to escape the figure of Man.[40] Not being Man entails a collective practice of envisioning and enacting 'imaginable epochs to come' and promises to reduce the subjugation of human and nonhuman life.[41] Such epochs would be facilitated by 'primate vision', Haraway's shorthand for the prosthetic technologies and representative processes that constitute our perception of reality.[42] 'Primate vision', aligned with the 'partiality, irony, intimacy, and perversity' of the cyborg, jams the metaphysical machinery of Man, exposing humanity as a mere participant in the multi-agential networks of the natural world, constituted by prostheses, and without a pre-determined identity or end.[43] Humans are, Haraway writes, forced to confront the fact that '"we" are permanently mortal, that is, not in "final" control'.[44] Agency is redistributed; matter is no longer perceived as passive until acted upon by humans. Haraway coins a new, agential figure for the earth, that of the coyote, which serves to remind us of the 'always potent tie of meaning and bodies'.[45]

This displacement of Man undermines the elevated figure of the human storyteller who names, taxonomises and immaterialises his material surroundings. However, Haraway insists on the potential for fiction – unbounded by fact, and free to perform, invent and recreate – to negotiate human–nonhuman relations in ways that science, restricted by the myth of its own neutrality and compelled to conceal its performativity, cannot. As Joseph Schneider notes, 'fact hides or "masks the generative deed or performance," whereas fiction, so to speak, wears that performance on its sleeve'.[46] Such a practice of storytelling must, however, be a cross-species undertaking, a space in which the identities of humans and nonhumans are co-constituted. Stories 'must listen to the practices of interpretation of the primate order in which the primates themselves – monkeys, apes, and people – all have some kind of "authorship"'.[47] Stories, as we have seen, are not pagebound distractions but facilitate different ways of life. Fiction suggests an active form of being (unlike facts, which are perceived as inert and unchangeable) that permits access to other ways of being; in it we hear 'vision, inspiration, insight, genius', as well as 'the act of fashioning, forming, or inventing'.[48] According to Haraway, narrative and material co-constitution and coexistence are not clearly separable; rather 'species is about the corporeal join of the material and the semiotic'.[49] As readers and writers, we are responsible for rewriting anthropocentric histories – for example that of canine domestication – and constructing alternative cross-species futures, not authored by Man under the misapprehension that language and aesthetic production separate humans from the natural world, but fully alert to the fleshiness of the word.[50]

ASSESSING ANTHROPOMORPHISM

The opening pages of Andrew Miller's 2011 novel *Pure* position the reader in the Palace of Versailles. According to the protagonist Jean-Baptiste, the palace is reported to contain an elephant: 'A great, melancholy beast that lives on Burgundy wine. A gift from the king of Siam.'[51] Jean-Baptiste wonders whether the elephant, and the house dogs which bark incessantly after the elephant's arrival, might be 'figures in a parable'.[52] An unseen yet immense backdrop, the elephant haunts Miller's novel, unnoticed until the final pages when we glimpse 'something grey and vast and lonely', too large to be viewed in its entirety, 'the great death-swollen bulk of it in its nest of empty wine bottles, one dull eye big as a soup plate, the delicate veined edge of an ear, a curving yellow tusk'.[53] Miller illustrates the tragic consequences of taking the human as cross-species measure: not only are our descriptive tools hampered – the elephant's spectacular eye reduced to a 'soup plate' – but here anthropomorphism leads to death, the elephant slowly poisoned by wine. Resolutely turning away from the dead creature, Jean-Baptiste's emotional response to cross-species kinship is mixed, his 'terrible brotherly pity' ultimately overshadowed by 'terrible brotherly disgust'.[54]

Anthropomorphism is a broad term which covers varied processes and disciplines. It has been subdivided, variously, into scientific and creative, 'interpretive' and 'imaginative',[55] and 'cold' and 'hot'.[56] Tom Tyler distinguishes three distinct forms:

> With decreasing regularity it is employed in its very literal sense to refer to the practice of attributing physical human *form* to some non-human being, as did the Christian anthropomorphite heretics. Secondly, it refers to the over-enthusiastic ascription of distinctively human *activities and attributes* to real or imaginary creatures, a practice frequently encountered, for instance, in children's stories [. . .] The third use is the one most frequently encountered in scientific and philosophical literature, and refers to the practice of attributing *intentionality, purpose or volition* to some creature or abstraction that (allegedly) does not have these things. This particular charge of anthropomorphism is frequently levelled at doting animal behaviourists or sloppy evolutionary theorists who are careless in the terminology they employ.[57]

In the Introduction, we saw both the vehemence with which some philosophers look to avoid the latter charge, insisting, in Tom Regan's case, on 'a concerted effort not to indulge our emotions or parade our sentiments',[58] and the ways in which this approach reinforces a long-standing, highly problematic philosophical 'somatophobia'.[59] Scientists have been similarly wary of the accusation of anthropomorphism, given that it is 'usually applied as a term of reproach, both intellectual and moral',[60] which implies naivety and delusion,[61] and carries with it 'the stale dust of nineteenth century anecdotal evidence for the continuity of humans with nonhuman animals'.[62] For Eileen Crist, responses to anthropomorphism are telling, revealing that late twentieth- and early twenty-first-century accounts of the human remain locked between a human exceptionalism rooted in Cartesianism, and the Darwinian belief in a continuum of all living beings.[63] The sharp break with, and distrust of, anthropomorphism that characterised twentieth-century positivism and behaviourism has, however, ceded to a resurgence of interest in anthropomorphism, attributable, Sandra D. Mitchell argues, to two factors: the rise of cognitive ethology and the development of new forms of environmental ethics.[64]

The most famous ethological advocates of anthropomorphism are Marc Bekoff and Frans de Waal, who aim to recuperate anthropomorphism from its association with 'sloppy thinking' and to challenge the assumption that scientific language should always adopt an objective, depersonalised, passive voice.[65] In *Minding Animals*, Bekoff describes himself as 'carefully anthropomorphic', contending that 'anthropomorphism allows other animals' behaviour and emotions to be accessible to us'.[66] He insists on the possibility of being '*biocentrically anthropomorphic* and do[ing] rigorous science'.[67] Frans de Waal's defence of anthropomorphism proceeds from the claim that the differences between humans and other primates are differences of degree, not of kind; qualities, therefore, are 'scaleable' between different primates. Accordingly, in *Chimpanzee Politics* de Waal visually and rhetorically frames the chimpanzees' social groups as if they were human, arguing that chimpanzee personalities 'can only be portrayed accurately by using the same adjectives as we use for our fellow humans'.[68] As a tool for the scientist, anthropomorphism figures as an intuitive or affective engagement, an instinctive empathy, which leads to cognitive examination and empirical testing; it functions as a 'means to get at the truth, rather than as an end in itself'.[69] The framing of anthropomorphism as an anecdotal, affective or imaginative starting point which then leads to critical thought is also advanced by Gordon Burghardt, who espouses a 'critical anthropomorphism' that filters intuitive responses through accepted philosophical and/or scientific approaches and methodologies.[70]

Denunciation of anthropomorphism is often rooted in anthropodenial, the rejection of the fact that humans are animals, and, accordingly, of methodologies that proceed from biological similarities and the assumption of 'similar causal mechanisms' across species.[71] Of his methodology, de Waal writes:

> I personally adhere to a different law of parsimony, according to which, if two closely related species act the same under similar circumstances, the mental processes behind their behavior are likely the same, too. The alternative would be to postulate that, in the short time since they diverged, both species evolved different ways of generating the same behavior. From an evolutionary standpoint, this is a convoluted proposal.[72]

According to the philosopher Martha Nussbaum, the stakes of anthropodenial are high; it is 'not simply a pernicious intellectual position', she contends, but also 'a large cause of moral deformity'.[73] For Nussbaum, comparisons of human and nonhuman life tend to be rooted in 'continuities' and 'good discontinuities', where the human outperforms the nonhuman.[74] This approach, she argues, elides other discontinuities where the nonhuman outperforms the human. One instance of this, she suggests, is compassion, as human compassion 'is profoundly uneven and unreliable' and sometimes makes animals look like 'morally superior beings'.[75]

Although Tyler proposes a clear distinction between the second type of anthropomorphism (literary) and the third (scientific or philosophical), such a distinction reinforces the model of science – unfailingly rational, objective and disembodied – that Haraway, as well as de Waal and Bekoff, disavow. Their alternative models challenge the opposition between narrative and truth; Susan McHugh, for example, notes:

> de Waal's insistence that narrative has been an integral part of the structures and methods through which ethologists gain credit for breaking up the human monopoly on culture by the end of the twentieth century; in other words, that story becomes a means of negotiating alternatives to nature/culture, animal/human, and related hierarchic dualisms in thought itself.[76]

Like that of Haraway, such ethological positions also recognise nonhumans as narrative agents whose lives are 'meaningful and authored'.[77]

The most significant challenge posed to anthropomorphism from within animal studies is the charge of anthropocentrism. Here anthropomorphism, like empathy, is perceived as an imaginatively limited procedure that reinforces existing hierarchies and relations. As Lorraine Daston and Gregg Mitman write: 'humans project their own thoughts and feelings onto other animal species because they egotistically believe themselves to be the center of the universe'.[78] Anthropomorphism is anthropocentric because the human continues to be both the starting point and the measure; rather than thinking '*with* animals', anthropomorphism remains a thinking *of*, where the thinking process is

untroubled by other cognitive or affective modes.[79] This is the position from which Stephen Jay Gould argues; anthropomorphism, he
claims, is a 'genuine barrier' to understanding the 'different worlds' of
other species as it necessitates projection on to other species; we pull
them into the human orbit, rather than encountering them on their
own terms.[80] While the danger of anthropocentrism should continue
to discomfit anthropomorphism, anthropomorphism should not be
discarded on the grounds that any kind of cross-species comparison
betrays the singularity of 'different worlds'. As we saw in the case of
compared atrocities in Chapter 1, singularity is always compromised
by the generalising effects of comparison and communication; we must
proceed carefully and pragmatically.

A more interesting challenge to the work of comparison inherent in
anthropomorphism proceeds from an examination of the assumption
that the terms are fixed, in other words, that the 'human' has a clear,
fixed identity. As Tyler writes:

> Anthropomorphism, both as term and concept, imprudently starts with the
> human, even though the whole question of the nature of the human has yet
> to be determined. Anthropomorphism as a notion is, in short, anthropo-
> centric, in a particular sense. This variety of anthropocentrism is not one
> that necessarily implies human superiority [. . .] But by invoking anthro-
> pomorphism as a term, one is inevitably committed to thinking humanity
> *first*. By relying on anthropomorphism as a concept, one places the human
> *foremost*.[81]

Not only does anthropomorphism begin with the human, it mistakenly presupposes that the human has an essence which pre-exists its
relations with nonhuman life, rather than emerging through them. It
is also, Tyler suggests, unhelpfully proprietorial about qualities; it is
'dangerous and misleading to suppose that attributes or behaviours
"belong" to the creatures who display them'.[82] In the next section, I
shall argue that we should advocate for a dynamic and selective anthropomorphism which does not presuppose fixed definitions of the human
and its others.

PRIMATOLOGICAL FICTION: *WE ARE ALL COMPLETELY BESIDE OURSELVES*

In *Primate Visions*, Haraway aims to disturb the association between
language and human mastery by demonstrating that tests of nonhuman
primates' linguistic capacities are scientifically flawed and by advancing
the construction of cross-species fictions. This aim is complemented by
Derrida's notion of the 'animality of writing', a provocative reminder

that writing – dispersed, disruptive and inhuman – challenges rather than reinforces the sovereignty of Man.[83] If Man is the paradigm of propriety, sameness and self-identity, writing is improper and untamed. In Karen Joy Fowler's 2013 novel *We Are All Completely Beside Ourselves*, it is, to use Derrida's phrase, the 'animality of writing', its creative, non-instrumental value, rather than its communicative use, which is explored and endorsed.[84] The functional value of language, the protagonist Rosemary notes, is limiting; language 'does this to our memories', she discloses, 'simplifies, solidifies, codifies, mummifies'.[85] It is an 'imprecise vehicle' (*WAACBO*, 85). That language has creative potential, both for cross-species play and in defying sedimented conceptual structures, is revealed by the 'idioglossia' (*WAACBO*, 100) constructed by Rosemary and Fern, the chimpanzee raised as her sister. When Fern is removed from the family, a dismayed Rosemary realises that 'all of my verbosity had been valuable only in the context of my sister. When she left the scene, no one cared anymore about my creative grammars, my compound lexemes, my nimble gymnastic conjugations' (*WAACBO*, 108).

Fowler's novel, a fictional rewriting of the 1970s practice of raising infant chimpanzees within human families to assess animal language acquisition, advances a critique of primatology – as cruel, unreflective and reinforcing an inaccurate account of the human – alongside an alternative history of its victims which, in inspiring cross-species empathy, 'a process or procedure by which a person *centrally imagines* the thoughts, feelings, and emotions (what I will call the *narrative*) of another person', might be used to ground a different future.[86] Fowler contends with the challenge of rewriting, or at least pluralising, an anthropocentric history without reducing nonhuman animals to literary tropes, ventriloquising them, or reproducing the kind of 'simian Orientalism' that Haraway identifies. To this end, she experiments with anthropomorphism and zoomorphism. If she succeeds, it is by sustaining ambiguity, generating multiple meanings of the text by resisting a definitive focus, either human or nonhuman. For the critics, however, there is no ambiguity. Just as decades of critical readings of Kafka's short story 'A Report to an Academy', the inspiration behind Fowler's novel, attempted to stabilise this unruly and disturbing text by confining it to allegory, Fowler's critics tend to impose humanistic readings on her novel.[87] In the critics' conservative hands, the text, whose very title, *We Are All Completely Beside Ourselves*, challenges the 'metaphysical heritage' of Man as sovereign and self-identical, becomes unmistakable as a novel about human life: 'a provocative take on family love' and 'a story of Everyfamily'.[88]

These reductive readings disregard Fowler's resistance to clarifying or restricting the focus of the novel. Like the 'Fern/Rosemary Rosemary/Fern study' (*WAACBO*, 99) itself, in which Rosemary suspects that she too is an object of study, Fowler renders the tragically separated siblings biologically, conceptually and ethically inseparable. One cannot understand human-chimp Fern aside from chimp-human Rosemary, and synecdochally, one cannot understand nonhuman primates without human primates. Fowler reflexively reproduces primatological methodology, which conceals its primary purpose – the understanding and development of a narrative of the human – beneath its secondary purpose – the study of nonhuman primates – by demonstrating that the two goals are inextricably linked. Indicting the myopia of scientific practice and its attachment to the figure of Man, Fowler tartly observes that 'the thing ostensibly being studied is rarely the thing being studied' (*WAACBO*, 99). While the critics frame Fowler's novel as a fictional exploration of familial ties and human capabilities, when the human is the primary focus it is subjected to a cold, critical gaze, both in terms of its cognitive limitations – 'research at Kyoto University has demonstrated the superiority of chimps to humans at certain short-term memory tasks' (*WAACBO*, 301) – and its lack of empathy or compassion – 'some scientist had observed all that, had actually watched a chimp raped 170 times and kept count. Good scientist. Not me' (*WAACBO*, 275–6). Like the audience facing Red Peter in Kafka's story, unnerved when their ostensible object of study brands humanity *his* 'specimen', as Fowler's readers we are disturbed to find that it is human, not nonhuman, behaviour that is subjected to unsentimental interrogation.[89] Both Kafka's audience and Fowler's readers, exposed to the myth of human beneficence and the artifice of human behaviour – the act of *aping* as constitutively human – are forced to see the human as 'beside itself'. Fowler explains of her novel's title: 'Though she [Rosemary] has lived an extreme version of being beside herself, still, it affects us all [. . .] The line between us and not-us is a blurry one: that's what the title is trying to say.' And she voices a philosophical position espoused from Kant to Haraway, but seemingly ignored by primatology: 'This is partly because we are incapable of seeing anything that isn't transformed into us by the mere act of seeing it.'[90] Here we are invited to consider the double-bind in which Fowler's text is caught: it is ethically responsible for bearing witness to nonhuman life, but in speaking for the 'other', it cannot always avoid intrusion or misrepresentation.

The separation of Fern and Rosemary is presented as an act of brutality (precipitated by human arrogance and stupidity) from which neither recovers. The coupling of their stories, in the – inevitably

elliptical – text that Rosemary feels compelled to write is presented as
an act of witnessing, a story 'for Fern too, Fern again, always Fern'
(*WAACBO*, 304), which painstakingly attempts not to intrude, over-
step or imperialise, by speaking on behalf of Fern. Accordingly, the
novel is constructed around the specularity of the pair; in Haraway's
parlance, they are co-constituted, not least because they began to mould
each other before they had 'gotten to be themselves' (*WAACBO*, 107).
In their infancy, neuroplasticity ensures that their neural development
is mirrored (*WAACBO*, 101), and, later, they experience similar social
and sexual estrangement because of their upbringing – Rosemary
cannot leave behind her 'chimp nature' (*WAACBO*, 221) and Fern is
convinced of her own humanity. Fern's loss is experienced by Rosemary
viscerally, 'a hunger on the surface of my skin' (*WAACBO*, 107).
Historically, the mirror has served as a marker of human difference and
superiority: Jacques Lacan's 'mirror stage' marks an important step in
the establishment of subjectivity; the mirror self-recognition test, developed in 1970, assesses the extent to which nonhuman animals conform
to human expectations of intelligence and awareness. In addition, as
Cynthia Willett states:

> Theories that rely upon mirror metaphors, as in the measurement of self-
> awareness through the mirror recognition test and theorizing empathy
> through mirror neurons or abstract sameness, inadvertently reinforce atom-
> istic models of the self as bound and separate rather than attuned to, and
> immersed with, others in a biosocial web with its larger energy flows.[91]

It is exactly this atomisation and isolation, perceiving selves as
objects of study, that causes Fern and Rosemary irreversible emotional
damage. Fowler, however, is not content to dispense with mirror
imagery altogether; rather she looks to supplant the kind of one-sided
mirroring in which one term is fixed and instrumentalised, the 'animal
mirror' of primatological history,[92] with a type of mutual mirroring, in
which both sides, 'Fern/Rosemary Rosemary/Fern', reflect, adapt and
learn from each other. The misguided attempt by their grandmother
to console Rosemary – 'You just remember you were the one made in
God's image' (*WAACBO*, 67) – is rendered absurd; Fern and Rosemary
are moulded in each other's image, leaving neither space for God nor a
distinguishable divine imprint on Rosemary. In fact, the intrusion of the
nonhuman in the development of human subjectivity does not confirm
human superiority – the '*good discontinuities*' which we are keen to
identify between ourselves and other animals – but human limitations.[93] Rosemary is the 'monkey-girl' (*WAACBO*, 128) with 'boundary issues' (*WAACBO*, 30), whereas Fern has superior vocal ability and
a more agreeable temperament. Fowler's account of mirroring allows

both for species difference and for cross-species co-constitution. The most noticeable effect of species difference is that it dictates the limits of commodification. This is recognised even by the infant Rosemary who observes: 'There was something NotSame about Fern and me, Fern could be bought and sold' (*WAACBO*, 213).

That the figure of Man is a fiction, a 'failure to read', or a formalisation of a misrecognition, and that this results in an isolated species fantasising about its re-naturalisation, is insistently reiterated by Fowler's novel. The destabilisation of the category of the human is exemplified by Rosemary's own 'mirror stage': 'My own face in the mirror', she describes, 'a badly lit mug shot, egg-white and staring. I reject it entirely' (*WAACBO*, 169). A disjunction between the experience of fragmentation and the totality of the perceived image is constitutive of the 'mirror stage'; the Imaginary, which constitutes me as a subject, is 'the notion of the Symbolic as having a relation to the real', Colebrook writes.[94] Here, Rosemary resists identification; without Fern, she is an 'egg', unborn, incomplete. This scene contrasts with the ending of the novel, also a mirror scene, but one in which both Rosemary and Fern are present, each of them leaning their head on the glass barrier which divides them. Rosemary explains: 'I didn't know what she was thinking or feeling. Her body had become unfamiliar to me. And yet, at the very same time, I recognized everything about her. My sister, Fern. In the whole wide world, my only red poker chip. As if I were looking in a mirror' (*WAACBO*, 308). In this scene Rosemary attains the recognition earlier denied, with her disjointed self-experience reflected by Fern, whom she sees 'only in teary, floating pieces' (*WAACBO*, 308). This, however, can only be a temporary closure of the distance between them, a momentary suspension of their alienation.

Haraway contends that 'response cannot emerge within relationships of self-similarity', that responsible behaviour is not facilitated by specular logics.[95] In this, Haraway is aligned with thinkers for whom empathy, 'in contrast to emotional contagion, entails the capacity to experience what others do experience, while being able to attribute these shared experiences to *others* and not to the self'.[96] Fowler's novel, however, is ambivalent about specularity; while it is a symptom of the instability of human identity often leading to cross-species irresponsibility, it can also be employed imaginatively to foreground the 'semiotic materiality' that we share with other beings.[97] We can read this in terms of the text's treatment of empathy: the affective force of the novel is grounded in its self-conscious evocation of cross-species empathy, both between its characters and from reader to text. Fowler's anthropomorphisation of Fern is not a comic projection or literary escapism, but a serious reflection on scientific evidence. Its aim, therefore, is to extend our understanding of chimpanzees beyond the literary, to 'stir societally effective empathy'. Although our practical experiences of chimpanzees might be limited, it is clear from the novel that Fern is 'not humanized into a caricature', but 'bring[s] forth' a particular form 'of animality in ways that enable recognition'.[98] We empathise with Fern when she is separated from her family, mistreated and, finally, incarcerated. In her experience of temporary incarceration, we witness Rosemary's empathetic engagement with Fern's condition. Empathy is a challenge for Rosemary as it entails 'a practice of self-empathy' to which, as a consequence of her guilt and shame, she is extremely resistant.[99]

In its framing of the mistreatment of female animals, the text highlights the political precedence of sexual difference over species difference, that 'women and animals are similarly positioned in a patriarchal world', in order to mobilise empathy and, thus, female solidarity.[100] Yet empathy, like anthropomorphism, must be other-focused to lead to understanding in cross-species relationships. Critiquing the sentimental tendencies of literary anthropomorphism, Fowler reminds us that focusing on similarity at the expense of difference is naive and dangerous. In the most striking example of Fern's difference, Rosemary watches as Fern takes the kitten Rosemary has handed her, swings him against a tree trunk, and finally 'opened him with her fingers like a purse' (*WAACBO*, 250). Shock and horror (at the actions of both Fern and Rosemary) here supersede empathy as our affective response to this incident. Herein lies the uncanniness of human and nonhuman primate relations: the 'uncanny valley' (*WAACBO*, 102) response is generated not just by cross-species similarity, but by difference. Nonhuman primates (and Rosemary too, when she fails to perform her humanness effectively) are uncanny because they are never quite convincing as humans. As Cora Diamond reminds us, it is morally perplexing that the 'sense of its being impossible that we should go and *eat* them [animals]' is combined with 'feeling how powerfully strange it is that they and we should share as much as we do, and yet also not share'.[101]

For Fowler, specularity, and thus anthropomorphism, need not be narcissistic or appropriative, but might facilitate a dynamic negotiation between one's own and others' identities. This is illustrated by Rosemary's conception of 'a sort of reverse mirror test' which would 'identify those species smart enough to see themselves when they look at someone else. Bonus points for how far out the chain you can go. Double bonus for those who get all the way to insects' (*WAACBO*, 201–2). This suggestion that such refigured anthropomorphism is a triumph of imagination, and of sympathy beyond similarity, is advanced throughout the novel, with Lowell critiquing his father's resistance to anthropomorphism. 'Dad was always saying that we were all animals', he reveals, 'but when he dealt with Fern, he didn't start from that place of congruence. His methods put the whole burden of proof onto her [. . .] It would have been more scientifically rigorous to start with an assumption of similarity' (*WAACBO*, 202). Lowell's identification of the 'distorting parameters' of animal experiments and endorsement of a selective anthropomorphism is consistent with the work of Bekoff and de Waal.[102] We cannot wholly escape our own conceptual frameworks; however, we can treat them reflexively; in the case of primatology, this might entail a shift from the ranking of cognitive ability 'for approximation to the human form', to identifying and valuing other modes and manifestations of intelligence, thus broadening our definition of the latter.[103]

   To accept and encourage anthropomorphism, science must acknowledge the roles of approximation and storytelling within its practices, rather than performing or feigning detached neutrality. Haraway suggests that reading scientific practice through the lens of science fiction and vice versa might be one way of achieving this.[104] Representing the intransigent rejection of anthropomorphism, the Cooke father is an ambivalent figure in the novel. The initiator of Fern's adoption, he is hopelessly naive and obstructively detached; highly invested in the belief that 'a neutral language exists, or can be constructed, and that this will yield incontestably objective accounts of animal behaviour', he is emotionally disengaged both from his family and from Fern's suffering.[105] An instantiation of too little empathy, their father is contrasted with both Lowell and their mother, whose guilt and shame – reinforced by empathetic over-engagement with Fern – leads to mental breakdowns for both, the mother becoming 'vaporous' (*WAACBO*, 60), incapable of caring for herself or her other children. One must navigate a path, Fowler suggests, between too little and too much empathy. Without self-care and self-empathy, productive empathy becomes impossible; 'reflective empathy', Elisa Aaltola insists, must aim 'primarily towards learning more of oneself in order to know the other'.[106]

   Fowler's novel employs anthropomorphism judiciously, safeguarding against Tom Tyler's concern that 'the designation of any quality or attribute as distinctively human, a designation required by the concept of anthropomorphism, is unwarranted',[107] by emphasising Fern's mastery of qualities usually perceived as human, her skills a 'mountain' in comparison to Rosemary's 'molehill' (*WAACBO*, 82). Appropriately, given the literal co-constitution of the siblings, the anthropomorphisation of Fern is accompanied by an animalisation of 'monkey girl' Rosemary. Like Haraway, Fowler's anthropomorphism does not conflate the human with the 'anthropos', with a pre-existing essence and end. The human is not a fixed point in Fowler's novel, a scale against which we can measure nonhuman difference. Rather, the novel demonstrates that anthropomorphism is a clumsy but useful tool for understanding kinship and difference once we have exploded the myth of scientific neutrality. While anthropomorphism derives from a genuine curiosity and desire to understand other living beings, it also seems to issue from a desire to expunge our own strangeness by projecting it outside ourselves and by abusing the beings on to which we project. The human becomes, like Red Peter, unable to express its own animal nature for fear of cracking the façade, rather embodying the 'ethos of disavowal' which characterises the human.[108]

The lesson of Fowler's novel is not that we can transcend the strangeness of other animals but rather that we are also strange, that this odd mixture of distance and kinship which characterises human relationships with nonhumans parallels the relationships they have with themselves. For this reason, Fowler both invokes anthropomorphism, which is essential for the affective impact of the book, and questions it. The latter occurs both at a basic narrative level – Fern's adoption is predicated on a misguided anthropomorphism – and more subtly, as Fowler displays a range of distancing emotions – anger, shock, 'shame at being human' – that counter the limitations of empathetic anthropomorphism.[109] Nor does Fowler reassert anthropocentrism by confining the novel's ethical concerns to the specular relationships between human and nonhuman primates. Her concerns are broader: the laboratory rats that Lowell releases, the insects that defy anthropomorphism, and even the Thanksgiving turkey, whose transmission of Tryptophan, 'rumored to make you sleepy and careless' (*WAACBO*, 21), is the ultimate instantiation of Haraway's cross-species co-constitution.

Alert to the limitations of anthropomorphism, Kay Milton proposes an alternative: 'egomorphism'. Beginning from mutuality and difference, rather than from hierarchised difference (so often presupposed by anthropomorphism), egomorphism is designed to stimulate cross-species empathy, to avoid the projections of anthropocentrism, and to understand nonhuman experience on its own terms. She explains:

> [Anthropomorphism] assumes that 'human-ness' is the primary point of reference for understanding non-human things; a more reasonable assertion, I suggest, is that the 'self' or 'ego' (in the general rather than the Freudian sense) is the primary point of reference for understanding both human and non-human things.[110]

Egomorphism parallels an empathetic mode which 'provides access to the suffering of the other' by recognising a meaningful distinction between self and other: it permits an affective response without the total collapse of critical distance and subjective boundaries, both of which are at least pragmatically necessary for the construction of a cross-species ethics.[111]

'CHIMPED-UP' WRITING: THE CHALLENGE OF CROSS-SPECIES AUTHORSHIP

In J. M. Coetzee's *The Lives of Animals*, the protagonist Elizabeth Costello assesses two modes of addressing nonhuman animal life: the philosophical and the poetic. The first, exemplified by philosopher Tom Regan's claim that we can only advance the cause of nonhuman animals 'by making a concerted effort not to indulge our emotions or sentiments',[112] endeavours to be 'cool rather than heated, philosophical rather than polemical'.[113] While it accords value to the Great Apes and to certain other mammals, this approach remains yoked to an anthropocentric scale in which nonhuman animals are valued only for the qualities they share with humans, thus ultimately reinforcing a story in which 'man is godlike, animals thinglike'.[114] To thinking, Costello opposes 'fullness, embodiedness, the sensation of being', a cross-species experience defined not by deficiency but plenitude, and expressed better by the poets than the philosophers, the latter largely unwilling to countenance that reason might be 'neither the being of the universe nor the being of God' but merely 'the being of a certain spectrum of human thinking'.[115] To deviate from the figure of Man is to reject reason as that which controls or integrates human subjectivity, which rather, as Schneider highlights, incorporates 'quite disparate, shifting, and often contradictory parts'.[116] The alternative, for Costello, is 'the sympathetic imagination' which enables us to imaginatively identify with other beings, perhaps, she suggests, without limit.[117] That we are in possession of a 'sympathetic imagination' clearly testifies to the malleability and dynamism of the human subject, rather than the self-identity of Man. The sympathetic imagination is an aesthetic faculty with ethical implications; evil is the result of a failure of empathy, 'that the killers', in the case of the Holocaust, 'refused to think themselves into the place of their victims'.[118] On the shared nature of being – accessible to imaginative, rather than rational, faculties – Costello and Fowler are aligned. Living animals and living humans are both 'full of being',[119] with chimpanzees teaching their human companions 'that in the phrase *human being*, the word *being* is much more important than the word *human'* (*WAACBO*, 158). The approach that Costello proposes would entail a dramatic shift in our social and cultural priorities; 'if empathy rather than rationality is genuinely universal', James Mensch posits, 'then literature [...] becomes our common language' and 'owns the public space uniting different cultures'.[120] Other critics are less convinced; Richard Holton and Rae Langton conclude that 'imaginative identification will get us nowhere'.[121]

Less clear than the aims of the 'sympathetic imagination', however, is how this kinship, the 'heavily affective sensation' shared by human and nonhuman primates 'of being alive to the world', might be employed to derail the figure of Man and suggest alternative cross-species stories.[122] For Fowler, familiar forms must be rejected; her invocation of the fairy tale 'once upon a time' (*WAACBO*, 58) is swiftly curtailed, this didactic mode framing nonhuman animal being as something to be corrected. Rosemary starts decisively 'in the middle' (*WAACBO*, 2) of the story, resisting the conventions of linear storytelling that presuppose the mastery of the human storyteller, a representative of stable and pre-determined Man. Even language, the 'imprecise vehicle' employed by Rosemary to express Fern's suffering, is regarded with suspicion. Attentive to the discrepancy between 'the happening and the telling' (*WAACBO*, 48), as well as to the ethical dangers of using individuals – herself, Fern, Lowell – to mount a broader critique of primatological practice, Rosemary persists, propelled by familial solidarity. 'What this family needs now is a great talker' (*WAACBO*, 304), she asserts. In her 'chimped-up' (*WAACBO*, 79) family, however, her loyalties are inevitably divided between her father, responsible for Fern's predicament, and Fern herself. While Rosemary attends meticulously to Fern's story, she also bears witness to some of the real chimpanzees placed in Fern's position by including a short excursus in which each is named and described. In this instance, fiction is complemented by facts, with the aim of exposing human failures.

That the figure of Man is constructed by violent exclusion, by a 'simian Orientalism' which is explicitly gendered, is unmistakable in Fowler's novel. At the heart of Rosemary's – misplaced – guilt towards her sister is the belief that Fern was failed, not by their father, but by the women who should have supported her: 'my mother, the female grad students, me – none of us had helped. Instead, we had exiled her to a place completely devoid of female solidarity' (*WAACBO*, 166). Unable to perceive the complicity between patriarchy and primatology, that 'misogyny is built into the objects of everyday life in laboratory practice'[123] and 'anthropodenial is thus linked with an aggressive and potentially violent misogyny', Rosemary acquits the real culprits, recognising only her own complicity.[124] At times, her writing feels like an act of penance, albeit one with no promise of redemption. To compensate for the instrumentalisation of Fern, Rosemary instrumentalises herself, becoming, through her writing, a tool 'for remembrance' (*WAACBO*, 11), bearing witness to Fern's mistreatment. That there might also be therapeutic gains for Rosemary, her writing transgressing her father's dislike for psychoanalysis by clearly staging the analytic process to facilitate the re-emergence of repressed experiences and emotions, is never explicitly acknowledged. Having witnessed the extreme subjugation of nonhuman needs in service of human curiosity, she is unable to acknowledge that the telling of Fern's story – a compensatory act – might be of benefit to her too. Rosemary's lack of self-empathy, her estrangement from her '*own* inner life', is a deficiency, not a strength.[125]

Accordingly, Fowler does not unequivocally endorse the ethical purism espoused by Rosemary and Lowell, the latter entirely disavowing his humanity. Rosemary states: '*They*, my brother said, whenever he talked about humans. Never *us*. Never *we*' (*WAACBO*, 232), earlier having disclosed that 'his mental condition is not good' (*WAACBO*, 305). Lowell's over-identification with nonhuman animals ultimately hampers his ability to function, and it is noticeable that Fowler does not cultivate such over-identification among her readers but emphasises species and individual difference. Accordingly, 'self–other differentiation allows the reader to simultaneously simulate the character's psychological states and experience her own separate psychological states'.[126] Rosemary and Lowell's upbringing results in their flight to the peripheries of human community; both are constitutionally unsuited for human interaction and appalled by the human violence they have witnessed. Rosemary is unwilling even to acknowledge that it is her human qualities, the language with which she wonders why we 'bother' (*WAACBO*, 85), that enables her to publicly vouch for Fern. As readers, however, we might ask of Rosemary and Lowell, as Elinor Marx asks of Elizabeth Costello: 'Are you not expecting too much of humankind when you ask us to live without species exploitation, without cruelty?'[127] It is telling that Fowler chooses to focus on Rosemary more than Rosemary herself would permit; Fowler's is a cluster of cross-species stories, not an act of confession. Co-constitution and coexistence, while not necessitating the extremes of cruelty exhibited in the novel, are messy and require, contra Lowell's abolitionism, that we 'learn to live responsibly within the multiplicitous necessity and labor of killing'.[128] Acknowledging the specificity of human responsibility does not necessarily lead to exceptionalism.

Recognising the complexity of cross-species relations requires resisting the appeal of a penitent 'anthropos' who, confirmed in its identity by the damage it has caused, promises to correct and atone. Such a vision denies both the human compulsion to instrumentalise its surroundings and the possibility of nonhuman agency. The distinction between stories which reinforce the 'anthropos' in this recuperative mode and those which identify and facilitate nonhuman agency is captured by Haraway's distinction between 'a politics of representation' and 'a politics of articulation'.[129] The former, in which nonhuman life is represented without being invited to participate, is a preliminary step in the recognition of nonhuman interests; however, its sphere of engagement remains singularly human. This is a danger for poetic accounts of nonhuman life, which run the risk of operating 'within an entirely human economy in which the animal has no share'.[130] Nonhuman tropes, while inviting us to escape 'inherited boxes', also risk substituting for the articulation of nonhuman life.[131] Fowler's novel shuttles between representation and articulation, with Rosemary endeavouring to limit her mediation of Fern's 'authorship' and deflate the myth of the deified human author. Writing of Albert Camus's polemic against the guillotine, motivated by the childhood trauma of witnessing the slaughter of a chicken, Coetzee's Costello asks: 'Who is to say, then, that the hen did not speak?'[132] Fowler, too, asks us to be more attentive to nonhuman authorship, particularly to the 'stealthily influential' (*WAACBO*, 299) Fern, who we might credit for Rosemary's writing. Fowler contends that aesthetic production is not unique to humans, describing in detail the paintings that Fern produces, supporting evidence for philosopher Elizabeth Grosz's contention that 'art isn't primarily or solely conceptual, that what it represents is the most animal part of us rather than the most human part of us'.[133]

In *Of Grammatology*, Derrida argues that the history of man is the history of supplementarity:

> Man *calls himself* man only by drawing limits and excluding his other from the play of supplementarity: the purity of nature, of animality, primitivism, childhood, madness, divinity. The approach to these limits is at once feared as a threat of death, and desired as access to a life without *différance*. The history of man *calling himself* man is the articulation of all these limits among themselves.[134]

Anthropomorphism, as a stabilising instance of 'man calling himself man' through the conduit of other beings, always risks disruption at the hands of other, *différantial* forces. The figure of 'Man' requires fixed borders; as soon as these borders become porous, his identity begins to disintegrate. The pluralisation of the human/animal border, the work of 'limitrophy, for the complication of the limit that grows', is thus both the philosophical and political aim of *The Animal That Therefore I Am*.[135] This aim is realised imaginatively in Fowler's novel through the 'limitrophe existence' of Rosemary and Fern.[136] Their liminality, Matthew Calarco argues, destabilises the 'anthropological difference and the metaphysical assumptions and dogmas that ground such a project'.[137] Instead of a recuperation of the 'anthropos', enlightened and revivified by the damage it has caused, Fowler exposes humanity as disunified, non-identical, 'beside itself'. This is a source of unease and discomfort, but also an opportunity for transformation, cross-species engagement and a broadening of the ethical sphere. Shelley's celebrated indictment of human narcissism, 'Ozymandias', itself impeded by its restriction to a singularly human economy, is comically transformed by its re-situation in a genuinely cross-species context, recited when Lowell's snow-ant is accidentally destroyed by Fern. On reuniting with Fern after a 22-year separation, Rosemary writes that 'no words are sufficient' (*WAACBO*, 307). Rosemary's fear is that words reduce the plural to the singular, shrink being into stasis, and impose mastery on those who articulate otherwise. Fowler's novel continuously resists such reduction, sustaining numerous stories and endorsing a language not of mastery or instrumentality, but of ambiguity and animality; this is articulated by the infant Rosemary, whom we see speaking, with all her chimp-human verbosity, in 'extravagant abundance' and with 'inexhaustible flow'. 'The point of the movie isn't the words themselves' (*WAACBO*, 2), but that Rosemary's loquacity is nonsensical without Fern. Without Fern, she is partial and incomplete.

Comparing herself to Kafka's Red Peter, Coetzee's Costello presents herself, as 'an animal, exhibiting yet not exhibiting, to a gathering of scholars, a wound, which I cover up under my clothes but touch on in every word I speak'.[138] In both Coetzee's and Fowler's texts, the human is not synonymous with Man, but is partial, wounded, prosthetic. This is both a point of cross-species similarity, the vulnerability of which Derrida, Butler and others speak, and a reminder of the contamination between the material and the social; the body, whether human or nonhuman, is always already 'marked', a 'critical locus of cultural and political contestation' central both to languages of liberation and those of domination.[139] This social and physical vulnerability is also an ontological vulnerability: the human wound is its lack of essence, and the anxieties emerging from this have long licensed cross-species abuse. We might refigure this wound, however, that which makes us 'beside ourselves', both as liberation – the human is no longer determined by its 'ends' – and as a route to cross-species empathetic interaction. Facilitating the cultivation of the 'sympathetic imagination', literature has a key role to play; the figurative can transform the conceptual. Fowler's text undermines Tyler's distinction between literary and philosophical anthropomorphisms; it clearly performs philosophical work.

A deconstructive thinking of Man must resist the temptation to claim, as some posthumanists do, that we can escape the recuperative play of 'Man' between anti-humanism and humanism.[140] Rather, Derrida cautions against attempts to make an 'absolute break', to think wholly outside the existing conceptual schema, on the grounds that they risk inhabiting the inside more strictly and naively than ever; such are 'false exits'.[141] Alternatively, a deconstructive 'weaving and interleaving' might consist of a continuous critique of Man in conjunction with the ongoing employment of its resources, including the benefits of anthropomorphism. Fowler's text employs such a manoeuvre, cultivating empathetic anthropomorphism while undercutting the very grounds of this anthropomorphism (both the philosophical and political sovereignty, and ethical superiority, of the human species), and transforming the notion of anthropomorphism from within. Hence, Fowler's reader is 'moved by the cognitive-perceptual state and concerns' of the human and nonhuman characters.[142] Fowler both advocates a model of cross-species co-authorship and highlights the political potential of fiction; in our fictional co-imaginings, we conceive of, and begin to bring forth, other worlds. Adopting a Levinasian-Derridean vernacular, Calarco appeals for 'careful and generous attention to radical alterity, in which the other's interiority is understood as never being fully present, providing only oblique signs and traces'.[143] While false empathy critics highlight the 'self-congratulatory delusions of those who incorrectly believe that they have caught the feelings of suffering others from a different culture, gender, race or class' (or, we might add, species), Calarco frames this as an ontological, rather than a cultural issue.[144] The 'sympathetic imagination' may be limited, but it is only by employing, inhabiting and questioning empathetic anthropomorphism that it can be transformed or even surpassed.

NOTES

1. Jacques Derrida, 'The Ends of Man', in *Margins of Philosophy*, trans. Alan Bass (Chicago: University of Chicago Press, 1972), pp. 111–36 (p. 136).

2. Timothy Clark, *Ecocriticism on the Edge: The Anthropocene as a Threshold Concept* (London: Bloomsbury, 2015), p. 9.

3. Tom Cohen and Claire Colebrook, 'Preface', in *The Twilight of the Anthropocene Idols*, ed. Tom Cohen, Claire Colebrook and J. Hillis Miller (London: Open Humanities Press, 2016), pp. 7–19 (p. 9).

4. Cohen and Colebrook, 'Preface', p. 7.
5. Eileen Crist and H. Bruce Rinke, 'One Grand Organic Whole', in *Gaia in Turmoil: Climate Change, Biodepletion, and Earth Ethics in an Age of Crisis*, ed. Eileen Crist and H. Bruce Rinke (Cambridge, MA: MIT Press, 2010), p. 330.
6. Cohen and Colebrook, 'Preface', p. 7.
7. Cohen and Colebrook, 'Preface', p. 91.
8. Haraway, 'Anthropocene', p. 160.
9. Bruno Latour, 'Waiting for Gaia. Composing the Common World through Arts and Politics', a lecture at the French Institute, London, November 2011, http://www.bruno-latour.fr/sites/default/files/124-GAIA-LONDON-SPEAP_o.pdf (accessed 18 February 2019), p. 2.
10. Cohen and Colebrook, 'Preface', p. 17.
11. Claire Colebrook, 'What is the Anthropo-Political?', in *The Twilight of the Anthropocene Idols*, ed. Tom Cohen, Claire Colebrook and J. Hillis Miller (London: Open Humanities Press, 2016), pp. 81–125 (p. 86).
12. Colebrook, 'What is the Anthropo-Political?', p. 86.
13. Derrida, 'The Ends of Man', p. 115.
14. Derrida, 'The Ends of Man', p. 128.
15. Derrida, 'The Ends of Man', p. 123.
16. Derrida, 'The Ends of Man', p. 135.
17. Colebrook, 'What is the Anthropo-Political?', p. 100.
18. Derrida, 'The Ends of Man', p. 134.
19. Where theory is understood as 'an acceptance of a distinction between a strong sense of the inhuman (that which exists beyond, beyond all givenness and imaging, and beyond all relations) and an unfounded imperative that we must therefore give ourselves a law'. Colebrook, *Death of the PostHuman*, p. 31.
20. Haraway, *Primate Visions*, p. 8.
21. Colebrook, 'What is the Anthropo-Political?', p. 93.
22. Timothy Morton, *Ecology Without Nature: Rethinking Environmental Aesthetics* (Cambridge, MA: Harvard University Press, 2007), pp. 175–6.
23. Haraway, *Primate Visions*, p. 125.
24. Donna Haraway, *Simians, Cyborgs and Women: The Reinvention of Nature* (New York: Routledge, 1991), p. 11.
25. Haraway, *Primate Visions*, p. 132.
26. Haraway, *Primate Visions*, p. 11.
27. Robin Dundar, 'The Apes as We Want to See Them', *The New York Times*, 7 January 1990, https://www.nytimes.com/1990/01/07/books/the-apes-as-we-want-to-see-them.html (accessed 18 February 2019).
28. Haraway, *Primate Visions*, p. 11.
29. Haraway, *Primate Visions*, p. 62.
30. Haraway, *When Species Meet*, p. 18.
31. Haraway, *Primate Visions*, p. 377.
32. Haraway, *Simians, Cyborgs and Women*, p. 188.

33. Haraway, *Simians, Cyborgs and Women*, p. 106.
34. Andrews and Gruen, 'Empathy in Other Apes', p. 208.
35. Donna Haraway, 'Situated Knowledges: The Science Question in Feminism and the Privilege of Partial Perspective', *Feminist Studies*, 14.3 (1988), 575–99 (p. 588).
36. Haraway, *Simians, Cyborgs and Women*, p. 198.
37. Derrida, *The Animal That Therefore I Am*, p. 39.
38. Haraway, *Primate Visions*, p. 139.
39. Haraway, *Manifestly Haraway*, p. 52.
40. Haraway, *Manifestly Haraway*, p. 57.
41. Haraway, 'Anthropocene', p. 160.
42. Haraway, *Simians, Cyborgs and Women*, p. 195.
43. Haraway, *Manifestly Haraway*, p. 9.
44. Haraway, *Simians, Cyborgs and Women*, p. 201.
45. Haraway, *Simians, Cyborgs and Women*, p. 201.
46. Schneider, *Donna Haraway: Live Theory*, p. 38.
47. Haraway, *Primate Visions*, p. 8.
48. Haraway, *Primate Visions*, p. 3.
49. Haraway, *The Companion Species Manifesto*, pp. 15–16.
50. Haraway, *The Companion Species Manifesto*, p. 100.
51. Andrew Miller, *Pure* (London: Sceptre, 2011), p. 6.
52. Miller, *Pure*, p. 7.
53. Miller, *Pure*, pp. 341, 342.
54. Miller, *Pure*, p. 342.
55. John Andrew Fisher, 'The Myth of Anthropomorphism', in *Readings in Animal Cognition* ed. Marc Bekoff and Dale Jamieson (Cambridge, MA: MIT Press, 1995), p. 5.
56. Lorraine Daston, 'Intelligences: Angelic, Animal, Human', in *Thinking with Animals: New Perspectives on Anthropomorphism*, ed. Lorraine Daston and Gregg Mitman (New York: Columbia University Press, 2005), pp. 37–58 (p. 51).
57. Tom Tyler, 'If Horses had Hands…', in *Animal Encounters*, ed. Tom Tyler and Manuela Rossini (Leiden: Brill, 2009), p. 14.
58. Tom Regan, cited in Bailey, 'On the Backs of Animals', p. 2.
59. Elizabeth Spelman, cited in Bailey, 'On the Backs of Animals', p. 3. It is worth noting Elisa Aaltola's defence of this approach: 'It is not difficult to see why Singer and others decided to favour reason. By the twentieth century, "sentimentalism" had become a term shrouded in a heavy, unforgiving layer of negative connotations. In Western analytic philosophy, emotions had become empty conveyors of ambivalent responses towards the external world that had little or nothing to do with "truth" – a suggestion that was robbing emotion-based morality of credibility.' Aaltola, *Varieties of Empathy*, para. 7.3.
60. Loraine Daston and Gregg Mitman, 'The How and Why of Thinking with Animals', in *Thinking with Animals: New Perspectives on*

Anthropomorphism, ed. Lorraine Daston and Gregg Mitman (New York: Columbia University Press, 2005), pp. 1–14 (p. 2).

61. Crist writes that '[a]nthropomorphism is presented to be a naïve view, an illusion generated through superficial analogies between human and animal behaviour, a deluded projection of the wealth of human experience onto a world that is putatively less rich'. Eileen Crist, *Images of Animals: Anthropomorphism and Animal Mind* (Philadelphia: Temple University Press, 1999), p. 152.

62. Sandra D. Mitchell, 'Anthropomorphism and Cross-Species Modeling', in *Thinking with Animals: New Perspectives on Anthropomorphism*, ed. Lorraine Daston and Gregg Mitman (New York: Columbia University Press, 2005), pp. 100–17 (p. 100).

63. Crist, *Images of Animals*, p. 1.

64. Mitchell, 'Anthropomorphism', p. 100.

65. Daston and Mitman, 'The How and Why', p. 3.

66. Marc Bekoff, *Minding Animals: Awareness, Emotions, and Heart* (Oxford: Oxford University Press, 2002), p. 49.

67. Bekoff, *Minding Animals*, p. 48.

68. de Waal, *Chimpanzee Politics*, p. 41.

69. Frans de Waal, *Good Natured: The Origins of Right and Wrong in Humans and Other Animals* (Cambridge, MA: Harvard University Press, 1996), p. 63.

70. Gordon Burghardt, 'Animal Awareness: Current Perceptions and Historical Perspective', *American Psychologist*, 40 (1985), 905–19 (p. 917).

71. Mitchell, 'Anthropomorphism', p. 114.

72. Frans de Waal, *The Bonobo and the Atheist* (New York: W.W. Norton, 2013), p. 145.

73. Martha C. Nussbaum, 'Compassion: Human and Animal', in *Species Matters: Humane Advocacy and Cultural Theory*, ed. Marianne DeKoven and Michal Lundblad (New York: Columbia University Press, 2012), p. 140.

74. Nussbaum, 'Compassion', p. 142.

75. Nussbaum, 'Compassion', p. 156.

76. Susan McHugh, *Animal Stories: Narrating Across Species Lines* (Minneapolis: University of Minnesota Press, 2011), p. 214.

77. Crist, *Images of Animals*, p. 49.

78. Daston and Mitman, 'The How and Why', p. 4.

79. Daston and Mitman, 'The How and Why', p. 5.

80. Stephen Jay Gould, 'A Lover's Quarrel', in *The Smile of a Dolphin: Remarkable Accounts of Animal Emotions*, ed. Marc Bekoff (London: Discovery, 2000), pp. 13–17 (p. 17).

81. Tyler, 'If Horses had Hands', p. 23.

82. Tyler, 'If Horses had Hands', p. 21.

83. Haraway, *When Species Meet*, p. 52.

84. The novel follows the adult protagonist Rosemary as she tries to come to terms with a childhood in which she was raised alongside a human sibling, Lowell, and a chimpanzee, Fern. It tracks Rosemary's guilt following Fern's removal from the family, her estrangement from the animal activist Lowell, and her own inability to fully integrate into human society. Delaying the revelation that Fern is a chimpanzee, not a human sister, the novel invites us to consider the ethical consequences of primatological studies in light of our own kinship with nonhuman primates.

85. Karen Joy Fowler, *We Are All Completely Beside Ourselves* (London: Serpent's Tail, 2013), p. 48. Subsequent references will be given in parentheses in the text.

86. Peter Goldie, 'How We Think of Others' Emotions', *Mind and Language*, 14.4 (1999), 394–423 (p. 409).

87. See, for example, Naama Harel's litany of allegorical readings of 'A Report to an Academy': 'an allegory to the assimilation of Jews in Europe, European colonialism in Africa, conformism, a common person who cannot find spirituality, the loss of innocence, the condition and values of humanity, education as a form of brainwashing, or art as inferior imitation'. Naama Harel, 'Deallegorizing Kafka's Ape: Two Animalistic Contexts', in *Kafka's Creatures: Animals, Hybrids, and Other Fantastic Beings*, ed. Marc Lucht and Donna Yarri (Lanham, MD: Rowman and Littlefield, 2010), pp. 53–66 (p. 43).

88. Liz Jensen, '*We Are All Completely Beside Ourselves* review – "A Provocative Take on Family Love"', *The Guardian*, 20 March 2014, https://www.theguardian.com/books/2014/mar/20/completely-beside-ourselves-family-love-review (accessed 18 February 2019); Barbara Kingsolver, 'The Other Sister: Karen Joy Fowler's *We Are All Completely Beside Ourselves*', *New York Times*, 6 June 2013, http://www.nytimes.com/2013/06/09/books/review/karen-joy-fowlers-we-are-all-completely-beside-ourselves.html (accessed 18 February 2019).

89. Margot Norris, 'Darwin, Nietzsche, Kafka and the Problem of Mimesis', *MLN*, 95.5 (1980), 1232–53 (p. 1246).

90. Karen Joy Fowler, *The Science of Herself* (Oakland: PM Press, 2013), p. 64.

91. Cynthia Willett, *Interspecies Ethics* (New York: Columbia University Press, 2014), p. 6.

92. Haraway, *Simians, Cyborgs and Women*, p. 21.

93. Nussbaum, 'Compassion', p. 142.

94. Colebrook, 'What is the Anthropo-Political?', pp. 107–8.

95. Haraway, *When Species Meet*, p. 71.

96. Gallese, 'Embodied Simulation', p. 11.

97. Haraway, *When Species Meet*, p. 72.

98. Aaltola, *Varieties of Empathy*, para. 9.36.

99. Koehn, *Rethinking Feminist Ethics*, p. 60.

100. Carol Adams, *The Sexual Politics of Meat: A Feminist-Vegetarian Critical Theory* (New York: Continuum, 1999), p. 168.

101. Diamond, 'Difficulty of Reality', p. 14.

102. Sara Waller, 'Science of the Monkey Mind: Primate Penchants and Human Pursuits', in *Experiencing Animal Minds: An Anthology of Animal–Human Encounters*, ed. Julie A. Smith and Robert W. Mitchell (New York: Columbia University Press, 2012), pp. 78–94 (p. 87).

103. Haraway, *Primate Visions*, p. 76

104. Haraway, *Primate Visions*, pp. 368–82.

105. Crist, *Images of Animals*, p. 209.

106. Aaltola, *Varieties of Empathy*, para. 13.27.

107. Tyler, 'If Horses had Hands…', p. 21.

108. Ziad Elmarsafy, 'Aping the Ape: Kafka's "Report to an Academy"', *Studies in Twentieth Century Literature*, 2 (1995), 159–70 (p. 166).

109. Matthew Calarco, 'Boundary Issues: Human–Animal Relationships in Karen Joy Fowler's *We Are All Completely Beside Ourselves*', *Modern Fiction Studies*, 60.3 (2014), 616–35 (p. 617).

110. Kay Milton, 'Anthropomorphism or Egomorphism? The Perception of Nonhuman Persons by Human Ones', in *Animals in Person: Cultural Perspectives on Human–Animal Intimacies*, ed. John Knight (London: Berg, 2005), pp. 255–71 (p. 255).

111. Agosta, *Empathy in the Context of Philosophy*, p. 75.

112. Tom Regan, *The Case for Animal Rights* (Berkeley: University of California Press, 1983), p. xii.

113. Coetzee, *The Lives of Animals*, p. 120.

114. Coetzee, *The Lives of Animals*, p. 121.

115. Coetzee, *The Lives of Animals*, pp. 131, 121.

116. Schneider, *Donna Haraway: Live Theory*, p. 161.

117. Coetzee, *The Lives of Animals*, p. 133.

118. Coetzee, *The Lives of Animals*, p. 132.

119. Coetzee, *The Lives of Animals*, p. 131.

120. Mensch, 'Empathy and Rationality', p. 17.

121. Richard Holton and Rae Langton, 'Empathy and Animal Ethics', in *Singer and his Critics*, ed. Dale Jamieson (Oxford: Blackwell, 1999), pp. 209–32 (p. 225).

122. Coetzee, *The Lives of Animals*, p. 131.

123. Haraway, *Primate Visions*, p. 238.

124. Nussbaum, 'Compassion', p. 161.

125. Gary Olson, *Empathy Imperiled: Capitalism, Culture and the Brain* (New York: Springer, 2013), p. 7.

126. Coplan, 'Empathetic Engagement', p. 148.

127. Coetzee, *The Lives of Animals*, p. 152.

128. Haraway, *When Species Meet*, p. 80.

129. Schneider, *Donna Haraway: Live Theory*, p. 160.

130. Coetzee, *The Lives of Animals*, p. 148.

131. Haraway, *Manifestly Haraway*, p. 124.

132. Coetzee, *The Lives of Animals*, p. 160.

133. Elizabeth Grosz, 'The Creative Impulse', interview, 14 August 2005, http://www.abc.net.au/rn/legacy/programs/sunmorn/stories/s1435592.htm (accessed 18 February 2019).

134. Jacques Derrida, *Of Grammatology*, trans. Gayatri Spivak (Baltimore: Johns Hopkins University Press, 1976), pp. 244–5.

135. Turner, 'The Animal Question in Deconstruction', p. 5.

136. Calarco, 'Boundary Issues', p. 618

137. Calarco, 'Boundary Issues', p. 619.

138. Coetzee, *The Lives of Animals*, p. 124.

139. Haraway, *Simians, Cyborgs and Women*, p. 210.

140. Derrida, 'The Ends of Man', p. 13.

141. Derrida, 'The Ends of Man', p. 135.

142. John, 'Empathy in Literature', para. 40.22.

143. Calarco, 'Boundary Issues', p. 628.

144. Keen, *Empathy and the Novel*, p. 159.

3. Telling Nonhuman Stories: 'The secret contours of objects'

Story is a parasitical entity that in its familiar forms clearly depends on humans, but story is also itself a living thing and not necessarily dependent upon language to be conveyed.

Jeffrey Jerome Cohen[1]

Writing of the world envisioned by Roger Caillois, Marguerite Yourcenar identifies 'an inverted anthropomorphism in which man, instead of attributing his own emotions, sometimes condescendingly, to all other living beings, shares humbly, and yet with pride, in everything contained or innate in all three realms, animal, vegetable and mineral'.[2] Caillois's projection depends on a counter to the tendency, identified by Tom Tyler in the previous chapter, to regard characteristics as possessions or unexchangeable markers of a fixed species identity, as well as to the assumption that we are the only parties doing any meaningful thinking, acting or being. On the contrary, Timothy Morton assures us, humans are not the only 'morphisers'. Thus, anthropomorphism 'is not a prison without windows, because as I anthropomorphize this bunch of grapes, the grapes are grape-morphizing my fingers and my mouth, causing me to handle them just so'.[3] Finding the language of perception inadequate for nonhuman and inter-objective encounters, the philosopher Graham Harman, like Morton, searches for an alternative terminology. Prehension, a term adopted from A. N. Whitehead, is a better fit for purpose, he decides.[4]

As we have seen, the failure of philosophy to acknowledge agency, *ipseity* or interactive capacities beyond the human is well documented. Anna Lowenhaupt Tsing, however, optimistically suggests that the contemporary moment marks an intersection between three forces which may, between them, facilitate 'new ways of telling true stories beyond civilizational first principles'.[5] For Tsing, these forces – the drive to limit anthropogenic environmental destruction, the increase in biological

understanding of interspecies interactions which undermines the primacy of the human, and improved awareness of a diversified human
body whose interests do not all coincide with those of the Western
male – effectively challenge a post-Enlightenment philosophy which
situates a sovereign human subjectivity against an inert backdrop. The
upbraiding of philosophy's 'post-Cartesian genealogy' for its misrepresentation of nonhuman life undertaken by Derrida and others has
generated a thinking which acknowledges the vulnerability of sentient
nonhuman life through empathetic engagement.[6] This is complemented
by a literary storytelling which, understanding the implications of
perceiving nonhuman animals as 'mere tropes', frames them as active
participants.[7]

   This book is about animals, but it is also about the metaphorical
nature of perception and the complex relations between perception,
imagination and cognition in our dealings with the nonhuman. These
relations are foregrounded in a striking scene from Jim Crace's novel
Signals of Distress, in which Aymer Smith, Crace's bumbling protagonist, turns a corner on his walk to encounter a view which, at
first, defies his comprehension. We follow the enraptured Aymer as he
progresses from dazzled bewilderment to understanding, to the bathos
of his realisation – Crace's parody of pastoral conventions – that 'the
field was full of fish'.[8] Here is the passage in full:

> It looked at first like a landscape of ten thousand lakes; the mountains were
> the ridges in the earth; the valleys, furrows; the narrow pools, each shaped
> like icy mouths, reflecting all the silver in the sky. Again, it looked as if some
> fairy silversmith had dropped a cargo of brooches, or tried to plant the soil
> with polished metal leaves [. . .] The field was full of fish. The sea was taking
> everyone away, and putting fish on land. There were no leaves or lakes or
> brooches, just one star-gazy pie with a four-acre crust of earth and a shoal
> of pilchards staring at the moon, their eyes as dead as flint, their scales like
> beaten tin, their fraying fins and tails like frost, their flesh composting for the
> next year's crop. The field was absolutely still. The fastest movements were
> the snails and slugs which were enamelling the fleshy silverwork with their
> new saliva trails. (*SD*, 186–7)

Smith's habitation in a village sustained by fish has given his imaginative repertoire a distinctly piscine note, his fantasy about the amorous
newlyweds he meets framed, rather incongruously, as bodies 'embrac-
ing, wrapping, bending like a pair of fish: a stringy eel, a plump and
mottled salmon' (*SD*, 59). It is ironic, therefore, that when Smith is
literally faced with a 'field full of fish', his imagination ranges across
the natural world and human artistry before alighting on the truth.
Smith's simultaneous disorientation and aesthetic pleasure are shared
by the reader. As described, Smith's experience resists our assumptions

about human agency and passive materiality. While Smith's experience is presented historically, the interwoven histories are cross-species histories: the seasonal cycle of surplus fish nourishing the soil for next year's crops, and the history of industrialisation, whose products, the fish which Smith mistakes for 'polished metal leaves', are no more intrinsically valuable than the snails' 'saliva trails'. The agency here is nonhuman, exhibited by the 'fairy silversmith', the movements of the sea, and the usually reviled gastropods, whose trails appear as 'fleshy silverwork'. Understanding the forces at work requires us to consider, in the words of Jane Bennett, 'a more *distributive* agency' in which activity and order are not restricted to the human, or even the living.[9]

Tsing reminds us that, historically, it was left 'to fabulists, including non-Western and non-civilizational storytellers, to remind us of the lively activities of all beings, human and not human'.[10] For the philosophers who shelter under the 'loose umbrella' of Speculative Realism,[11] brought together, Steven Shaviro writes, by 'a common commitment [. . .] to metaphysical speculation and to a robust ontological realism', this is testament to an ongoing philosophical failure, a consequence of what Quentin Meillassoux deems 'correlationism'.[12] This failure, which, according to Meillassoux and others, persists in contemporary 'continental' thought, proceeds from the Kantian split between noumena and phenomena, and consists in the belief that 'we only ever have access to the correlation between thinking and being, and never to either term considered apart from the other'.[13] The perceived effects of 'correlationism' are manifold: we can never have access to things in themselves; we cannot conceive of the world without humans; and we cannot philosophically address interactions in the world that do not involve human beings, and thus abandon these to natural science rather than philosophy. For the Speculative Realists, this is unsatisfactory as it leads, in Graham Harman's words, to philosophy's self-imposed 'curfew in an ever-tinier ghetto of solely human realities',[14] and, for Ian Bogost, to a misguided set of priorities: the valuation of the 'oval-headed alien anthropomorph' over 'the scoria cone, the obsidian fragment, the gypsum crystal, the capsicum pepper, and the propane flame'.[15] Correlationism is the insistence of the anthropo-theological by another name; thus, for Harman, we must deny 'that the special features of human consciousness are built into the heart of ontology at all'.[16]

While Harman despairs of a philosophy which 'has gradually renounced its claim to have anything to do with the world itself', like Tsing he speculates that we may have arrived at a turning point:

Will philosophy continue to lump together monkeys, tornadoes, diamonds, and oil under the single heading of that-which-lies-outside? Or is there some possibility of an object-oriented philosophy, a sort of alchemy for describing the transformations of one entity into another, for outlining the ways in which they seduce or destroy humans and non-humans alike?[17]

This chapter will put the novels of Jim Crace, distinguished, one commentator notes, by an 'occultish grammar of objects – beetles, stones, cracks in wood', in conversation with Graham Harman's brand of Speculative Realism, Object-Oriented Philosophy. Beginning with a discussion of the development of OOP in contradistinction to Bruno Latour's Actor Network Theory, it will outline and assess the claims made by Harman for the superiority of OOP over contemporary relational ontologies, such as that espoused by Jane Bennett. Turning to Crace, the chapter will argue that Crace's fiction enacts a sustained movement away from anthropocentrism, demonstrating the collaborative nature of storytelling and absenting the human from a variety of different landscapes. It will argue that, in their examination of the 'allure' of objects, these novels espouse a position closer to Harman than Bennett. Finally, the chapter will interrogate Harman's presentation of aesthetics as first philosophy, asking whether this claim might illuminate the interruptive nature of affect.

ACTOR NETWORK THEORY AND VITAL MATERIALISM

Taking aim at Heidegger, in 1993 Bruno Latour expressed a similar frustration to that which we have seen in Harman and Bogost. He questioned:

And yet – 'here too the gods are present': in a hydroelectric plant on the banks of the Rhine, in subatomic particles, in Adidas shoes as well as in the old wooden clogs hollowed out by hand, in agribusiness as well as in time-worn landscape, in shopkeepers' calculations as well as in Hölderlin's heart-rending verse. But why do those philosophers no longer recognize them?[18]

Latour's work inspired Speculative Realism, with the Actor Network Theory espoused by Latour in the 1980s and 1990s serving as a model against which Harman's Object-Oriented Philosophy would come to define itself. Latour's work refuses to accept as primary the divisions around which philosophy has grown. For Latour, distinctions such as nature/culture, human/nonhuman and subject/object are 'less interesting than the complete chain along which competences and actions are distributed'.[19] In fact, the relations and networks are much more complex, and the agency more diverse, than such terms suggest. As Ian

Hodder says, 'agency is simply the ever-present force of things: the life force of humans and all organic things, and the forces of attraction, repulsion, etc. of all material things and their interactions'.[20] It is for this reason that Latour prefers the word 'actant' to designate a node in an agential network, rather than the anthropocentric 'subject'. As we see in the following example from the essay 'On Interobjectivity', the interaction between humans and nonhumans problematises what we commonly understand as reflective human agency.

> As a common shepherd all I have to do is delegate to a wooden fence the task of containing my flock – then I can just go to sleep with my dog beside me. Who is acting while I am asleep? Me, the carpenters, and the fence [. . .] Are the sheep interacting with me when they bump their muzzles against the rough pine planks? Yes, but they are interacting with a me that is, thanks to the fence, disengaged, delegated, translated and multiplied.[21]

Through empirical examination of human/nonhuman networks, Latour concluded that the practical workings of agency demanded a modification both of our understanding of objects and of action.[22] By emphasising process and relationality, Latour demonstrates not only that accepted divisions are 'less interesting' but, more profoundly, that they are effects of relational networks, 'belated results that no longer suffice to designate the other dimension', rather than realities that pre-exist them.[23] One of the implications of this, as Harman observes, is Latour's 'refusal to focus on a single magical gap between thinking, practical, moody humans on the one hand and stupefied inanimate clods of matter on the other'.[24] In neither Latour nor Harman does this manifest as the collapsing of the perceived gap between the human and the material; rather, both look to a proliferation of gaps and differences which, when considered collectively, challenge the divisions along which institutional structures have sedimented.

According to Latour, the most pervasive and yet fallacious conception of the human–nonhuman relation arrives with modernity, a designation which, in his landmark text *We Have Never Been Modern*, he exposes as comprising two contrasting impulses:

> The hypothesis of this essay is that the word 'modern' designates two sets of entirely different practices which must remain distinct if they are to remain effective, but have recently begun to be confused. The first set of practices, by 'translation,' creates mixtures between entirely new types of beings, hybrids of nature and culture. The second, by 'purification,' creates two entirely distinct ontological zones: that of human beings on the one hand; that of nonhumans on the other [. . .] The first set corresponds to what I have called networks; the second to what I shall call the modern critical stance.[25]

Latour claims that modernity is constructed upon a disavowed hybridity which is inconsistent with modernity's ideology of human exceptionalism. The result is not only a perceived divide between nature and culture but also between Western culture – as it identifies itself by contradistinction from nature – and all other cultures that do not self-identify in this way. In response to these issues, Latour advocates an acknowledgement of the hybrid connections that have facilitated the West's success, turning to Michel Serres's notion of the quasi-object, neither singularly natural nor singularly social, to express them. Gesturing towards Kant's so-called 'Copernican Revolution', Latour foresees 'a Copernican counter-revolution' which names 'a movement that makes both object and subject revolve around the practice of quasi-objects and mediators'.[26] Through this account, power and agency are dramatically reframed.

Inspired by the relationality of ANT and by Latour's replacement of subjects with actants, in *Vibrant Matter* Jane Bennett looks to outline 'a more *distributive* agency'. Like Latour, Bennett perceives traditional philosophical conceptions of agency and subjectivity as flawed, rooted, ultimately, in an anachronistically theological account of human sovereignty. While the implications of the change she advances are political, the change itself requires an ontological shift, superseding a model of 'passive, mechanistic' materiality, distinct from and determined by human action, with a vital materiality.[27] Here she looks to Spinoza to understand that which is shared by human and nonhuman bodies alike, perceiving a 'conative nature', a persistency or vitality in each body's being, which deposes the human from its privileged position.[28] Human agency, Bennett contends, is simply another kind of 'thing-power', a notion that spreads agency 'across a wider range of ontological types' and articulates a 'more horizontal representation' of human–nonhuman relations, which would account for interspecies entangling.[29] Bennett argues that vital materiality 'better captures an "alien" quality of our own flesh', the human body always already a host for numerous other organisms.[30] This explains the gap that we experience between the theory of the human as sovereign and self-identical, and lived bodily experience.

Both the fragility of Latour's 'modern critical stance' and the need for a different account of agency are demonstrated by Crace's novel *Signals of Distress*, which recounts the impact of a shipwreck, in 1836, on the villagers of Wherrytown. The constitutive tension of modernity, as Latour frames it, emerges in the discrepancy between the persistent solitariness of the painfully comic protagonist Smith, who 'didn't voyage in the multitude' and 'knew that he was destined to a life alone'

(*SD*, 170), and the cross-species entangling which he cannot escape, not least in his financial dependence on a fortune built on soap made from kelp. The contamination of the human by the nonhuman, or rather the constitution of the human by means of nonhuman prostheses, is repeatedly illustrated: by the kelp soap (soon to be replaced by artificial chemicals) that explains Smith's presence in Wherrytown; by the global topography enabled by sea travel; and by the Wherrytown residents' total reliance on fish. Smith is utterly disarmed by the life, agency and mobility of the latter, who, 'tumbling like molten lead' (*SD*, 83), could themselves have leaped from Bennett's pages. The porosity of the boundary between human and nonhuman is staged all too literally in the death of the sailor Nathaniel Rankin, and the description of his physical disintegration; 'a man who's marinated in the sea for two days is bound to swell', we are told. 'His flesh becomes porous and water enters him. He begins to peel and split. He loses shape. His margins flake' (*SD*, 130).

Smith's preoccupations – the placing of the human in a world where faith is lost, and the products of industry and technology – lead him to ask: 'Where was the order in the universe?' (*SD*, 187). While the novel itself is ordered by Smith's walks across Wherrytown, these do not deliver Smith a sense of clearly mapped and conceptualised territory. Rather, Smith's metaphysical uncertainty is expressed topographically in the fall of Cradle Rock. The inability of Wherrytown's inhabitants to keep pace with a world whose parameters are shifting – the local now inflected by the global – is represented by the escaped slave Otto; the villagers, we are told, 'weren't used to this topography' (*SD*, 12). Smith represents a humanity whose self-perception is, ultimately, deluded. His attempts to restore order – to return Otto to the 'deeper green and yellow' (*SD*, 272) which he perceives as Otto's natural landscape – are fantasies, as we see in his somnolent attempt to restore Cradle Rock to its position above the village. Smith represents the futility of human attempts to impose order, as well as the limitations of the perspectives they take to be universal. Like Aymer, who, Philip Tew notes, 'significantly misinterprets agency in others', we, as readers, cannot orient ourselves or determine the origins or circulation of agency.[31]

The climax of the novel, which sees *The Belle of Wilmington* sunk with the loss of all of its passengers, Cradle Rock dislodged, and Smith violently assaulted, destabilises any assumption of human control or mastery. Smith's attempt to impose order is thwarted. We can, however, in Latour's terms, perceive a network of quasi-objects and quasi-subjects: Cradle Rock, the *Belle*, Whip the dog, the vast force of the ocean and the fish within it, the kelp. These are all both tangible and discursive; as Latour writes: 'collective because they attach us to one another, because they circulate in our hands and define our social bond by their very circulation. They are discursive, however; they are narrated, historical, passionate, and peopled with actants of autonomous forms.'[32] While Latour and Bennett provide a theoretical framework through which to understand 'the shaping force of nature'[33] that pervades Crace's novels, there is a sense in which the objects that emerge from his texts, notable, as Tew writes of the seaweed which strikes Smith, for their 'ontological intensity', cannot be sufficiently explained as actants.[34] To understand these objects, we turn to the work of Graham Harman.

GRAHAM HARMAN I: OBJECT-ORIENTED PHILOSOPHY AND TOOL-BEING

Although Harman concedes the influence of Latour on his work, he clearly differentiates his own Object-Oriented Philosophy both from Actor Network Theory and from the 'new materialisms' which have proliferated in recent years. For Harman and others, the problem with such new materialisms is twofold: on the one hand, as Latour writes, they often proceed from 'a rather idealist definition of matter';[35] on the other, the term has become so diffuse that it has little to do with matter, simply meaning, as Levi Bryant notes, 'that something is historical, socially constructed, involves cultural practices, and is contingent'.[36] Harman distinguishes himself from the work of Bennett, who, for him, 'vividly but wrongly'[37] describes the vital materiality of the 'throbbing whole'.[38] While Bennett perceives the belief that the world is constituted by fixed objects as a heuristic employed in order 'to live',[39] for OOP this narrative is ontologically accurate. While there are clear distinctions between new materialism – in all its diversity – and Latour's ANT, they share a focus on relationality which Harman rejects. On this, Harman contends: 'The claim of object-oriented philosophy, which I advocate, is that the primacy of relations over things is no longer a liberating idea (since it reduces things to their pragmatic impact on humans and on each other).'[40] This political objection to materialism supplements a philosophical objection. According to Harman, materialisms cannot 'account for true *emergence* at levels other than the most basic one'; in other words, if objects are exhausted by their relations, then there is nothing held in reserve which might facilitate change.[41] Recent years have seen productive interactions between Harman and Bennett, with the latter proposing a middle ground:

But perhaps there is no need to choose between objects or their relations. Since everyday, earthly experience routinely identifies some effects as coming from individual objects and some from larger systems (or, better put, from individuations within material configurations and from the complex assemblages in which they participate), why not aim for a theory that toggles between both kinds or magnitudes of 'unit'? One would then understand 'objects' to be those swirls of matter, energy, and incipience that hold themselves together long enough to vie with the strivings of other objects, including the indeterminate momentum of the throbbing whole.[42]

While Harman supports Bennett in the need to account for both objects and relations, he argues that her proposal for doing so already assumes the pre-eminence of relations. Rather, he claims, it is OOP that counters current prejudices in favour of relations to provide a 'balance' which incorporates 'this twofold fate of objects as both communicating and non-communicating'.[43]

Harman is closer than Bennett to Latour, whom he sees as retrieving individual objects from the 'primitive, vibrant continuum' which characterises new materialism, and permitting 'all entities an equal claim to participating in its theory: human and non-human, natural and cultural, real and imaginary'.[44] Both ANT and OOP emphasise the agency of objects; they are not static or inert; rather, they are 'set loose into the world like wild animals: just as enchanting, and every bit as deadly'.[45] ANT's great limitation, however, according to Harman, is its unremitting focus on action, which clashes with the first founding rule of OOP: '*Objects, not actors*'.[46] For OOP, objects cannot be reduced to their actions.

To understand Harman's claim here, we must suspend our assumption that an object is inert and static, awaiting the influence of a subject. The most useful definition of objects in Harman's work is as 'unified realities – physical or otherwise – that cannot fully be reduced either downwards to their pieces or upwards to their effects'.[47] This definition is counter-intuitive; to objectify is to reduce to its components or its effects, to instrumentalise. Instead Harman claims that objects cannot be reduced to the sum of their parts. Useful here is Harman's insistence – contra self-flagellating humans – that it is not only humans that objectify things. Rather, all relations – even those between objects – are objectifying, because each entity only has a necessarily limited experience of the other entity. Unexpectedly, it is Heidegger to whom Harman turns to explicate his theory of objects, focusing on the account of equipment in the opening chapter of *Being and Time*. Heidegger's work here, Harman claims, offers 'a theory of objects' which leads us to 'nothing less than a metaphysics of reality'.[48]

Central to this 'theory of objects' is tool-being, which describes the transitions between readiness-to-hand (*Zuhandenheit*) and presence-to-hand (*Vorhandenheit*) in our experience of equipment. The former, readiness-to-hand, describes our experience when equipment functions so smoothly as to be submerged in a network of relations. This is more primordial than presence-to-hand, which refers to the kind of theorised interaction we have with an object when it breaks or fails to function efficiently. The example Heidegger gives is of a hammer, whose presence we do not notice (*Zuhanden*) when it is operating correctly, but which comes to our notice (*Vorhanden*) when something goes wrong. The novelty in Harman's reading of Heidegger is to suggest that tool-being is not confined to tools, used by human beings to perform a particular function, and therefore as antithetical to *Dasein*. Rather, he contends that 'the meaning of being is tools'.[49] This means that we can understand all objects (entities that are irreducible to either components or effects) in this way, where tool-being refers to a fracture or oscillation between *Zuhandenheit* and *Vorhandenheit*.

Harman cautions against several misreadings of tool-being. He explains:

> The description of equipment does not serve as a regional ontology that could be limited to the order of hatchets, drills, and pulleys. Instead, tool-being is the name for a fundamental dualism that rips through the heart of everything that is: not just the tools in the limited sense, but also plants, animals, numbers, machines, rocks, and even people.[50]

So, tool-being is not specific to tools; 'the tool isn't "used"; it *is*'.[51] Nor can the difference between *Zuhandenheit* and *Vorhandenheit* be mapped on to the distinction between subject and object, or on to different types or classes of object. Rather, these terms describe 'a universal dualism found in all entities'[52] which can best be understood, as Shaviro clarifies, as a double movement consisting of 'retreat and eruption'.[53] Important to note about both movements is that they defy reduction to conceptual categories. While Harman repeatedly reminds us that tool-being is neither a mark of usability nor restricted to tools, it remains significant that the structure of tool-being, the 'ontology of things', is revealed by tools. In Harman's words: 'When objects fail us, we experience a negation of their accessible contours and become aware that the object exceeds all that we grasp of it.'[54]

Harman's reading of Heidegger is extremely unorthodox, repurposing the notion of tool-being to critique anthropocentrism and holism within and beyond Heidegger. Unsurprisingly, therefore, critical responses have been forceful, ranging from the ambivalent, such as Nathan Brown, who reviewed *Tool-Being* as 'a philosophical effort worthy of attention' which 'took a disappointing turn', to Peter Wolfendale's unrelenting book-length critique of Harman, *Object-Oriented Philosophy: The Noumenon's New Clothes*.[55] Wolfendale's challenge to Harman's reading of Heidegger is, at times, convincing, particularly his criticism of Harman's 'disastrous misreading' of the figure of 'world' as 'a complete totality of entities rather than a phenomenological horizon within which entities appear'.[56] There are also problems with Harman's methodological approach.[57] These, however, are beyond the scope of this study, which aims both to consider the ways in which Harman's work exposes the unbalanced emphasis on relationality in current scholarship, and to address the ways in which his focus on objects corresponds with the fiction of Jim Crace.

Harman's refiguration of tool-being illuminates the world that Crace articulates in *The Gift of Stones*. While the novel ostensibly tracks the historical progression from the Stone Age to the Bronze Age – the supersession of one set of tools by another – there is a clear tension between the anthropocentric human narrative and a fascination with objects as portals to other, nonhuman histories. As Jeffrey Jerome Cohen detects, 'stone's time is not ours'.[58] Criticism that presupposes the primacy of the subject–object division falls short of Crace's text. Tew, for example, writes that 'Craceland amplifies both the meaning of the objective and its ability to mirror the subject's experience of events [...] articulating subjective–objective empathy', an account which, while realising that objects are important for Crace, can only frame this significance anthropocentrically and cannot think how empathy might translate into a nonhuman context.[59] Objects are, therefore, inert mirrors, with 'mythopoeic possibilities', rather than active, interruptive agents or entities.[60] Similarly, identifying the ways in which Crace's protagonists often experience 'an ontological and epistemological displacement from the world', a consequence of their employment of 'the wrong interpretative parameters', Richard J. Lane reads this sense of displacement as a narrative device to emphasise the individual experience of historical change.[61] Although historical shifts are central to Crace's fiction, the disjunctive human–nonhuman relationships also speak of an ontological displacement that is constitutive of experience *per se*, not just at times of historical change.

Jane Bennett restates a familiar question faced by the vital materialist or posthumanist: is there not a 'performative contradiction' in the advancement of vital materialism in language?[62] Isn't language the very instantiation of human exceptionalism and therefore ill-suited to the development of avowedly non-anthropocentric perspectives? This, of course, depends on whether we understand human language as simply another form of natural adaptation. Rather than a creative act passed from God to Man, Crace depicts storytelling as a compensation for human frailty. Here, there is no omniscient, omnipotent narrator whose word is law, but rather an oral, communal approach to storytelling which results in a disjointed narrative, often interrupted by Doe's daughter, who is 'tempted to infiltrate [her] own concocted version of these moments in the past'.[63] The storyteller himself is not elevated or glorified, a disembodied voice who draws structure and posterity from the dynamic landscape that surrounds him. Rather, we are introduced to him via his disfigurement. 'My father's right arm ended not in a hand but, at the elbow, in a bony swelling', Doe's daughter insouciantly informs us. 'Think of a pollard tree in silhouette. That was my father's stump' (GS, 1). It is no accident that the storyteller's disfigurement is of his right hand, the writer's primary tool. Explicitly framed as a kind of symbolic castration, this act of cross-species description does not simply undermine human exceptionalism, healing the rift between humans and the natural world. Rather, the storyteller's disfigurement represents the ontological displacement that Lane identifies. With his weeping wound oozing what appears to be 'wasted and unsummoned semen' (GS, 1), the storyteller presents the human as a distortion of the natural order, rather than its apex. While we are introduced to the storyteller as a diminished figure, unsuited to the world around him, we later become aware of his capacity to shape a different world for which he would be a better fit. As Doe's daughter recounts: 'we know that when he spoke he shaped the truth, he trimmed, he stretched, he decorated. He was to truth what every stoney was to untouched flint, a fashioner, a god' (GS, 56). He captivates his listeners, and his approach to storytelling is to acknowledge the malleability of truth and to remind us that historical changes occur through the transformation of familiar stories.

The novel depicts a people for whom human–nonhuman interactions are not determined by the chauvinism of the 'modern critical stance'. Human characteristics are often described with reference to the natural world: 'the anthill' (GS, 30) of the working village, and 'the arc of flesh which hangs like cobwebs from the bone' (GS, 4). These comparisons are mutually illuminating. They celebrate the parallel rather than denigrating either term and depict a community whose frames of reference, and therefore imaginative resources, are predominantly nonhuman. Therefore, we see 'the jackdaw shoulders, the insect hands' (GS, 107), human flesh which had 'turned the inner blue of mussel shells' (GS, 28), and people whose 'skin was bark' and 'blood was sap' (GS, 110). On occasions where the comparison involves violence or force, we are invited to interrogate our own speciesist tendencies. A mass slaughter of geese entails a 'deadly stew of temper which, in young men, is called exuberance and which in wolves is known as brutishness' (*GS*, 95). The beauty and elegance of the geese, 'a buoyant, stately fleet [. . .] in such rhythmic unison' (*GS*, 77), is contrasted with the violence and disorder of the human response. Human skill is established by its likeness to 'the force and delicacy of owls' (*GS*, 22). Nonhuman life provides a model for human learning: it is 'the geese [which] had taught the baby how to walk [. . .] Her arms [. . .] bony wings' (*GS*, 83).

There is a tension in Crace's novel between the tendency to linger on the things themselves, like Crace himself transfixed by the 'incredibly beautiful' flints in the British Museum that would inspire the text, and to regard them as markers of human history.[64] Tew's reading is interested only in the latter, in the ways in which Crace's objects represent 'trans-historically how people humanize themselves from the substance of their unmediated pre-civilized origins'.[65] This, more orthodox, reading nonetheless enables us to perceive the tangling of the material and the ideological, with the bronze arrow-head, a sign from the future that kills Doe, a paradigm of Latour's quasi-object, puncturing not only Doe's physical body but also the community's 'sense of what was true' (*GS*, 158). Reading Crace through Tsing, we can also recognise this moment, 'the advent of modern capitalism', as the inception of the Anthropocene, which 'entangles us with ideas of progress and with the spread of techniques of alienation that turn both humans and other beings into resources'. Tsing maintains that 'such techniques have segregated humans and policed identities, obscuring collaborative survival'.[66] This is clearly illustrated by the figure of Doe, the subjugated victim of the capitalist economy. We are reminded that 'she was the merchandise as well' (*GS*, 150), her only remaining choice whether 'to be the helpless beetle on its back or else the working beast' (*GS*, 123).

It is through apparently inert objects, the stones of Crace's title which provide the villagers with an occupation, that Crace makes the strongest challenge to our assumptions about human–nonhuman relations. The power and potential of first stone, then bronze, 'perfect and [. . .] beautiful' (*GS*, 158), belies their apparent stability. Stones are not static objects awaiting human agency but conversants in dialogue with the human; stone is 'a catalyst for relation, a generative substantiality through which story tenaciously emerges'.[67] Jeffrey Jerome Cohen identifies a linguistic deficit, his work in search of 'a word we have yet to invent, a word stone wants to convey its movement-effects'.[68] When the stones that Doe is lifting resist her, they are depicted as animate, they 'had life. They crept. They nestled. They muttered in the wind and heat' (*GS*, 117). This exemplifies 'tool-being' as Harman styles it, the 'eruption' and 'retreat' of the object, which we see most clearly in our attempts to utilise entities. Crace further challenges the conception of stone as immobile and inert by demonstrating its figurative malleability. At one moment, it represents unchangeable longevity: 'when everybody's dead [. . .] There'll still be stone' (*GS*, 100), and at another, change and humanity: 'People are like stones. You strike them right, they open up like shells' (*GS*, 48). We tend to use stone as a symbol of coldness or distance in human beings, but here using stone, making flints, is 'what gave them [the community] heart' (*GS*, 35). It becomes a sign of strength and fortitude, not inhumanity.

While *The Gift of Stones* is, for the most part, preoccupied with human–nonhuman relations, there are moments in which the possibility of a relationality without humans, even a world without humans, is glimpsed. Even Crace's storyteller knows the limitations of his power, noting that after humans 'crabs and flies and carcass shrubs' (*GS*, 100) will remain. The final words of the novel depict a world in which human projections fail, and only nonhuman entities remain: 'He [the storyteller] tried to fill the air with human sounds. But all he saw were horses in the wind, the tide in loops upon the beach, the spray-wet rocks and stones reflecting all the changes in the sky, and no one there to notice or applaud' (*GS*, 170). Crace's experiment, an exercise in humility, feels particularly prescient within an Anthropocene context where our usual historicising practices are disrupted by the genuine possibility of our own extinction. As Dipesh Chakrabarty writes, following Alan Weisman's provocatively titled book *The World Without Us*,

we have to insert ourselves into a future 'without us' in order to be able to visualize it. Thus, our usual historical practices for visualizing times, past and future, times inaccessible to us personally – the exercise of historical understanding – are thrown into a deep contradiction and confusion.[69]

GRAHAM HARMAN II: AESTHETICS AS FIRST PHILOSOPHY

Crace's understated concluding gesture can be read as a response, like that of Harman, to the habitual neglect of nonhuman relations. If we endeavour to think the 'ontological displacement' which Lane identifies in Crace beyond Crace's human protagonists, Harman and Crace are brought even closer together. Returning to Kant, Harman contends that it is not the identification of things-in-themselves that makes Kant problematic, but rather 'his notion that they haunt human beings alone, so that the tragic burden of finitude is shouldered by a single species of object. What Kant failed to note', Harman claims, 'is that since any relation fails to exhaust its *relata*, every inanimate object is a thing-in-itself for every other as well.'[70] This is the inevitable consequence of Harman's insistence that tool-being is shared by all objects, a position that rejects the fetishisation of human consciousness and the preoccupation with cognition as determinant of an entity's value. Accordingly, as Shaviro insists, 'epistemology must be deprivileged',[71] in turn necessitating a shift in our understanding of humans, which become, in Harman's words, '*ingredients* in a symbiosis rather than just privileged observers'.[72] Whitehead's notion of prehension is useful for Harman here; without the privileging of sense-data, prehension is not limited to human, or at least animal, perception, and thus we can conceive of objects prehending each other without any human involvement. Bennett, Latour and Harman agree that the subject/object division proceeds from an erroneous ontology. For Harman, 'this tiresome pair of terms yields an impoverished conception of objects that must be abandoned' because it propagates the idea of an active, reflective subject acting upon a passive, unchanging object.[73] Rather than collapsing the gap into the continuum of vital materiality, however, Harman multiplies the gaps, arguing that 'instead of a single privileged gap between human and world, around which philosophy would have to be locked in permanent orbit, there are actually trillions of gaps: or rather, an infinite number'.[74] The most philosophically interesting of these is not between subject and object, but within the object itself, the 'triple interplay between an object and its accidents, relations, and qualities'.[75] While he argues that we only see objects partially, he distinguishes his position from the Kantian schism between phenomena and noumena by insisting that the partiality he describes is not a condition of human experience, but of all relationality.[76] He describes the relations between objects as 'vicarious' because they 'never directly encounter the autonomous reality of their components'.[77] Rather, they experience each other by proxy, by sensuous representations. This means that relations are asymmetrical: as a real object, I can only experience a sensual one.

In his archaeological history of objects, Ian Hodder describes the ways in which objects momentarily defy the instrumental frame we have imposed on them. Writing, like Harman, via Heidegger, his account parallels the 'retreat' and 'eruption' which, for Harman and Shaviro, constitutes tool-being. Hodder writes:

> As social actors we tend to see things in ego-centred ways, in terms of what they can do for us. We hardly look at them. Our interests are in the effects for us, aesthetic, social, scientific, psychological and so on. But every now and then we actually look at the thing itself, as a whole object, a thing in

its own right. We explore its grain, feel its weight, note its colour in different lights, marvel at its balance and delicate detail. Of course our interest
remains self-serving, and often nostalgic, but there is sometimes a moment
of realization that in order to understand the thing we have to look harder,
anew, deeper, more fully.[78]

Obviously, for Harman, we can never understand the thing fully, only
the sensuous object we encounter, but what is shared by their two
accounts is a sense of the discretion and autonomy of the object. Jane
Bennett too, despite her focus on relations, describes an encounter
with objects in a similar way; she experiences 'a nameless awareness
of the impossible singularity of *that* rat, *that* configuration of pollen,
that otherwise utterly banal mass-produced plastic water-bottle cap'.[79]
The descriptions given by Bennett and Hodder recount distinctively
aesthetic experiences, and for Harman, the aesthetic is key to understanding the nature of tool-being. He expresses this in terms of 'allure',
the aesthetic experience of the sensual object whereby I realise that the
real object far exceeds the sensual object that I experience. Reflecting
Bennett's stress on the singularity of the object, Harman explains:

> Aesthetics is about the singularity and supplementarity of things: it has to do
> with things insofar as they cannot be cognized or subordinated to concepts
> and also insofar as they cannot be utilized, or normatively regulated, or
> defined according to rules.[80]

Although, as yet, this is only outlined in Harman, there is a sense in
which, as Shaviro says, allure is 'the engine of change within the world'
by virtue of interrupting the prevailing conceptual framework and
disrupting the construction of meaning.[81]

While rejecting the anthropocentrism that he perceives therein,
Harman employs the work of Emmanuel Levinas to underpin the
subsequent claim that aesthetics, not ethics as Levinas would have it, is
'first philosophy'.[82] Harman relates:

> As Levinas teaches us, the real problem of metaphysics is not how beings
> interact in a system: instead, the problem is how they withdraw from that
> system as independent realities while somehow communicating through the
> proximity, the touching without touching, that has been termed allusion
> or allure. If we identify this event with 'aesthetics' in the broadest sense of
> the term, it becomes clear why first philosophy is aesthetics, not ethics. The
> ethical relation to other humans is merely a special case of substances com-
> municating without touching. Aesthetics is first philosophy, because the key
> problem of metaphysics has turned out to be as follows: how do individual
> substances interact in their proximity to one another?[83]

Harman acknowledges that this framing challenges the traditional
understanding of aesthetics, which restricts aesthetic qualities to

animate elements of the natural world that are perceived as beautiful, and aesthetic experience to humans alone. However, he argues that the limitations of experience are not unique to human experience, but rather that allusion, a fleeting experience of the reality of another being through sensual experience, is shared by all nonhuman entities. Its consequence, for Harman, is not solely aesthetic; 'allure is not just a theory of art', he contends, 'but a theory of causal relations in general. Levinas is the accidental mentor of a new metaphysics of causation.'[84] Aesthetics, as I will stress later, is also an affective experience. Irrespective of the persuasiveness of Harman's reading of Levinas, he raises an important question about the significance of the aesthetic: what is aesthetic experience and what function does it serve? Does it expose ontological structures, as Harman contends? The final section of this chapter returns to Jim Crace, reading the objects in his novels *Harvest* and *Quarantine* through Harman's OOP and addressing Harman's claims about the relationship between aesthetics and ontology.

FROM AESTHETICS TO ONTOLOGY: OBJECTS IN *HARVEST* AND *QUARANTINE*

We have already seen that, for Crace, objects are not inert components of structural and symbolic frameworks, lifeless repositories of human meaning or markers in human history; they too *act*. Crace's worlds are constituted by interconnected objects, beings and forces, and his human characters symbiotically engage with their living and non-living surroundings. With Crace, the perceived difference between the natural world and technological advancement is destabilised, as Crace both recasts the human technological impulse as natural – as we have seen, for example in *The Gift of Stones* – and exposes the nonhuman technologies of the natural world. In this, Crace's fiction remains poised: on the one hand, critiquing the objectification of nature, the fetishisation of technology and the linear narrative of progress; and on the other, rejecting nostalgic pastoralism, looking afresh at 'objects' and at 'nature'. Tew notes that an 'underlying sense of a primeval, natural quality of the environment recurs throughout Crace's fiction, permeating his symbolic sense of the objective world' and emerging through objects, such as Cradle Rock in *Signals of Distress*, which counter 'the anthropomorphic view of the human world'.[85] He continues: 'For Crace landscape represents an opportunity for the reorientation of human wonderment of the world.'[86] While this is partly true, evidenced even by Smith's strange fish-sighting in *Signals of Distress*, to reduce the landscapes and objects in Crace's fiction to the purpose of human aesthetic refreshment is to overlook his radical presentation of objects. They are not solely symbolic, but speak of themselves too, shaking free, at times, of anthropocentrism; we can see this in some of the key objects in *Harvest* and *Quarantine*.

Like many of Crace's novels, *Harvest* is situated at the uneasy cusp of a new era and constellates around a series of fiercely powerful objects: a luxurious velvet scarf, a wooden cross and a piece of vellum, made from the skin of a slaughtered calf, on to which the old and new maps of the village are to be inscribed. The symbol of the future is the sheep, representing a village due to be carved into land for pasture; 'the sheaf', the narrator informs us, 'is giving way to sheep'.[87] Here it is not the past that haunts, but an unknown future, which brings with it 'the weird and phantom bleats of sheep' (*H*, 80), an unmappable 'sheepscape' (*H*, 129). Whereas in *The Gift of Stones*, Doe represented the commodification of the human, here all the villagers are instrumentalised and objectified; 'I think he means to shear us all, then turn us into mutton' (*H*, 159), notes Master Kent. The women, of course, are first to be sacrificed, with a small party taken hostage and brutally treated. The narrator Walter Thirsk's lover Kitty Gosse is subjected to 'fiercer questioning' when 'the inquisitors had discovered on her naked body her warts and lumps and judged them perfect teats on which the Devil readily might suck' (*H*, 159), and Lizzie Carr, a child chosen as Gleaning Queen, is abandoned by her family on the grounds that 'a farmer knows to gate the herd before he hunts the stray' (*H*, 173). Rather than intervening, Thirsk himself retreats into a dream world which revivifies his deceased wife Cecily; 'my thrush was there', he recounts, 'my Cecily, full-throated and alive again' (*H*, 238). Representative of both a disenfranchised past and the perceived female 'witchery' (*H*, 155) on to which the villagers project their worst fears is a velvet shawl worn by Mistress Bedlam, 'an expensive lordly weave in heavy Turkish mauve and silver thread' (*H*, 27), which reappears at crucial points in the narrative. The last we hear of the shawl is its reflection in 'the mauvish scarf of smoke' (*H*, 240) which marks the immolation of the village and, with it, the traditional way of life.

Like *The Gift of Stones*, *Harvest* retells a history that is not uniquely human, and imagines a future in which human–nonhuman ties are destined to be severed or disavowed. In the earlier world, animals are 'backyard brethren' (*H*, 35) and history is marked by the longevity of the nonhuman, 'the grizzled oak [. . .] so old it must have come from Eden to our fields' (*H*, 196). The villagers acknowledge that 'each step we've taken since the last frost at winter's end – an age ago – has left its imprint on our earth' (*H*, 60). This is a model of stewardship that will be rent by the future, signalled by an imminent 'storm of reckoning' (*H*, 86). The changes in human history, the underlying potential of human violence and the human relationship with the earth are all brought together in the figure of a wooden cross that stands in the village. Thirsk describes:

> our wooden cross, our neglected pillory, standing at the unbuilt gateway of our unbuilt church. It's slightly taller than a normal man, oak built. The two hinged boards which form its wings and provide two stations for its prisoners are wider and a little longer than its upright. That makes our cross more muscular and far reaching than the usual, narrower crucifix. The orifices which in a crueller place would more regularly provide a fitting for the necks and wrists of miscreants have lately been a useful space for us to hang prayer rosaries or love chains made from flowers. (*H*, 37)

Thirsk's description occurs at the very point at which the village becomes this 'crueller place', the cross on the very next page housing two men, 'left to sag for seven days' (*H*, 38). The role of the oak, elsewhere described as 'trustworthy' (*H*, 229), is ambiguous. The cross has human qualities – it is 'muscular' – and yet it is subject to the whims of human feeling and implicated in human history, forming both a space for celebration and serving as a tool of human violence and punishment.

Towards the end of the novel, Thirsk walks to the boundary of the village, a place he confesses to having avoided for some years, as it seemed 'too precarious' (*H*, 270). In *The Gift of Stones*, the storyteller's role was to bring order to events and structures that were mysterious or whose disorder made the villagers uneasy. He spoke of the past to unify the present, eventually demonstrating both the necessity of storytelling and its futility and fragility; it can impose order only temporarily before its words are crushed. In *Harvest*, Thirsk befriends Mr Quill because he hopes that the map-maker might bring him a different future. Quill is murdered before his map is completed. Like Quill, Thirsk is also an interloper, his body not joined to the land like those of the villagers. His experience of migrancy, like those of the storyteller in *The Gift of Stones* and of the geese pelted to death by angry villagers, points to the inescapable core of lived experience. Our attempts to understand, to write stories, to create order are only provisional. It is fitting, therefore, that at the end of the novel Thirsk carries a blank map: 'My vellum is an unmarked sheet. It could be anywhere' (*H*, 271).

The vellum which Thirsk tortuously moulds by hand is perhaps the most resonant of the novel's symbols, bringing together the earth, nonhuman life and the human desire to impose order and structure through a craftsmanship – like the production of flint knives or bronze arrows in *The Gift of Stones* – that is inescapably destructive.

> Now I can see the puckering where that little hand-reared animal, which was so moist and succulent for us at our gleaning feast, was cut along the spine, peeled off the ribs and then spread out for butchering. Her twin flanks are still joined at the girth, along an uneven edge of skin [. . .] The skin is not yet leathery. I should say vellumy. It's far too coarse still, and resistant. I should have soaked it for a week or more. I have to limber it. I will not say it's easy work. I will not say I enjoy being this intimate with an animal I've known and liked (and eaten, actually). (*H*, 128)

In a world in which a slaughtered man and a dead horse are both flung into the same pit, and the young veal calf and the immature human Gleaning Queen have a similarly terrible fate, distinctions cannot be cleanly drawn along species lines. In his account of the disorder that the village witnesses, Thirsk classifies the 'Innocent' as 'including beasts' (*H*, 202). The perception of the calf's skin as a blank slate or page upon which the human story can be mapped is undermined by Thirsk's description. The calf's skin already maps in detail human–animal relations: the tension between the vulnerability of the 'little hand-reared animal' and its 'succulent' flesh upon which the villagers feasted; Thirsk's uneasy intimacy with the remnants of a 'liked' animal in whose death he was complicit. This aerial view of a set of relations, predicated on domination – 'slowly I can feel the calfskin surrendering to my hand' (*H*, 129) – makes us, as readers, uncomfortable voyeurs. The resistance of the calfskin reveals the experience of allure which Harman describes; Thirsk suddenly realises that he cannot possibly understand the depths of this non-sentient object, that his perspective is incomplete. Alert to the gravity of killing, yet unrepentant, Thirsk's position reflects that of Haraway; 'in order to be *for* some ways of living and dying and not others', she asserts, 'I/we must kill'.[88]

Quill's 'scratchy charts and drawings' appear derivative, undermining the belief that only human beings are capable of meaningful inscriptions. Thirsk notes that he recognises 'their intrigue and their sorcery'.

> I've seen equally compound patterns, no less ineffable than these, when I've peeled back bark on dying trees, or torn away the papering on birches. I've seen them sketched by lichens on a standing stone, or designed by mosses in a quag, or lurking on the under-wing of butterflies. (*H*, 133)

Not only is agency, order and aesthetic significance here attributed to nonhuman objects, but it is also clear that these inscriptions are 'ineffable'; in other words, that Thirsk can never fully apprehend them.

In an early essay in *Towards Speculative Realism*, Harman uses OOP to reimagine an image of Friedrich Nietzsche sitting at his desk. His description begins:

> Each of the objects in Nietzsche's room rumbles in its depths, unleashing powerful forces in its ceaseless duels and friendships with the others. The bulky table sustains a sheet of paper that compresses the table ever so lightly in return. The legs of the chair dig into the floor as if to wound it, ungrateful for the support they receive, thankless toward the ground that stops them from plummeting to the center of the earth. Photons ricochet off Nietzsche's pale hands like bullets, reflected in an instant towards the coldest reaches of distant space.[89]

When viewed properly as objects – which cannot be reduced to either components or effects – rather than through the 'tiresome' subject/object binary, the entities that surround Nietzsche are brought to life. There is a comparable passage in Crace's novel *Quarantine* in which the beleaguered character Miri, whose human relations, her marriage, have proved 'inflexible and empty',[90] finds in the wilderness a rich and yielding welcome:

> It [the wilderness] gave its hospitality to her [. . .] It would use what little skills it had to make her life more comfortable, to keep her bedding free from scorpions, her skin unsnagged by thorns, her sleep unbroken. And if it could, it would direct some rainfall to her tent or save her billy from a fall or drive gazelles towards her traps. It would be the one – hooded in a brown mantle – whose breathing twinned with hers. It would be the one, mistaken for a thorn bush or a breeze, that rustled at her side. It would be her shoulder-blades, and then the one that brushed the sand-flies from her lips and eyes. It was bewitched by her already, if that is possible, if the land can be allowed a heart. [. . .] The earth was showing kindness to the flesh. (*Q*, 8–9)

While it could be argued that this anthropomorphic vivification of the nonhuman is here detailed in its service of the human character, this would not be entirely accurate. Miri's perspective on the land is set against prevailing human perspectives. For Marta and Jesus, the land is inhospitable, godless. Jesus compares it unfavourably to Galilee, which was 'full of god at that time of the year – new crops, flowers on the apricot, the lambs, the warmer nights' (*Q*, 22). He concludes that 'Creation was unfinished here' (*Q*, 22), using it as an environment against which he will test his faith, searching and failing to find God's 'fingerprints' (*Q*, 77), because a land without vegetation must be, he decides, godless: 'The stones were sinners. And the scree was hell' (*Q*, 77). In contrast, through Marta's eyes, we see plenitude and fertility, a litany of creation: 'Swag flies, mud wasps and fleas blistered the surface of the water, dipping their bodies at both ends; one dip to drink and one to drop a line of eggs. Centipedes and millipedes, lonely lovers

of the damp, gathered at the edges of the cistern in rare communion'
(*Q*, 56). Marta, however, is 'repulsed' (*Q*, 56). Yet, ultimately, we
dismiss these perspectives; Jesus is a figure of immaturity, not wisdom,
and the worn anti-heroine Miri flourishes where Marta struggles.
In fact, Miri, distinct from the labours of Jesus and Marta, and the
mercenary perspective of Musa, becomes a window through which
we can perceive nonhuman interactions as if humans did not exist.
Crace begins to frame Miri, in Harman's words, as an '*ingredient* in
a symbiosis rather than just [a] privileged observer'.[91] She 'became a
porcupine, became percussion in the scrub' (*Q*, 14). Through Miri's
eyes, the earth becomes a strange, moving, living organism. We are
told that:

> no wild land is ever entirely still and silent. It has its discords and its deto-
> nations. Earth collapses with the engineering of the ants: lizards smack the
> pebbles with their tails; the sun fires seeds in salvos from their pods; pigeons
> misconnect with dry branches; and stones, left loosely to their own devices,
> can find the muscle to descend the hill. (*Q*, 14)

In this passage, Crace comes closest to depicting nonhuman 'allure',
the 'discords and detonations', the 'misconnect', representative of the
partiality of all interactions, a gesture towards nonhuman aesthetic
experience which points towards Object-Oriented Philosophy.

Crace caricatures the figure of Jesus and undermines the notion of a
transcendent, interventionist God, encouraging us to look downwards
rather than upwards for beauty and divinity; as Aphas says: 'My god
is not a holy king, an emperor in heaven. He's immanent in everything'
(*Q*, 53). No divine logic emerges in the text, only the unrelenting force
of Musa, the keen-eyed, bargaining capitalist who cashes in on Jesus's
death, unhindered by any sense of divine justice. Scriptural religion
feels absurd in this landscape. It is only in his famished delirium that
Jesus comes to see the sky above as 'like the scriptures' (*Q*, 135),
and feverishly scrawls the name of God over every object in his cave,
disturbed because he can no longer perceive the imprint of God in creation. In his final hours, he becomes the text, 'a dry, discarded page of
scripture' (*Q*, 193), with Crace exploiting the ambiguities in scriptural
history to give an alternative account of Jesus's life. The story of Jesus
is merely a subplot, however, the novel's life deriving not from the dry
pages of scripture but from the unprepossessing landscape, in the scrub
which, despite itself, offers 'something sustaining, unselfish, fertile even'
(*Q*, 219). It is the energy of the natural landscape, as mediated by the
attentive Miri, which enlivens the novel. We are told that she 'listened
to the conversation of the gnats, the dry remarks of crumbling soil. It
had seemed that she could hear the living rocks around the healer's

cave, breathing, humming to themselves, praying even' (*Q*, 115). Should divine retribution take place, it will be delivered not from on high, but from the workings of the earth; Musa's brutal donkey-killing, for example, is witnessed by 'three hawks [. . .] arcing high above the scrub' (*Q*, 34).

The passing of Shim's impressive spiralled walking stick to Musa signifies a shift in power to the latter, breaking the symbiosis between Shim and staff. 'Shim would not be safe or comfortable without his staff', we are told. 'It was not Greek or logical, but he loved the twisting wood, each curl a cycle of his life. It was as much a part of him as curls cut from his head' (*Q*, 98). When this phallic representation of masculine power changes hands, it becomes sinister and suspicious; in Jesus's eyes,

> It was the twisted wood that should be thrown out or burned. It was so fractured by the distance and heat that it seemed to curve in spirals like the demon's baton [. . .] The sort of stick that could strike flames into a bush, split rocks, become a snake, turn wine to water with a single touch, turn holy bread back into stone again, make brothers fight and mothers chase their sons from home. (*Q*, 111)

The different perceptions of the staff reinforce Harman's claim that the tool-being of an object means that it can never be fully perceived as it really is.

Less imposing but no less extraordinary is Miri's loom, an object whose significance is not exhausted by its function. Inherited from her mother, the loom provides for Miri a temporary escape from Musa and nurtures a companionship between herself and Marta which will eventually facilitate her permanent escape. Miri 'sat cross-legged before the loom. She rubbed the beams with her fingertips, exactly as her mother had, exactly as her daughter would. She plucked the warp. She played it like a harp' (*Q*, 107). Here, an encounter with a functional object becomes an aesthetic experience. The mat too, produced by the loom, acquires magical properties; Miri believed that 'finishing the mat would free her of the man. Perhaps she'd fly away on it, her baby sitting neatly in her lap' (*Q*, 166). *Quarantine* upends existing hierarchies: the narrative diverts from Jesus, a figurehead of patriarchal power, to the lowly peasant woman Miri, and the objects and landscape with which she interacts. The understated utopia that Crace gifts Miri at the close of the novel is one in which she is simply one being among others, all alike in their ontological intensity.

> Quite soon, they'd share a table in a room, colourless except for candle flame and the orange and the purple of their mat. They would be dining well

on fish [. . .] If there was something in the world that was bigger, stronger than their table-top, they would not care. It had not spoken to them yet. They were not listening. They were contented with their grainy universe of candlelight and wood and wool. (*Q*, 238)

OBJECTS AS THE 'ENGINE OF CHANGE': BETWEEN ALLURE AND AFFECT

In *The Mushroom at the End of the World*, Anna Tsing asserts that 'over the past few decades, many kinds of scholars have shown that allowing only human protagonists into our stories is not just ordinary human bias; it is a cultural agenda tied to dreams of progress through modernization'.[92] Tsing reinforces Latour's claim that modernity has entailed a disingenuous disavowal of nonhuman agency, rooted in a 'modern critical stance' which remains residually theological. This stance conceptualises progress as increased separation from, and domination over, the natural world. A similar critique underpins much ecological thought, for example, the ecofeminism of Val Plumwood, which interrogates the ways in which Western thought has understood progress through 'the contrast of civilisation (reason) versus primitivism (barbarism and savagery)'.[93] Similarly fantastical and equally damaging are Romantic depictions of Nature as the locus of idealistic harmony. In these, Timothy Morton perceives a thoroughgoing narcissism: 'putting something called Nature on a pedestal and admiring it from afar does for the environment what patriarchy does for the figure of Woman', he writes. 'It is a paradoxical act of sadistic admiration.'[94] As Chakrabarty acknowledges, the Anthropocene brings with it a material erosion of our conceptual categories; the first to go is 'the age-old humanist distinction between natural history and human history'.[95]

Tsing proposes an alternative to these destructive, anachronistic poles, looking to identify 'disturbance-based ecologies in which many species sometimes live together without either harmony or conquest'.[96] Given our tendency to project the latter narrative, Tsing's task is less modest than it first appears. Her goal, however, to cultivate an awareness of 'multispecies worlds', an acknowledgement that 'making worlds is not limited to humans', resonates with Crace's constructed worlds.[97] These are landscapes which, as Miyahara Kazunari says, 'are in flux, teeming with life, sensitive to interconnections between living things', and are always characterised by an attentiveness to the nonhuman that destabilises anthropocentrism.[98] For both Latour and Tsing, we must set aside the modern narrative of progress and embrace hybridity. Tsing advocates 'abandoning progress rhythms to watch polyphonic assemblages' and perceiving 'contamination as collaboration'.[99] Latour suggests that we recognise and pursue the disavowed quasi-objects of modernity, identifying ourselves as 'amoderns' for whom there is neither culture nor nature, but 'only natures-cultures'.[100] For Latour, humans are not the source of meaning or order, but mere 'latecomers' who have landed 'on a movement, a passage – literally a pass, in the sense of this term as used in ball games'.[101] Given the limitations of the 'modern critical stance', it is no accident that many of Crace's novels explore eras informed by different constructions of human–nonhuman relations.

These thinkers regard philosophy as particularly culpable in a series of processes that have facilitated our self-enclosure and authorised long-term anthropogenic environmental damage, the extent of which is only now coming to light. Their solutions, however, are never merely philosophical, but interdisciplinary: social, cultural, political and eco-logical. Graham Harman's divergence from these figures is threefold: first, in stubbornly remaining with philosophy and philosophical prob-lems, rather than subjugating these to politics; secondly, in focusing on objects rather than relations; and finally, in beginning to interrogate the relationship between aesthetics and ontology. Harman's is an altogether bolder and more disarming project, both because it 'puts the affairs of human consciousness on exactly the same footing as the duel between canaries, microbes, earthquakes, atoms and tar', and because it cannot fall back on our apparently intuitive preference for living beings to ground its appeal.[102]

Harman's *Guerrilla Metaphysics* contains a chapter, 'Metaphor and Humor', in which, via José Ortega y Gasset's account of metaphor, he develops his notion of allure. We have already seen the ways in which allure exposes the limitations of our experience of a real object through the sensual object. Here, metaphor (as opposed to simile, which is always attached to a particular property of an object or objects) gestures beyond current conceptual framings (which always proceed from the sensual, therefore limited, presentation of objects) to the construction of new objects. Although at first glance, metaphor appears uniquely human, Harman argues otherwise; it is shared by animals who perform, use tools and extrapolate. Metaphor permits Harman to combine an anti-realist epistemology with a realist ontol-ogy.[103] Given that objects are never fully realised in their sensual inter-actions, they are always open to novelty. By looking to 'globalize the rift between a thing and its features', we capitalise on the way in which allure renders objects the 'engine of change'.[104] The scene from *Signals of Distress* with which I opened this chapter appears to capture this kind of moment. Through his contention that the aesthetic has privileged access to the ontological, and his disengaging of the aesthetic from the human, Harman challenges both our assumptions about how to do philosophy and the sense that the aesthetic is the pinnacle of human achievement.

In the Introduction, I commented upon the domestication of Spinozan *affectus* into individualised, unmediated emotional experience. Disappointingly, Eugenie Brinkema reports, 'theories of affect offer all repetition with no difference'.[105] Resisting such accounts of affect which presuppose a classical account of human interiority, Brinkema proposes that affect is 'non-intentional, indifferent, and resists the given-over attributes of a teleological spectatorship with acquirable gains'.[106] Harman does not use the term 'affect' in relation to his accounts of aesthetics and allure, but doing so might help us to think Brinkema's notion of affect non-anthropocentrically. Rejecting panpsychism as residually anthropocentric by virtue of its continued prioritisation of cognition, Harman lightheartedly proposes the term 'pan-allurism' to signify the existence of allure 'in all reality, including the inanimate sphere'.[107] Given that allure is an essential component of causation, Harman provides a way of understanding how we might think affect outside cognition. As Shaviro says,

> the failure of epistemological cognition does not mean the impossibility of ontological interaction. Aesthetic modes of expression correspond to 'vicarious' (in Harman's sense) as well as to noncognitive (in a Whiteheadian sense) modes of interaction – they are ways of positively expressing 'what we cannot speak about'.[108]

We might say that allure names affective relations with and without the human, a move that enables us to think outwith the ontological projection of the human on to the world (of which Harman perceives panpsychism guilty) and to imagine animate and inanimate things as participants in 'the principle of revolution as such'.[109]

Reading Harman and Crace alongside each other demonstrates the tensions that emerge when elements of OOP are put into practice: Crace's novels contain an inescapable oscillation between the conventions of anthropocentric storytelling, and both investigations into nonhuman relations and the sheer dazzlement at the ontological intensity of objects. In previous chapters, it has been easy to identify an ethical or political demand in both literary and philosophical texts: the ethical responsibilities of literature in its accounts of sentient life, for example. While there are moments of ideological critique in Crace's fiction, and his landscapes consist of 'multispecies worlds' which undermine the destructive notion of human exceptionalism, the advancement of a political position is neither their primary aim nor effect. The same is true of Harman; unlike so much of contemporary philosophy, new materialisms included, whose principal aim is political, Harman's goal is a philosophical one, to 'reopen the Kantian settlement and renegotiate it in a way that distributes its terms differently'.[110] The clear alignment between Crace's literary texts and Harman's work, however, reinforces the claim that the aesthetic – as a new juxtaposition of the surfaces of substances – gives access to the ontological, and necessitates a recognition of dynamism beyond the living; that allure permits 'the object to manifest itself as something more than all of its current effects in our world'.[111] While no ethical or political programme is explicitly encoded in these texts, they offer richer potential than the superficial politics of 'new materialism' for attentiveness to different ways of seeing, and being in, the world. In the next chapter, I shall return to existing structures used for ordering the world, focusing on the gendered history of entomological collecting.

NOTES

1. Jeffrey Jerome Cohen, *Stone: An Ecology of the Inhuman* (Minneapolis: University of Minnesota Press, 2015), p. 36.
2. Marguerite Yourcenar, 'Introduction', in Roger Caillois, *The Writing of Stones*, trans. Barbara Bray (Charlottesville: University of Virginia Press, 1985), pp. xi–xix (p. xii).
3. Timothy Morton, *Humankind: Solidarity with Nonhuman People* (London: Verso, 2017), p. 129.
4. Steven Shaviro's discussion of this is particularly illuminating. Steven Shaviro, 'Object Oriented Aesthetics?', 8 November 2009, http://www.shaviro.com/Blog/?p=810 (accessed 18 February 2019).
5. Anna Lowenhaupt Tsing, *The Mushroom at the End of the World: On the Possibility of Life in Capitalist Ruins* (Princeton: Princeton University Press, 2015), p. vii.
6. Derrida, *The Animal That Therefore I Am*, p. 88.
7. Mario Ortiz Robles, *Literature and Animal Studies* (London: Routledge, 2016), p. 19.
8. Jim Crace, *Signals of Distress* (London: Picador, 2008), p. 186. Subsequent references are given in parentheses in the text.
9. Bennett, *Vibrant Matter*, p. ix.
10. Tsing, *Mushroom at the End of the World*, p. vii.
11. Graham Harman, *Towards Speculative Realism: Essays and Lectures* (Winchester: Zero Books, 2010), p. 1.
12. Steven Shaviro, *The Universe of Things: On Speculative Realism* (Minneapolis: University of Minnesota Press, 2014), p. 5.

13. Quentin Meillassoux, *After Finitude: An Essay on the Necessity of Contingency*, trans. Ray Brassier (London: Continuum, 2008), p. 5.

14. Graham Harman, 'On Vicarious Causation', *Collapse*, II (2007), 171–205 (pp. 190).

15. Ian Bogost, *Alien Phenomenology or What It's Like to Be a Thing* (Minneapolis: University of Minnesota Press, 2012), p. 3.

16. Graham Harman, *Guerrilla Metaphysics* (Chicago: Open Court, 2004), p. 243.

17. Harman, *Towards Speculative Realism*, pp. 94, 95.

18. Latour, *We Have Never Been Modern*, p. 66.

19. Latour, 'Where Are the Missing Masses?', p. 165.

20. Ian Hodder, *Entangled: An Archaeology of the Relationships between Humans and Things* (Malden, MA: Wiley-Blackwell, 2012), p. 215.

21. Bruno Latour, 'On Interobjectivity', *Mind, Culture, Activity*, 3.4 (1996), 228–45 (p. 239).

22. Latour, 'On Interobjectivity', p. 237.

23. Latour, *We Have Never Been Modern*, p. 137.

24. Graham Harman, *Prince of Networks: Bruno Latour and Metaphysics* (Melbourne: re.press, 2009), p. 35.

25. Latour, *We Have Never Been Modern*, pp. 10–11.

26. Latour, *We Have Never Been Modern*, p. 79.

27. Bennett, *Vibrant Matter*, p. xiii.

28. Bennett, *Vibrant Matter*, p. 2.

29. Bennett, *Vibrant Matter*, pp. 10, 9, 98.

30. Bennett, *Vibrant Matter*, p. 112.

31. Philip Tew, *Jim Crace* (Manchester: Manchester University Press), p. 94.

32. Latour, *We Have Never Been Modern*, p. 89.

33. Tew, *Jim Crace*, p. 95.

34. Tew, *Jim Crace*, p. 102.

35. Latour, cited in Graham Harman, *Immaterialism: Objects and Social Theory* (Cambridge: Polity, 2016), p. 19.

36. Bryant, cited in Harman, *Immaterialism*, p. 13.

37. Harman, *Immaterialism*, p. 20.

38. Jane Bennett, cited in Harman, *Immaterialism*, p. 20.

39. Bennett, *Vibrant Matter*, p. 58.

40. Harman, 'Art Without Relations'.

41. Graham Harman, 'Materialism is Not the Solution: On Matter, Form and Mimesis', *The Nordic Journal of Aesthetics*, 47 (2014), 94–100 (p. 96).

42. Jane Bennett, 'Systems and Things: A Response to Graham Harman and Timothy Morton', *New Literary History*, 43 (2012), 225–33 (p. 227).

43. Harman, 'Materialism is Not the Solution', p. 99.

44. Harman, *Immaterialism*, p. 96.

45. Harman, *Towards Speculative Realism*, p. 33.

46. Harman, *Immaterialism*, p. 114.

47. Harman, 'Art Without Relations'.

48. Harman, *Towards Speculative Realism*, pp. 23, 45.

49. Harman, *Towards Speculative Realism*, p. 10.

50. Harman, *Towards Speculative Realism*, p. 46.

51. Harman, *Towards Speculative Realism*, p. 25.

52. Harman, *Towards Speculative Realism*, p. 27.

53. Shaviro, *The Universe of Things*, p. 52.

54. Harman, 'On Vicarious Causation', p. 193.

55. Nathan Brown, 'The Nadir of OOO: From Graham Harman's Tool-Being to Timothy Morton's *Realist Magic: Objects, Ontology, Causality* (Open Humanities Press, 2013)', *Parrhesia*, 17 (2013), 62–71 (p. 62).

56. Peter Wolfendale, *Object-Oriented Philosophy: The Noumenon's New Clothes* (Falmouth: Urbanomic, 2014), p. 43.

57. Wolfendale, *Object-Oriented Philosophy*, p. 299.

58. Cohen, *Stone*, p. 16.

59. Tew, *Jim Crace*, p. 28.

60. Tew, *Jim Crace*, p. 28.

61. Lane, cited in Tew, *Jim Crace*, p. 30.

62. Bennett, *Vibrant Matter*, p. 120.

63. Jim Crace, *The Gift of Stones* (London: Vintage, 1997), p. 22. Subsequent references are given in parentheses in the text.

64. Crace, cited in Tew, *Jim Crace*, p. 61.

65. Tew, *Jim Crace*, p. 62.

66. Tsing, *Mushroom at the End of the World*, p. 19.

67. Cohen, *Stone*, p. 33.

68. Cohen, *Stone*, p. 131.

69. Dipesh Chakrabarty, 'The Climate of History: Four Theses', *Critical Inquiry*, 35.2 (2009), 197–222 (pp. 197–8).

70. Harman, *Immaterialism*, p. 29. Wolfendale rejects Harman's claims about OOP's relationship to Kant, arguing that ultimately OOP is 'a consolidation' of the 'central tenets' of correlationism. Wolfendale, *Object-Oriented Philosophy*, p. 6.

71. Shaviro, *The Universe of Things*, p. 3.

72. Harman, *Towards Speculative Realism*, p. 54.

73. Harman, *Towards Speculative Realism*, p. 146.

74. Harman, *Towards Speculative Realism*, p. 115.

75. Harman, *Towards Speculative Realism*, p. 147.

76. See Harman, 'On Vicarious Causation', p. 188.

77. Harman, 'On Vicarious Causation', p. 189.

78. Hodder, *Entangled*, p. 2.

79. Bennett, *Vibrant Matter*, p. 4.

80. Shaviro, *The Universe of Things*, p. 53.

81. Shaviro, *The Universe of Things*, p. 53.

82. Graham Harman, 'Aesthetics as First Philosophy: Levinas and the Non-

Human', *Naked Punch*, 2012, http://www.nakedpunch.com/articles/147 (accessed 14 July 2016).

83. Harman, 'Aesthetics as First Philosophy'.
84. Harman, 'Aesthetics as First Philosophy'.
85. Tew, *Jim Crace*, p. 7.
86. Tew, *Jim Crace*, p. 67.
87. Jim Crace, *Harvest* (London: Picador, 2013), p. 42. Subsequent references will be given in parentheses in the text.
88. Haraway, *Manifestly Haraway*, p. 236.
89. Harman, *Towards Speculative Realism*, p. 51.
90. Jim Crace, *Quarantine* (London: Picador, 2010), p. 7. Subsequent references will be given in parentheses in the text.
91. Harman, *Immaterialism*, p. 54.
92. Tsing, *Mushroom at the End of the World*, p. 155.
93. Val Plumwood, *Feminism and the Mastery of Nature* (London: Routledge, 1993), p. 107.
94. Morton, *Ecology Without Nature*, p. 5.
95. Chakrabarty, 'Climate of History', p. 201.
96. Tsing, *Mushroom at the End of the World*, p. 5.
97. Tsing, *Mushroom at the End of the World*, p. 22.
98. Kazunari, cited in Tew, *Jim Crace*, p. 121.
99. Tsing, *Mushroom at the End of the World*, pp. 24, 27.
100. Latour, *We Have Never Been Modern*, pp. 90, 104.
101. Latour, *We Have Never Been Modern*, p. 129.
102. Harman, 'On Vicarious Causation', p. 189.
103. Harman, *Guerrilla Metaphysics*, p. 101.
104. Harman, *Guerrilla Metaphysics*, p. 152.
105. Brinkema, *Forms of the Affects*, p. xiii.
106. Brinkema, *Forms of the Affects*, p. 33.
107. Harman, *Guerrilla Metaphysics*, p. 244.
108. Shaviro, 'Object Oriented Aesthetics?'
109. Harman, *Guerrilla Metaphysics*, p. 244.
110. Shaviro, *The Universe of Things*, p. 69.
111. Harman, *Guerrilla Metaphysics*, p. 245.

4. *The Sexual Politics of Nature Writing and Lepidoptery: 'The siren song of entomology'*

We both realized . . . that we were in a mausoleum and that the walls were lined with death, that those gorgeous pinned specimens, precisely arranged according to aesthetic criteria – color, size, shape, geometry – were not just dazzling objects; they were also tiny corpses.

Hugo Raffles[1]

Thus there is in the life of a collector a dialectical tension between the poles of disorder and order. Naturally, his existence is tied to many other things as well: to a very mysterious relationship to ownership, something about which we shall have more to say later; also, to a relationship to objects which does not emphasize their functional, utilitarian value – that is, their usefulness – but studies and loves them as the scene, the stage, of their fate. The most profound enchantment for the collector is the locking of individual items within a magic circle in which they are fixed as the final thrill, the thrill of acquisition, passes over them.

Walter Benjamin[2]

Benjamin is, of course, talking about books and it is perhaps unfair to transpose his account of unpacking his library and creating order from the 'disorder of crates that have been wrenched open' to a different type of collecting, to rows of flies, bees and butterflies pinned and labelled in cases and drawers.[3] And yet his descriptions of 'the thrill of acquisition' and of the pleasure of realising a particular order apply just as well to butterflies as books, to the pleasures of lepidoptery. Collecting is building a world; for Benjamin and his books, an attempt to 'renew the old world', for the entomologists and natural historians of yore, an attempt to bring forth the concealed order of the existing world, to make it visible.[4] That order is both given and hidden lies at the heart of natural history. As Michel Foucault writes, the presupposed 'continuity of nature' is complicated by its invisibility:

> experience does not reveal the continuity of nature as such, but gives it to us both broken up – since there are a great many gaps in the series of

values effectively occupied by the variables [. . .] and blurred, since the real, geographic and terrestrial space in which we find ourselves confronts us with creatures that are interwoven with one another, in an order which, in relation to the great network of taxonomies, is nothing more than chance, disorder, or turbulence.[5]

The perceived urgency and value of natural history – the bringing forth of order from disorder – derives from its framing as an expression of stewardship: Man names God's creation; Linnaeus is the 'second Adam'.[6]

Entomological collecting was once enfolded within natural history as species vocation, perceived as a 'worthy, sacred endeavour'.[7] In the late eighteenth and early nineteenth centuries, 'insects became attractive subjects precisely because of their apparent distance from humanity. They were less human and therefore more natural than quadrupeds.'[8] In its Victorian heyday, this association between insects and nature led to the employment of entomological research as grounds for theories of sexual politics, social order and, through ongoing studies of social insects such as bees in observation hives, the naturalisation of 'particular forms of governance'.[9] The application of entomological knowledge to pest control in European colonies led to great financial rewards. Understanding of and control over insects was understood as a significant species success, especially given that humans have been battling insects, as Richard Schweid notes, 'since making our appearance on this planet'.[10] However, greater awareness of anthropogenic environmental destruction has led to scepticism towards the project of 'benign stewardship' and a suspicion that natural history is 'a form of ideologically-loaded housekeeping'[11] that reinforces human mastery.[12] It is no surprise, therefore, that the reputation of the entomological collector, whose scientific value has clearly diminished, is much altered; he (and it is, almost invariably, a he) is now more likely to be viewed as a 'neurotic hoarder' than an 'intellectual conquistador'.[13] 'But how, in a few short centuries,' asks Marina Benjamin, 'did the heroic collector or naturalist adventurer, champion of exploration and scientific knowledge, end up shrivelling into the world-withdrawn wimp, humble curator, cataloguer and maker of lists?'[14]

The starting point for this chapter is the collector's belief that 'ownership is the most intimate relationship that one can have to objects'.[15] The chapter will consider the ethical and aesthetic implications of this claim when, as in the case of entomological collecting, the possessed objects are or were living beings. Arguing that the discourse of insect collecting is one of objectification and domination, and that entomological classification and practices continue to reflect concerns about sex and gender which were present in its eighteenth- and nineteenth-century instantiations, this chapter will align the objectification of women with that of insects. It will interrogate the notion of aesthetic disinterestedness as licence for such objectification, asking whether aesthetic disinterestedness permits an empathetic disengagement which, at its worst, leads to a sociopathic lack of ethical awareness. The chapter has three parts, focusing on John Fowles's *The Collector*, insects in contemporary nature writing and, finally, the role of lepidoptery in the fiction of Vladimir Nabokov. The closing section will interrogate the relationship between ethics and aesthetics, appealing for the joint necessity of cross-species empathetic engagement and a distancing that is alert to its own subjective positioning. This chapter is complemented by Chapter 5, which looks at insects which are neither suppressed nor domesticated, but literally and conceptually 'unpinned'.

LITERARY LEPIDOPTERY I: COLLECTING BUTTERFLIES AND WOMEN

In his discussion of natural history, Foucault recalls the 'great metaphor of the book' of nature, a book opened and studied so that one might 'know nature', assuming, of course, that its 'text' contains an underlying order that might be unearthed and articulated. If matter is inherently legible, then language must 'reside in the world, among the plants, the herbs, the stones, and the animals' and taxonomy should be understood as discovery rather than creation.[16] Originating in a theological worldview, this perspective assumes the existence of a creator, a teleological order within creation, and a uniquely human role of discerning (and maintaining) creaturely order. The trope of landscapes and their inhabitants as texts is familiar. Of butterflies chased into a thicket, Vladimir Nabokov records: 'I'm not collecting them, but only *rereading* them, because I know them in all these localities.'[17] Looking back over his entomological preoccupations, the Swedish naturalist Fredrik Sjöberg muses: 'All these species were a language, and now I knew so much vocabulary by heart that I could pay more attention to the grand narrative.'[18]

Sjöberg's account of the successful naturalist bypasses the elision he makes; his designation of insects as legible texts reinforces the dualism between active human (male) subjectivity and passive nature. The natural object is also feminised, with the seductions of entomology described as an irresistible 'siren song'. Sjöberg is partially alert to the gendering of entomology; 'no sensible person is interested in flies, or anyway no woman',[19] he quips, before explaining rather more honestly that there is 'something about the combination of insects and collecting that frightens women'.[20] His explanation, however, is perhaps too benign: collecting is merely *passé* and 'women have a good nose for sniffing out the musty scent of past centuries that clings to those solitary men who are more interested in punsch than poetry'.[21] Sjöberg's, albeit rather limited, attempt to grapple with the legacies of entomological history typifies a genre – contemporary popular entomology – which struggles to position itself in relation to a past towards which it is indebted and about which it is ashamed. Patrick Barkham's 2010 memoir, *The Butterfly Isles: A Summer in Search of Our Emperors and Admirals*, exemplifies this tension. Barkham disavows collecting as cruel and both despairs at the 'wearily familiar' way that lepidopterists 'have been cast as eccentrics and even sexual predators over the years',[22] and firmly distances himself from the practice of butterfly collecting which he admits is cruel, even 'creepy':

> There may be an element of double standards in my contemporary distaste for catching a rare butterfly in a net, squeezing its small body between finger and thumb until it is lifeless, poisoning it to make sure, pinning its body to a cork board and shutting it in a drawer. We may inadvertently slaughter far more butterflies than the collectors of old. But some of the ways in which butterflies were killed and preserved in the golden age of butterfly collecting were downright creepy.[23]

Aside from the historical exclusion of women from lepidoptery, Barkham speculates that the 'male inclination towards mania', which, he suggests, includes objects as varied as 'steam trains, racing cars, surfing or guitars', might explain male interest in lepidoptery. Noticing that there might be something different in collecting living beings to fixating on inanimate ones, he concludes that 'perhaps butterflies exert a particularly strong hold over the male gaze'.[24] That both women and butterflies might be subject to the male gaze perhaps accounts for the perception, which Barkham identifies but is unable to debunk, that 'a passion for butterflies' signified 'an alarming attitude to women, who must be pursued, possessed and pinned down'.[25]

Frederic Clegg, the protagonist of John Fowles's 1963 novel, *The Collector*, exemplifies the 'withdrawn wimp' with whom collecting had become associated by the mid-twentieth century, and enables Fowles to explore the shifting gaze of the emasculated collector from butterflies to women. Fowles's novel combines a long-held interest in the Bluebeard story with a passionate hatred of entomological collecting, which, he contends, offers 'endless opportunities [. . .] to indulge self-esteem and display vanity [that] have long brought out the very worst in man – and stifled the best, which lies in his saving ability to grasp the transience of being'.[26] 'Any one who still collects (i.e. kills) some field of living life just for pleasure and vanity', he insists, 'has all the makings of a concentration-camp commandant.'[27] At stake here are the connected assumptions that collecting is grounded in a discourse of mastery which presupposes that the role of the human is, in the words of Francis Bacon, 'to conquer and subdue [nature], to shake her to her foundations', and that the expression of mastery and domination over nature can be linked to an impulse to master other human beings which denies their agency, sentience and value.[28]

Clegg's inability to perceive the ethical implications of butterfly collecting – 'what difference would a dozen specimens make to a species?' he puzzles – is aligned with his failure to take responsibility for his incarceration of Miranda.[29] This, Bruce Woodcock contends, is the consequence of 'a constitutional self-centred egoism which is central to the social legacy of masculinity', and which legitimates his subjugation of the needs and desires of other beings to his own.[30] Woodcock is keen to stress the patriarchal context from which Clegg emerges, rather than diagnosing him as psychopathic, an approach that might prove depoliticising. However, it is clear that, as David Punter writes, Clegg both 'lacks any true empathy with others which might temper his behaviour' and has only a slim understanding of his own emotional responses.[31] Clegg offers an extreme example of the way in which a lack of empathy can 'impair human relationships and contribute to psychopathology'.[32] Indeed, Amy Coplan's definition of empathy as that which 'combines affective matching, other-oriented perspective-taking, and self–other differentiation' to generate 'experiential understanding' exposes the limits of Clegg's empathetic capabilities.[33] While Clegg has extreme self–other differentiation, he is incapable of either affective matching or other-oriented perspective-taking; in this sense, we can ascribe to him neither cognitive nor affective empathy and his moral failings are a direct consequence of his lack of empathy. Crucially, this empathetic deficiency – Clegg's inability to understand or feel the implications of the humanity of his victim – is equivalent to 'the loss of' his own humanity.[34]

Clegg frames his pursuit and capture of Miranda as an entomological expedition:

> It was like not having a net and catching a specimen you wanted in your first and second fingers (I was always very clever at that), coming up slowly behind and you had it, but you had to nip the thorax, and it would be quivering there. It wasn't easy like it was with a killing-bottle. And it was twice as difficult with her, because I didn't want to kill her, that was the last thing I wanted.[35]

This passage recalls Walter Benjamin's identification of 'the dialectical tension between the poles of disorder and order' in the collector's life. In this case, order is only fully achieved by the death of either the butterfly or the human 'specimen'. Miranda, fully trained in internalising the male gaze, realises that she has been collected, 'pinned [. . .] in this little room' as 'one in a row of specimens'.[36] That Miranda is all too alert to her objectified status testifies to John Berger's claim in *Ways of Seeing* that:

> men act and women appear. Men look at women. Women watch themselves being looked at. This determines not only most relations between men and women but also the relation of women to themselves. The surveyor of woman in herself is male: the surveyed female. Thus she turns herself into an object – and most particularly an object of vision: a sight.[37]

Miranda understands that Clegg's perception of her is inescapably ocularcentric and that he holds an impossible desire for her 'pinned' but not dead, purified of her own subjectivity, desires and thoughts. For Robert Huffaker, this reveals Clegg's fixation with the Jungian figure of the *anima*; 'this coincidental quality of hers prevents certain anima-obsessed men from regarding her as a real, conscious phenomenon', he notes.[38] While Clegg clearly exhibits psychopathic traits, the cultural normalisation of the objectification of women renders other-oriented perspective-taking almost impossible; if Clegg perceives himself as a subject and Miranda an object, this inhibits the possibility of empathy via imaginative identification.

In the same way that butterfly collectors display unease, even revulsion, towards living butterflies – typically with regard to sexual habits and gustatory preferences that belie their ethereal beauty – Clegg begins to despise the living Miranda. She realises: 'I'm meant to be dead, pinned, always the same, always beautiful. He knows that part of my beauty is being alive, but it's the dead me he wants. He wants me living-but-dead.'[39] As a consequence, Miranda's predicament, loaded with the Gothic claustrophobia that befits a retelling of the Bluebeard myth, is inevitable.[40] Her physical confinement reflects the confinement of female sexual subjects under patriarchy; 'they sulk if you don't give and hate you when you do', Miranda acknowledges.[41] The only space for recalcitrant women, for Miranda as 'existentialist heroine', is objectified and entombed.[42]

Miranda falls victim to the 'puritan and destructive power of sexual idealism confused with gentility and male power', in the form of Clegg's hybridisation of the language of courtly love and the erotics of pornography.[43] Here, Fowles anticipates Laura Mulvey's landmark analysis of cinematic scopophilia, 'Visual Pleasure and Narrative Cinema', in which she argues:

> In a world ordered by sexual imbalance, pleasure in looking has been split between active/male and passive/female. The determining male gaze projects its phantasy on to the female figure which is styled accordingly. In their traditional exhibitionist role women are simultaneously looked at and displayed, with their appearance coded for strong visual and erotic impact so that they can be said to connote *to-be-looked-at-ness*.[44]

Clegg's timidity and prudishness towards the conscious Miranda contrasts with his violation of her unconscious body which he styles and photographs without permission, preferring the images 'with her face cut off'.[45] The fury inspired by her advances towards him is only tempered when she is rendered passive by illness; 'not while she was living, but when I knew she was dead', he discloses, 'that was when I finally forgave her'.[46] Miranda is the victim of a misogyny in which all women, like potential butterfly specimens, are judged according to their attractiveness and sexual behaviour. Clegg explicitly conflates the human and the butterfly, describing a prostitute he visits as 'old and [. . .] horrible, horrible. I mean, both the filthy way she behaved and in looks. She was worn, common. Like a specimen you'd turn away from, out collecting.'[47] The comparison between women and butterflies does not, however, shrink the species gap, facilitating cross-species empathy, but enlarges the gap created by sexual difference; Miranda's otherness is such that she might as well be a different species. As readers, we are invited to critique Clegg's collecting and the society from which it emerges. However, the novel is disconcerting and disorientating, a text 'which can sometimes make us lose our bearings, become less than certain of what it means to be human', precisely because the critique depends upon the reader's growing awareness of his complicity with Clegg's objectifying gaze.[48] Fowles, too, Woodcock notes, cannot escape being

> a kind of Clegg, a collector of imagined women pursuing his own obsessions and, in the process, making available fantasies for reading. For Fowles, it is both an exercising and an exorcism of power: it is after all he who 'kills' Miranda to make way for another version of the fantasy woman in another novel.[49]

'Conceiving of an experimental subject as an inferior, "subhuman" other – as a "specimen" meant to serve – lightens the burden of justifying the infliction of pain and death', writes Lori Gruen, describing the process through which Clegg undermines empathetic engagement with others and distances himself from the deaths of his butterfly specimens and, ultimately, Miranda.[50] In a strategy designed to undercut Clegg's distancing, Fowles gives the reader direct access to Miranda through her diary, creating a 'dialectical effect' between Miranda and Clegg,[51] and enabling the reader to empathetically engage with Miranda via what Weik von Mossner calls 'the *insider perspective*'.[52] In drawing out the parallel between herself and Clegg's butterflies, Miranda facilitates cross-species empathy, highlighting both the specificity of the butterflies' vulnerability and their shared victimhood.

LITERARY LEPIDOPTERY II: ECOFEMINISM AND CONTEMPORARY NATURE WRITING

That women, animals and nature might all be subject to the male gaze and reduced to passivity has long been argued by ecofeminists, who contend that an intersectional approach is necessary to undercut patriarchal authority and the oppression it engenders. The premise of ecofeminism, Greta Gaard explains, 'is that the ideology which authorizes oppressions such as those based on race, class, gender, sexuality, physical abilities, and species is the same ideology which sanctions the oppression of nature'.[53] Patriarchy subsists on the devaluation and denigration of the feminine, and 'that Nature is feminine is a cultural given', asserts Louise Westling.[54] Such denigration upholds the perception of the unique rationality of the figure of Man, a perception which is rooted in anthropodenial and dependent upon the expulsion of all traces of the natural. These traces are projected on to 'woman', who is therefore understood as being closer to nature, with nature unruly, irrational and demanding domination.[55] As Carolyn Merchant observed in *The Death of Nature*: 'Disorderly woman, like chaotic nature, needed to be controlled.'[56]

In this formulation, animals, women and nature are exchangeable placeholders for disruptive and mysterious otherness. Expressed in the feminised figure of Mother Earth, we see nature conceptualised as nurturing, inscrutable and loving, and, in the case of James Lovelock's metamorphosis of Mother Earth into Gaia, terrifyingly vengeful.[57] Douglas Coupland's novel *Generation A*, a text in which the humans themselves become specimens, satirises the Romantic construction of an idealised Mother Nature which conforms to male desire. The protagonist Zack Lammle recalls:

When I was growing up, Mother Nature was this reasonably hot woman who looked a lot like the actress Glenn Close wearing a pale blue nightie. When you weren't looking, she was dancing around the fields and the barns and the yard, patting the squirrels and French kissing butterflies. After the bees left and the plants started failing, it was like she'd returned from a

> Mossad boot camp with a shaved head, steel-trap abs and commando boots, and man, was she *pissed*.[58]

Coupland's parody alerts us to the crudeness of Mother Earth imagery and to the dangers of the woman–nature association, through which 'nature is overpersonified and women are underpersonified'.[59] This association, Janis Birkeland contends, has led to 'tragic consequences' for women and the natural world, which will continue for as long as we construct relationships hierarchically and understand masculinity as a synonym for power.[60] That the perceived connection between woman and nature has sanctioned conceptual and literal violence is undisputed by ecofeminists, who then face a choice between rejecting this connection as a patriarchal construct or endorsing it (either essentially or strategically) to form a woman–nature coalition to counter patriarchal oppression.[61] The return of Mother Earth through the figure of Gaia marks an attempt, if a problematic one, to provoke a more affective response to anthropogenic devastation by environmentalists; the mechanistic view of nature that followed the Scientific Revolution, they argue, led to the misconception that human damage to the natural world was essentially victimless.[62]

Increasing ecological awareness has generated at least two distinct literary responses: the first turns to accessible science to facilitate a more transparent, and ultimately less damaging, relationship with the natural world; the second to a resurgence of nostalgic pastoralism in a largely escapist gesture under the guise of renewed respect for, and understanding of, nature. While the pastoral genre has an ancient legacy of transgression, as a space 'with new kinds of borders, demanding new kinds of behaviours, new codes, new relationships with both our potentialities, and our pollution', more recently it has served as a space of nostalgic comfort.[63] Writing of its functioning after the Industrial Revolution, Carolyn Merchant frames it as 'a model created as an antidote to the pressures of urbanization and mechanization'. She writes: 'it represented a fulfilment of human needs for nurture, but by conceiving of nature as passive, it nevertheless allowed for the possibility of its use and manipulation'.[64] The New Nature Writing, a phrase coined in 2008, incorporates both of these tendencies, engaging more and less critically with its own complex lineage as well as that of the pastoral. The most challenging and creative texts observe Richard Kerridge's demand that they be 'clearly differentiated from the conservative tradition and aware of its appeal and dangers', and combine an attentive ecological consciousness with aesthetic experimentation.[65] Other texts are largely unreflexive and unashamedly nostalgic – 'we did things differently then', laments Peter Marren – retracing and mourning elements of the conservative tradition.[66] Referring to post-apocalyptic fiction in particular, Claire Colebrook notes that it is easier to imagine apocalypse than to think outside 'the structuring fantasies of gender', and this is clear too in contemporary entomological writings, the threat of environmental destruction accompanied by social conservatism.[67]

Like Victorian entomologists, these authors prize insects for their proximity to nature, with butterflies serving either as 'a conduit into natural beauty' or a metonym for the natural world as a whole.[68] As ecofeminist Val Plumwood observes, within patriarchy nature implies passivity, 'the "environment" or invisible background conditions against which the "foreground" achievements of reason or culture (provided typically by the white, western male expert or entrepreneur) take place'.[69] This perspective strips nature of agency and sentience, placing it outside the empathetic realm. For writers such as Marren, writing in *Rainbow Dust: Three Centuries of Delight in British Butterflies* (2015), butterflies either signify a space unpoliced by the demands of masculinity or one in which an Oedipal battle is staged. Their stories open at the cusp of adolescence, at 'the frankly sensual moment in a child's life when the full force of nature is felt for the first time'.[70] While this intimate note and the trope of childhood discovery are characteristic of contemporary nature writing more broadly, they also situate these texts within a longer entomological history; 'the majority of entomologists over the last century', Charlotte Sleigh records, 'have made a point of tracing their interest in insects to an incident during their early youth'.[71] In the case of Michael McCarthy, writing in *The Moth Snowstorm: Nature and Joy* (2015), butterflies serve as a distraction from a deficient childhood, 'filling the space where my feelings should have been', and enabling him to acknowledge his anger towards his mother.[72] Dismayed by the current perception of the emasculated collector, these texts glorify their authors' entomological quests, extending what Annete Kolodny calls 'our continuing fascination with the lone male in the wilderness'.[73] With actual collecting outlawed, these writers must collect in other ways, with Barkham, for example, over whom butterflies had cast 'a mysterious curse', setting himself the task of spotting all of Great Britain's 59 native butterfly species in the course of a summer.[74] 'Wondrous in themselves, for their own will to survive', he writes, 'butterflies are also colourful canvasses for all our projections. A journey in search of every species of butterfly is about our need to celebrate and capture fleeting moments of wonder as we fly through our lives.'[75] McCarthy undertakes the same project, perceiving the butterflies as tools through which to resolve his troubled feelings towards his mother; on completing his task, he records: 'It was my gift to her [. . .] I gave her all the butterflies of my country. I gave her every one.'[76] Affective triggers, for these writers butterflies are tools or tropes rather than agents themselves.

That the human male is disarmed by insect (usually butterfly) beauty is a familiar figure in these texts, captured most provocatively by Sjöberg's depiction of 'the siren song of entomology'.[77] A similar disavowal of male power and responsibility is evident in Matthew Oates's mournful disclosure in *In Pursuit of Butterflies: A Fifty-Year Affair* (2015) that he relinquished collecting butterflies when he became 'too fond' of them. 'In effect', he claims, 'the butterflies had collected me, having infiltrated my soul.'[78] He adopts a nostalgic pastoralism, reading the butterflies as 'symbols of something precious that has been lost, some much-missed part of ourselves, of yesterdays gone by'.[79] This nostalgia is both for a bucolic idyll and, in the case of Marren, for the belief in nature as an inexhaustible resource. In an impassioned defence of 'the bogeyman collector' in the face of moral disapproval regarding collecting, Marren attests:

> There seems to be a moral imperative to it, beyond any ecological rationale. Could it be something to do with the birthday-card image of butterflies as icons of beauty and freedom; as if catching them is morally on the same level as taking a potshot at an angel? Or might it just be just another part of the over-protective nanny culture that tells us that nature must not be touched – which more or less guarantees that children grow up not knowing the names of flowers or trees or butterflies?[80]

Marren's outrage at being denied unlimited tactile access to nature, an access that he frames as a mode of loving and valuing nature, echoes the kind of Romantic language that facilitates the violation of 'Mother Nature' by means of her idealisation. As Chaia Heller explains in a passage which speaks both to Marren and to Fowles's character Clegg, 'romantic love naturalizes and glorifies social domination, making the relationships between oppressor and oppressed appear inevitable, desirable, and even "complementary"'.[81] Marren concedes that his love of butterflies takes the form of a 'wanting to possess them', and yet justifies entomological collecting by denying butterflies agency; without any supporting evidence, he makes a Kantian appeal that 'real butterflies are not "free" in any meaningful sense'.[82]

Like Marren an apologist for collecting, Fredrik Sjöberg is a competitive entomologist. He is a proud member of the *Callicera* Club – whose elite have the *Callicera* 'impaled on a pin'[83] – boasting of his tally of '202 species. Two hundred and two',[84] thinking in 'score-sheets',[85] and employing a collecting discourse which mixes the poetic and the predatory. 'We're talking about hunting for pleasure', he observes, 'nothing more', and jokes that flies are 'very compliant collectibles'.[86] Aware and unashamed that collecting is a pleasure of mastery, he observes: 'In exercising control over something, however insignificant and apparently meaningless, there is a peaceful euphoria, however ephemeral and fleeting.'[87] He concedes that it is a kind of 'fetishism' which eases anxiety.[88] His desire for poetry, escape and euphoria is, however, juxtaposed with a clinical violence, expressed in accounts of wing trimming and of aggressively wielding 'the poison bottle' to scare off mocking critics.[89] Illustrating his perception that insects are facets of nature rather than autonomous agents, he describes the insect-inhabited landscape as a kind of language, with entomology a mode of 'landscape literacy'.[90] But while he concedes that the flies are participants, 'telling stories of every kind within the framework of the grammatical laws set down by evolution and ecology', ultimately these tales are appropriated so that 'the entomologist becomes a story-teller'.[91]

These entomological texts look to defy the vilification of collectors as 'stigmatised outcasts'[92] in search of 'trophies of the field', reframing entomology as a celebration of natural beauty.[93] Sjöberg, for example, envisions his fly collection as 'a distillation of unthinking happiness':

> If it tells us anything at all, it is perhaps that freedom starts when we take a step to one side and, if only for a moment, do something that has no purpose beyond itself, something that is not done in vain pursuit of respect, appreciation, power, money, love, fame or honour.[94]

It is telling, however, that this freedom comes at the expense of the insects, which are subjected to the male gaze either as they are unnaturally pinned and displayed, or simply in the writers' sexualised, feminised and sometimes explicitly misogynistic descriptions. Oates abandons technical language when discussing the butterflies' sexual habits, noting that they are not 'artisans of the gentle art of courtship – smash and grab is more their style. There is no way that that clip could have been broadcast before the 9 pm watershed.'[95] In a moment of primness, he observes that 'it cannot have been the lady's first mating, for she was clearly worn', and elsewhere is amused that 'three of our butterflies are named after young ladies who were ravished by Zeus'.[96] More striking still is Michael McCarthy's total relinquishment of his earlier 'lepi-empathy' in this extraordinary description of a particularly attractive butterfly as:

> *glamorous* ... By glamour I suppose I mean something like beauty with built-in excitement. Clichés beckon. Movie stars. But there was undoubtedly something in this insect's appearance, in its banana-yellow slingback wings

slickly transected by bold jet-black stripes, which set it apart. Its was not a
calming colour scheme. It was flashy, it carried a hint of risk, even of danger,
and today, with innocence long gone, I might say there is even something
almost tarty about it, as if the pair of black needletails to the hindwings were
stiletto heels.[97]

McCarthy suggests that, divested of innocence, he can see the butterfly
more clearly; however, the passage reads as an absurd, even comic,
act of projection in which McCarthy externalises his own desire on to
the feminised animal, attributing to it a kind of 'built-in excitement'.
This recalls Mulvey's demonstration that woman is conceived as '*to-
be-looked-at-ness*', and her reminder that the visual 'object' is not an
agent, but a constructed fantasy. In these texts, objectification and identification are often unexpectedly allied. While Sjöberg is clearly seduced
by his collection, it also acts as his representative, and he experiences
vicarious arousal on realising that 'there won't be any flies in the whole
wide world that have been so close to so many beautiful women'.[98]

The eroticised voyeurism evident in these texts occasionally breaches
the monstrous, exemplified by Tim Dee's observation, in his account
of bird-watching, *The Running Sky*, of 'a carrion crow, like its raven
brother in Somerset' which 'was going in at the ripped arse-end of a
rabbit, the intact fluffy scut softly stroking the bird's black head, as it
dipped at the riches it found there'.[99] The desire to dissect and expose
the mysteries of the 'animal', ostensibly in service of a science ordained
by God or, at least, humanism, is further sharpened in the face of
insects, those 'utterly alien'[100] creatures, which are rather like 'these
pools of darkness in our own selves' which can never either be fully
eliminated or decoded.[101] In *The Cockroach Papers*, Richard Schweid
critiques the clinical discourse that licenses insect dissection as 'chilling', while relishing his own voyeuristic narrative which exposes, and
manipulates, insect bodies.[102] Recording an entomologist's observation
'that each cockroach has its own individual face', Schweid nonetheless
provides a graphic description of its dissection, using 'a single-edge
razor blade and tweezers to make a slice down the middle of the roach's
forehead and peel the flaps of skin back from it', exposing a 'pearl-gray
glob of brain'.[103] Much of Schweid's description is strangely sexualised and decidedly misogynistic; the layer of fat under a cockroach's
carapace 'may look like nothing more than creamy thick jism', he comments, and he retells an off-colour joke that 'the only thing uglier than
a German cockroach is a pregnant German cockroach'.[104] In Schweid's
accounts, both women and insects are reduced to their constituent
physical parts, which are rendered visible for inspection and assessment. The combination of the two is, for Schweid, explicitly erotic;

the reader is uncomfortably implicated, observing, through Schweid, dissector Missy Williams, 'lovely, tall, with short blonde hair, long legs, and flawless skin, wearing the tiniest of turquoise minidresses and with much more of her exposed than covered', as 'she pinned a roach on its back in a petri dish' and cut 'its abdomen with a tiny pair of scissors'.[105] By paralleling the lascivious gaze with the ostensibly scientific perspective, Schweid both disingenuously legitimises the former and nullifies any call for empathetic engagement with women or insects.

LITERARY LEPIDOPTERY III: NABOKOV AND INSECT AESTHETICS

'Natural history', Foucault writes, 'is nothing more than the nomination of the visible.' It presupposes an affinity between words and things, 'but it exists as a task only in so far as things and language happen to be separate. It must therefore reduce this distance between them so as to bring language as close as possible to the observing gaze, and the things observed as close as possible to words.'[106] In *Nabokov's Blues*, their 1999 account of Vladimir Nabokov's contribution to lepidoptery, Kurt Johnson and Steve Coates return to the trope of the natural historian as illuminating an obscure text through careful study:

> For taxonomists the dissection of a specimen is the equivalent of opening one of the books and reading it. Butterfly morphology, the study of the internal structures of Lepidoptera, specifically the genitalia, is tedious and exacting labor. It is also exhausting; willingness to tolerate the drudgery is a requisite for most laboratory taxonomists, for Nabokov no less than others. But the search for hidden information is the kind of detective work that brings rich rewards and reveals an unorthodox beauty. It is also the key to the third item on Nabokov's list of the joys of lepidoptery – the possibility of exploding an old taxonomic classification, upsetting the old scheme, and, as Nabokov put it, confounding its obtuse champions.[107]

That classification is a capricious fiction is clear to Foucault and to Charles Darwin too, who notes in *The Origin of Species* that species itself is a term 'arbitrarily given for the sake of convenience to a set of individuals closely resembling each other'.[108] Johnson and Coates, however, are credulous, framing taxonomy as advancement, by attentive reading, towards the expression of a pre-existing truth. Their account is a reminder of the proximity between physical mastery – the capture, killing and dissection of a 'specimen' – and conceptual mastery, the installation of one's own taxonomic schema. They are startlingly inattentive to the physical violence of dissection; describing a row of butterfly genitalia, they tastelessly joke: 'There was no structural coherence to the sample, even though all were supposedly in the same genus. It was like looking at a parking lot full of Cadillacs, Volkswagens, and dune buggies that a car dealer had assured you were all alike.'[109]

Nabokov's poem 'On Discovering a Butterfly' is a paean to the longevity of taxonomical achievement, combining the clinical language of the scientist with the luxuriant description of the aesthete. It typifies the kind of invasive, voyeuristic perspective that has characterised our entomological readings so far; here, the butterfly 'text' can only be deciphered after its dismemberment. 'My needles have teased out its sculptured sex', Nabokov puns, and then later, 'Smoothly a screw is turned; out of the mist/ two ambered hooks symmetrically slope,/ or scales like battledores of amethyst/ cross the charmed circle of the microscope'.[110] In Marie Bouchet's account of Nabokov's lepidoptery, she notes that 'naming a new species, and more specifically putting the butterfly into words via description, was more precious to Nabokov than literary fame', the equivalent of 'having the insect born to the world of science'.[111] This is reiterated in Nabokov's poem; 'I found it and I named it', he boasts of his conquest; seduced by the notion of collection as preservation, the butterfly, 'safe from creeping relatives and rust', will 'transcend its dust'.[112] He is not referring to the physical specimen – 'wide open on its pin (though fast asleep)'[113] in Carol Adams's phrase, the 'absent referent' of this poem, but to the longevity of the taxonomical discovery that it represents. The posterity that will outlive poetry is not the butterfly but the 'red label' it sports, a marker of Nabokov's achievement.

Nabokov's texts are littered with lepidopterological references and jokes; however, given Nabokov's infamous prickliness, 'the relationship between Nabokov's two lifelong passions – literature and lepidoptery – should', Ellen Pifer urges, 'be approached cautiously'.[114] Johnson and Coates are deferential to the point of obsequiousness, their book an elaborate piece of gatekeeping written to secure Nabokov's moral legacy as a family man and 'picture of steadfast faith', alongside his literary and taxonomical legacies.[115] Their anxiety surrounding Nabokov's morality extends to policing the readings of his literary texts. Following his lead, they rail against 'superficial readers' banal, symbol-obsessed considerations of butterflies in his writing – the presumption, together with the inevitable Freudian smirk, of having found psychological "insight," usually pruriently discreditable, into the author's fascination with Lepidoptera'.[116] Not only does Johnson and Coates's defence belie the subtlety and dynamism of Nabokov's work – sufficiently agile to rebut poor textual readings unaided – it reinforces the problematic rhetoric of the mastery of nature which we have already seen in Marren and others. Against this charge, Johnson and Coates's defence, that Nabokov's lepidopterological imagery is 'a minor motif to reinforce themes', does not hold.[117]

In Chapter 1, I criticised Spiegelman's use of animal tropes in *Maus*, arguing that the employment of nonhuman animals as 'an alibi for other themes' discounts nonhuman experience and suffering and mobilises the 'anthropological machine', which ultimately licenses human oppression.[118] I concluded that different types of suffering might be effectively and profitably compared as long as neither is elided or demoted in the process.[119] The same principle applies here: tropes, metaphors and allegories are necessarily comparative, but comparison should not entail instrumentalisation. While aspiring to an account of the aesthetic that is connected to ethics, ultimately Nabokov's fiction, most notably *Lolita*, is complicit with the aesthetic instrumentalisation of both human and nonhuman life. This, as Mario Ortiz Robles recognises, 'is not only a means to denigrate animals and humans alike; it is also to understate the power of tropes themselves. Tropes are the cognitive referents on the basis of which we make sense of the world.'[120]

For Nabokov's critics, the allegorical functioning of his fiction is a boon which facilitates an aesthetic defence against charges of immorality or obscenity. *Lolita*'s Dolores and her abuse should not be read literally, Gabriel Josipovici contends, but as 'a model of the relationship between the writer and his book and the reader and the writer'.[121] David Packman, too, encourages the dematerialisation of the abused female body in service of the aesthetic. 'One may speculate', he writes, 'that the nymphet's body is less important than the particular narrative end to which it is put. That is, her body is functional; it provides a springboard for the action of the narrative.'[122] Likewise, Johnson and Coates defend Nabokov's depiction of Van's voyeurism of Ada in *Ada, or Ardor* as 'wonderful fun', and explain that in *Lolita*, incest is 'a metaphor for narcissistic self-absorption'.[123] In a project that looked to recognise Nabokov's achievements as a lepidopterist by naming butterflies after his literary characters, Nabokov's followers continued his casting of both fiction and lepidoptery as mere games, making 'certain to place *humbert* in a separate genus and assigned to that name a species with a limited range living some fifteen hundred miles from where *lolita* might ever be found roaming'.[124] The presupposition shared by these critics, all of whom defend the fictional instrumentalisation of the abuse of women, is that the aesthetic is distinct from, and immune to, ethics. Yet the novel itself challenges this pitching of aesthetics against ethics, by sandwiching Humbert Humbert's account between hyperbolically polarised terms, in the form of ethics – John Ray Jr's moralising foreword (which the critics wisely discredit) – and aesthetics: Nabokov's disingenuous concluding note in which he casually announces that the novel 'has no moral in tow'.[125] In their attribution of full licence to the novel on aesthetic grounds, Rampton and Josipovici naively reproduce the latter, which Linda Kaufman astutely identifies as 'a sham' which 'simply extends the Humbertian aesthetic manifesto'.[126] Reinforcement of Humbertian aesthetic solipsism overlooks the text's attempts to actively distance itself from Humbert; it is no accident, for example, that Humbert 'is notoriously ignorant and dismissive of nature. He can't distinguish a butterfly from a moth, or a hawkmoth from a hummingbird.'[127]

Rampton contends that *Lolita* resists the polarisation of ethics and aesthetics by highlighting the dangers of fetishising the aesthetic and noting Nabokov's appeal to an aesthetics which responds to embodied experience with tenderness. He writes:

> *Lolita* is more than an impersonal artefact which gave its creator a certain amount of pleasure in the making, because it dramatizes the potential inhumanity of the kind of aesthetic attitude to experience that fails to make this kind of [ethical] commitment. But it doesn't simply express a preference for warm and vital human beings as opposed to cold and impersonal works of art. Humbert's description of Lolita at tennis is an exercise in the special art of seeing her as an object, an art that only aesthetic detachment makes possible. And his 'Confession,' the product of that detachment, is at the same time a study of its limitations. As Michael Bell points out in '*Lolita* and Pure Art', it is not 'that the awareness of others as "objects" is in itself wrong but that it has to find its proper place in our general sense of them.'[128]

Rampton's suggestion that we might separate Humbert the aesthete from Humbert the paedophile is tendentious, predicated both on the assumption that Humbert's crime derives from a category error (that corporeal possession is synonymous with aesthetic appreciation), and on the acceptance of a notion of aesthetic disinterestedness which has effectively been debunked by feminist criticism. Peggy Zeglin Brand, for example, claims that the affected neutrality of disinterestedness is neither possible nor desirable, and that 'denying one's identification and involvement with the work on a personal level' problematically 'seeks mastery even over one's own bodily responses'.[129] The historical use of aesthetic disinterestedness to corroborate and universalise the male gaze, and to vindicate the dehumanisation of women, is continued by Rampton's endorsement of Humbert who, in his inability to distinguish between fantasy and art, is incapable of aesthetic detachment. Even at the moment Rampton cites, when Humbert is watching Dolores play tennis, his detachment is replaced by cruelty and jealousy; describing

Dolores and her doubles partners, Humbert sees 'a fair angel among three horrible Boschian cripples'.[130] Rampton's call, via Bell, for a repositioning of objectification is dangerously de-historicised; objectification always takes place within a network of power relations where only certain bodies are perceived as objects. The appeal to disinterestedness underscores an empathetic detachment which diminishes the possibility of re-subjectification of the object. As Leland de la Durantaye writes: 'We are led astray because we are offered the wrong optic through which to see Lolita – *the optic of art*.'[131]

In appealing to 'aesthetic detachment', Rampton approvingly invokes a history of art in which women are marginalised or objectified. This is the same history from which Humbert draws to authorise and mythologise his abuse of Dolores; 'O Lolita', he declares, 'you are my girl, as Vee was Poe's and Bea Dante's.'[132] In reference to Poe, Humbert's first lost love, Dolores's 'prototype', is named Annabel Lee; the apparent substitutability between the two girls further inscribes Humbert's passion within the canon of 'the writer's ancient lust'.[133] Indeed, Humbert's empathetic disengagement from the living Dolores is underpinned by the strength of his attachment to the figurative 'eternal Lolita' and his attempts to recreate her, 'another, fanciful Lolita – perhaps, more real than Lolita [. . .] having no will, no consciousness – indeed no life of her own'.[134] It is no accident that both Annabel Lee and Dolores Haze are condemned to early deaths. As Elisabeth Bronfen observes, Dolores embodies 'the composite image of a lost beloved' and is inscribed into a citational history rich with 'the conjunction of femininity and death', where the beloved is '"killed" into the trope of muse'.[135] Indeed, it is not only Dolores's literal death that should concern feminist readers, but also the implications of the novel's alignment of Humbert's repentance with his literary inscription of Dolores. For Josipovici, for example, the conferring upon Dolores of 'the immortality of art' serves as a 'partial redemption' for her, which is facilitated by Humbert's progression from the desire to possess and consume to the wish merely 'to articulate'.[136] However, Humbert has simply exchanged one kind of possession for another; his unchanged aim, 'to fix once for all the perilous magic of nymphets', requires the effacement of Dolores's individuality.[137]

Lolita participates not only in a literary history which permits, even naturalises, the objectification of women and girls, but also in a similarly restrictive visual history. As Jenefer Shute observes:

> Description – especially of the female body – can never be neutral, never innocent. It partakes always, with varying degrees of self-consciousness, of prior codes: the nude, the portrait, the inventory, the striptease, and so on. Not only is the woman's body made into an object – as Nabokov's syntax

makes perfectly clear here – but it is an object defined by certain codes, an object of art.[138]

The text, as participant in these aesthetic histories, accedes to a disingenuous model of aesthetic distance, which in reproducing familiar modes of framing the female, fails to interrogate them. The issue here is not lack of reflexivity; as Kaufman notes, Nabokov knows that *Lolita* 'elides the female by framing the narrative through Humbert's angle of vision', because he directly comments upon it in its intertextual references.[139] The problem is that these references do not provide a critical perspective on this framing but reinforce and legitimise it; as such, *Lolita* actively participates in 'a canonical body of literature in which women's stories are taken away from them, in which all we get are men's stories'.[140] Given that the 'implied reader here – like the implied viewer in the Western tradition of the nude – is obviously male', the female reader is both alienated and interpellated into a 'projected community of voyeurs' where 'description becomes a kind of undressing'.[141] Judith Fetterley coins the term 'immas-culation' to describe this process, where the reader is invited to participate in an experience from which she is, by her nature, excluded, and which hampers the very construction of her subjectivity.[142] The novel's coding of the juvenile female body as an object for consumption is juxtaposed with Humbert's revulsion towards the adult females with their 'stale flesh' and 'dark, decaying forests'.[143] For Humbert, the mature female body is a 'coffin of coarse female flesh within which my [his] nymphets are buried alive'.[144]

Without a counter to the misogyny inculcated so deeply in the novel, it is hard for readers to empathise with the female characters. On the contrary, as Eileen John writes with reference to a moment when Humbert fears that Dolores has left him:

> I [. . .] expect that readers have many empathetic experiences aligned with Humbert. A reader, not in any sense 'on board' with his project of control and sexual exploitation of Dolores, still seems likely to register the deserted tennis court with a hint of Humbert's alarm and sense of emptiness. *Lolita* sets up a kind of worst-case scenario for achieving this kind of alignment – with a linguistically over-the-top paedophile as its first-person narrator – and still does it.[145]

John highlights Nabokov's manipulation of empathy, which depends upon unmediated access to Humbert's thoughts and feelings, and on the reader's susceptibility to Humbert's self-framed vulnerability. For the 'terrestrial women' with whom Humbert interacts, and who we perceive only through his misogynistic perspective, it is virtually impossible for the reader to cultivate empathy.[146] Rather, our affective responses are coloured by Nabokov's framing of them, without exception, as physically repulsive and intellectually vapid. Nabokov offers us no alternative to this view; accordingly we are more likely to feel revulsion than pity when, with Humbert, we encounter 'the mangled remains' of his wife, Charlotte Humbert.[147] While the reader is given a little more access to Dolores than to her mother, this amounts to 'scarcely a glimpse' of her thoughts and feelings.[148] As such, the lack of empathy exhibited by male critics towards Dolores is shocking but unsurprising; for Page Stegner, she is 'a rather common, unwashed little girl', and Josipovici judges her 'lack of imagination [. . .] horrifying'.[149] These perspectives reproduce, unchallenged, Humbert's reading of Dolores as 'a disgustingly conventional girl'.[150] Although Humbert is a master of self-pity, his self-deprecating descriptions of himself as 'abject' and a 'monster' imply a degree of self-awareness which, for the most part, he does not possess.[151] Rather, the moments when the narrative most effectively distances itself from Humbert's viewpoint are those of disjunction between his flippant tone and serious subject matter, when his empathetic deficiencies are genuinely shocking. These include his realisation that he is unable to kill Charlotte, not for her sake, but because, 'her ghost would haunt me all my life', and his planning for a future in which Dolores might give birth to a child for him to abuse.[152]

Linda Kaufman asks whether it is 'possible in a double movement to analyse the horror of incest by reinscribing the material body of the child Lolita in the text, and simultaneously to undermine the representational fallacy by situating the text dialogically in relation to other texts?'[153] While there are moments when the text achieves this 'double movement', they are seldom. More often, it is seduced by textual play, encoding the embodied Dolores as ill-fated beloved, alluring nude or immaterial 'nymph'. The latter, a term for the young of non-lepidoptera orders (such as damselflies and dragonflies), which, unlike lepidoptera, already resemble the adult, is a reference to Lolita's premature sexualisation. This, one of the 'delightfully amusing covert references to taxonomy and lepidoptery in the text', offers neither pedagogical value nor insight into insect existence.[154] Rather, as one of the relatively few instances where entomological vocabulary is applied to human females, it downplays the significance of Dolores's repeated rape, betraying 'the material body of the child Lolita'. Indeed the 'nymphing' of Dolores is an act of dematerialisation which is not adequately countered. In stressing the inhumanity of the 'nymph', who is either immaterial, 'not human, but nymphic', or animalised, displaying 'monkeyish nimbleness', Humbert hampers the reader's perception of her as an embodied female.[155] For Kaufman, Lolita requires the supplement of feminist criticism to expose how the 'textual body is *fabricated* – in both senses of the word – as a fiction and as a construct' and to liberate her from her relentless reduction to the role determined for her by Humbert: 'to reflect and satisfy the body of the father'.[156] However, while feminist criticism can reveal the construction of the text, it cannot replace Dolores's elided materiality.

Derek Matravers claims that 'empathy does not seem central to our appreciation of art or literature. This is because art and literature are more in the business of presenting us with a world to contemplate, rather than inviting us to construct a world for ourselves.'[157] In general, I disagree with Matravers's contention; the novels of Martel and Fowler, for example, offer clear invitations, via empathy and other tools, for the collaborative construction of alternative worlds. *Lolita*, however, represents the former tradition, reasserting the mastery of the author, rejecting the possibility of a democratic or discursive storytelling and, accordingly, snubbing 'folkloric or "Freudian" symbols that [take] off on their own wings and [fly] out of the control of the all-powerful author'.[158] Rather, Nabokov wields the utmost control over the text, exercising, Peter Marren writes, a 'mastery of language [which] seems at times to be deployed with the crisp decision of a pin through a thorax'.[159] Readers, characters and symbols are ordered like entomological specimens. Despite Nabokov's attempt to distance *Lolita* from Humbertian solipsism, playful yet calculating aestheticism overrides tenderness. Accordingly, for Nabokov, Dolores is 'like the composition of a beautiful puzzle – its composition and its solution at the same time, since one is a mirror view of the other, depending on which way you look'.[160] Nabokov's unsentimentalism towards lepidoptera – 'I let it go if it is old and frayed or if I don't need it for my collection'[161] – parallels Humbert's plan to 'get rid somehow of a difficult adolescent whose magic nymphage had evaporated'.[162] While this is precisely the kind of comparison against which Johnson and Coates caution, both examples reflect a striking empathetic deficiency. 'Throughout a narrative', Amy Coplan writes, 'it is possible for a reader to move in and out of different perspectives, those of different characters or different perspectives on the overall narrative.'[163] As we have seen, *Lolita* hinders this kind of empathetic mobility, identifying too strongly with Humbert to permit the other characters active subjectivities.

'On Discovering a Butterfly' follows 'the tradition of lifting nature's veil', presupposing that the 'specimen' must be examined, via expert dismemberment, in order to yield its truth.[164] Natural history and storytelling are allied in their extreme impulses to mastery; 'to order (in the sense of ordering the world)', Bruno Latour notes, 'is to order (in the sense of giving orders)'.[165] Dolores, for Kaufman the '*femme morcelée par excellence*', is visually dismembered by Nabokov's narrative,[166] yet even this is not sufficient exposure for Humbert, who desires further access, to 'her unknown heart, her nacreous liver, the sea-grapes of her lungs, her comely twin kidneys'.[167] Aesthetically framed, Humbert's engulfing desire for total possession of Dolores should teach us to distrust the desire for unlimited access to bodies of any sort, especially when this desire is articulated in aesthetic or scientific terms. His provocative description of the 'raped little table' when Charlotte takes his diary demonstrates how little he understands the violation precipitated by this desire for access.[168]

Much is made of Humbert's purported repentance in the final pages of the novel, notably his realisation 'that the hopelessly poignant thing was not Lolita's absence from my side, but the absence of her voice from that concord' of children playing.[169] Read generously, this sentimental display of affective empathy is a reminder of its potential for moral encouragement; as Elisa Aaltola observes: 'From the outlook of morality, affective empathy is the most vital ingredient due to the way in which it enables the immediate, experiential other-directedness necessary for noting the other's individuality and well-being as significant in their own right.'[170] Irrespective, however, of whether we find this performance convincing, Humbert's repentance remains too internalised, too literally hand-wringing, to perform the attentive work of empathising; it is a mere gesture beyond narcissism. Indeed, as we have seen with Anthropocene discourse, ostentatious repentance is a sure guarantor of deficient understanding and the replication of regressive logics. The texts in this chapter retell old stories of female and nonhuman animal domination as if they were the only stories; *Lolita* is in thrall to an aesthetic past which lionises these very stories. It tames the potentially disruptive reader who might challenge this narrative by exposing his complicity and lack of erudition; he is 'a sort of Humbert, frothing and panting, desiring only pleasure and beauty, overlooking the true complexity of the thing'.[171] We should not be bowed by this exposure of our complicity, but rather reassured by our knowledge that the recognition of complicity is the only grounds for the production of an aesthetic future in which the 'winged fugitive', in all its forms, will be permitted to speak and be heard.[172]

NOTES

1. Hugo Raffles, *Insectopedia* (New York: Pantheon Books, 2010), pp. 43–4.

2. Benjamin, *Illuminations*, p. 60.
3. Benjamin, *Illuminations*, p. 59.
4. Benjamin, *Illuminations*, p. 61.
5. Michel Foucault, *The Order of Things: An Archaeology of the Human Sciences* (London: Routledge, 2002 [1966]), p. 161.
6. That Linnaeus perceived himself as such was the accusation of his contemporary Albrecht von Haller. See Peter Harrison, 'Linnaeus as a Second Adam? Taxonomy as a Religious Vocation', *Zygon*, 44 (2009), 879–93.
7. Marina Benjamin, 'To Have and to Hold', in *Collectors' Items*, ed. Kate Salway (London: Pale Green Press, 1996), pp. 10–31 (p. 16).
8. J. F. M. Clark, *Bugs and the Victorians* (New Haven, CT: Yale University Press, 2009), p. 7.
9. Clark, *Bugs and the Victorians*, p. 79.
10. Richard Schweid, *The Cockroach Papers: A Compendium of History and Lore* (Chicago: University of Chicago Press, 1999), p. xiii.
11. Benjamin, 'To Have and to Hold', p. 16.
12. There are still numerous defenders of the notion (theological or secular) of stewardship. See, for example, Bryan L. Moore's invocation of humans' 'sacred responsibility to take care of and preserve our still-beautiful and only habitable planet, along with the million other species that share it with us'. Bryan L. Moore, *Ecology and Literature: Ecocentric Personification from Antiquity to the Twenty-First Century* (New York: Palgrave Macmillan, 2008), p. ix.
13. Benjamin, 'To Have and to Hold', p. 16.
14. Benjamin, 'To Have and to Hold', p. 16.
15. Benjamin, *Illuminations*, p. 67.
16. Foucault, *Order of Things*, p. 39.
17. Nabokov, cited in Laurence Talairach-Vielmas and Marie Bouchet, 'Introduction', in *Insects in Literature and the Arts*, ed. Laurence Talairach-Vielmas and Marie Bouchet (Brussels: P.I.E. Peter Lang, 2014), pp. 13–20 (p. 16).
18. Fredrik Sjöberg, *The Art of Flight*, trans. Peter Graves (London: Penguin, 2006), p. 538.
19. Fredrik Sjöberg, *The Fly Trap*, trans. Thomas Teal (London: Penguin, 2015), p. 11.
20. Sjöberg, *The Art of Flight*, p. 461.
21. Sjöberg, *The Art of Flight*, p. 461.
22. Patrick Barkham, *The Butterfly Isles: A Summer in Search of Our Emperors and Admirals* (London: Granta, 2010), p. 296.
23. Barkham, *Butterfly Isles*, p. 158.
24. Barkham, *Butterfly Isles*, p. 124.
25. Barkham, *Butterfly Isles*, p. 125.
26. John Fowles, 'Introduction', in *Collectors' Items*, ed. Kate Salway (London: Pale Green Press, 1996), pp. 8–9 (p. 8).

27. John Fowles, cited in Bruce Woodcock, *Male Mythologies: John Fowles and Masculinity* (Brighton: Harvester Press, 1984), p. 29.
28. Francis Bacon, cited in Benjamin, 'To Have and to Hold', p. 14.
29. John Fowles, *The Collector* (London: Vintage, 2004 [1963]), p. 55.
30. Woodcock, *Male Mythologies*, p. 29.
31. David Punter, 'Gothic and Neo-Gothic in Fowles's *The Collector*', in *John Fowles*, ed. James Acheson (Basingstoke: Palgrave Macmillan, 2013), p. 63.
32. Keen, *Empathy and the Novel*, p. 9.
33. Coplan, 'Understanding Empathy', p. 17.
34. Agosta, *Empathy in the Context of Philosophy*, p. xiv.
35. Fowles, *The Collector*, pp. 40–1.
36. Fowles, *The Collector*, pp. 44, 203.
37. John Berger, *Ways of Seeing* (London: Penguin, 2008 [1972]), p. 47.
38. Robert Huffaker, *John Fowles* (Boston: G. K. Hall, 1980), p. 81.
39. Fowles, *The Collector*, p. 203.
40. On Fowles and the Gothic, see Punter, 'Gothic and Neo-Gothic'.
41. Fowles, *The Collector*, p. 244.
42. Fowles, cited in Peter Conradi, *John Fowles* (London: Methuen, 1982), p. 38.
43. Conradi, *John Fowles*, p. 37.
44. Laura Mulvey, 'Visual Pleasure and Narrative Cinema', in *Issues in Feminist Film Criticism*, ed. Patricia Erens (Bloomington: Indiana University Press, 1990), pp. 28–40 (p. 33).
45. Fowles, *The Collector*, p. 110.
46. Fowles, *The Collector*, p. 274.
47. Fowles, *The Collector*, p. 14.
48. Punter, 'Gothic and Neo-Gothic', p. 65.
49. Woodcock, *Male Mythologies*, p. 40.
50. Lori Gruen, 'Dismantling Oppression: An Analysis of the Connection Between Women and Animals', in *Ecofeminism: Women, Animals, Nature*, ed. Greta Gaard (Philadelphia: Temple University Press, 1993), pp. 60–90 (p. 66).
51. Woodcock, *Male Mythologies*, p. 38.
52. Weik von Mossner, *Affective Ecologies*, p. 83.
53. Greta Gaard, 'Living Interconnections with Animals and Nature', in *Ecofeminism: Women, Animals, Nature*, ed. Greta Gaard (Philadelphia: Temple University Press, 1993), pp. 1–12 (p. 1).
54. Louise Westling, *The Green Breast of the New World: Landscape, Gender and American Fiction* (Athens: University of Georgia Press, 1996), p. 41.
55. See Marilyn French, *Beyond Power: Women, Men and Morals* (London: Abacus, 1985), p. 341: 'The reason for man's existence is to shed all animal residue and realize fully his "divine" nature, the part that *seems* unlike any part owned by animals – mind, spirit, or control.'

56. Carolyn Merchant, *The Death of Nature: Women, Ecology and the Scientific Revolution* (San Francisco: Harper, 1980), p. 127.

57. James Lovelock, *The Revenge of Gaia: Why the Earth is Fighting Back – And How We Can Still Save Humanity* (London: Allen Lane, 2006).

58. Douglas Coupland, *Generation A* (London: Windmill Books, 2009), p. 39.

59. Catherine Roach, 'Loving Your Mother: On the Woman–Nature Relation', *Hypatia*, 6.1 (1991), 46–59 (p. 51).

60. Janis Birkeland, 'Ecofeminism: Linking Theory and Practice', in *Ecofeminism: Women, Animals, Nature*, ed. Greta Gaard (Philadelphia: Temple University Press, 1993), pp. 13–59 (p. 19).

61. See Roach, 'Loving Your Mother'.

62. Merchant, *Death of Nature*, p. 2.

63. Terry Gifford, 'Afterword: New Senses of Environment', in *New Versions of Pastoral: Post-Romantic, Modern and Contemporary Responses to the Tradition*, ed. David James and Philip Tew (Madison, WI: Fairleigh Dickinson University Press, 2009), pp. 245–57 (p. 246).

64. Merchant, *Death of Nature*, p. 9.

65. Richard Kerridge, cited in Jos Smith, *The New Nature Writing: Rethinking the Literature of Place* (London: Bloomsbury, 2017), p. 11.

66. Peter Marren, *Rainbow Dust: Three Centuries of Delight in British Butterflies* (London: Vintage, 2015), p. 23.

67. Claire Colebrook, *Sex After Life: Essays on Extinction, Vol. 2* (London: Open Humanities Press, 2014), p. 150.

68. Barkham, *Butterfly Isles*, p. 89.

69. Plumwood, *Feminism and the Mastery of Nature*, p. 4.

70. Marren, *Rainbow Dust*, p. 3.

71. Charlotte Sleigh, 'Inside Out: The Unsettling Nature of Insects', in *Insect Poetics*, ed. Eric C. Brown (Minneapolis: University of Minnesota Press, 2006), pp. 281–97 (p. 287).

72. Michael McCarthy, *The Moth Snowstorm: Nature and Joy* (London: John Murray, 2015), p. 5.

73. Annete Kolodny, *The Lay of the Land: Metaphor as Experience and History in American Life and Letters* (Chapel Hill: University of North Carolina Press, 1975), p. 147.

74. Barkham, *Butterfly Isles*, p. 9.

75. Barkham, *Butterfly Isles*, p. 14.

76. McCarthy, *Moth Snowstorm*, p. 238.

77. Sjöberg, *The Fly Trap*, p. 72.

78. Matthew Oates, *In Pursuit of Butterflies: A Fifty Year Affair* (London: Bloomsbury, 2015), p. 41.

79. Oates, *In Pursuit of Butterflies*, p. 455.

80. Marren, *Rainbow Dust*, p. 74.

81. Chaia Heller, 'For the Love of Nature: Ecology and the Cult of the

Romantic', in *Ecofeminism: Women, Animals, Nature*, ed. Greta Gaard (Philadelphia: Temple University Press, 1993), p. 229.
82. Marren, *Rainbow Dust*, pp. 169, 173.
83. Sjöberg, *The Art of Flight*, pp. 340–1.
84. Sjöberg, *The Fly Trap*, p. 52.
85. Sjöberg, *The Art of Flight*, p. 316.
86. Sjöberg, *The Fly Trap*, pp. 53, 60.
87. Sjöberg, *The Fly Trap*, p. 49.
88. Sjöberg, *The Fly Trap*, p. 88.
89. Sjöberg, *The Fly Trap*, p. 19.
90. Sjöberg, *The Fly Trap*, p. 219.
91. Sjöberg, *The Fly Trap*, pp. 220, 118.
92. Oates, *In Pursuit of Butterflies*, p. 453.
93. Marren, *Rainbow Dust*, p. 35.
94. Sjöberg, *The Art of Flight*, p. 543.
95. Oates, *In Pursuit of Butterflies*, pp. 351–2.
96. Oates, *In Pursuit of Butterflies*, pp. 95, 61.
97. McCarthy, *Moth Snowstorm*, pp. 189, 191.
98. Sjöberg, *The Art of Flight*, p. 545.
99. Tim Dee, *The Running Sky* (London: Vintage, 2009), p. 200.
100. Clark, *Bugs and the Victorians*, p. 77.
101. Schweid, *Cockroach Papers*, p. xiv.
102. Schweid, *Cockroach Papers*, p. 166.
103. Schweid, *Cockroach Papers*, p. 94.
104. Schweid, *Cockroach Papers*, pp. 13, 64.
105. Schweid, *Cockroach Papers*, p. 41.
106. Foucault, *Order of Things*, p. 144.
107. Kurt Johnson and Steve Coates, *Nabokov's Blues: The Scientific Odyssey of a Literary Genius* (New York: McGraw-Hill, 1999), p. 83.
108. Charles Darwin, *On the Origin of Species*, ed. Gillian Beer (Oxford: Oxford University Press, 2008), p. 43.
109. Johnson and Coates, *Nabokov's Blues*, p. 96.
110. Vladimir Nabokov, 'On Discovering a Butterfly', *The New Yorker*, 15 May 1943, p. 26.
111. Marie Bouchet, 'Nabokov's Text Under the Microscope: Textual Practices of Detail in his Lepidopterological and Fictional Writings', in *Insects in Literature and the Arts*, ed. Laurence Talairach-Vielmas and Marie Bouchet (Brussels: P.I.E. Peter Lang, 2014), p. 94.
112. Nabokov, 'On Discovering a Butterfly', p. 26.
113. Nabokov, 'On Discovering a Butterfly', p. 26.
114. Ellen Pifer (ed.), *Vladimir Nabokov's Lolita: A Casebook* (Oxford: Oxford University Press, 2003), p. 5. Note, in particular, the treatment of Diana Butler in response to her article 'Lolita Lepidoptera'. Cited in Johnson and Coates, *Nabokov's Blues*, p. 298.
115. Johnson and Coates, *Nabokov's Blues*, p. 119.

116. Johnson and Coates, *Nabokov's Blues*, p. 302.

117. Johnson and Coates, *Nabokov's Blues*, p. 302.

118. Haraway, *The Companion Species Manifesto*, p. 5.

119. Davis, *The Holocaust and the Henmaid's Tale*, p. 4.

120. Ortiz Robles, *Literature and Animal Studies*, p. 19.

121. Gabriel Josipovici, *The World and the Book* (St Albans: Paladin, 1973), p. 211.

122. David Packman, *Vladimir Nabokov: The Structure of Literary Desire* (Columbia: University of Missouri Press, 1982), p. 52.

123. Johnson and Coates, *Nabokov's Blues*, pp. 302, 301.

124. Johnson and Coates, *Nabokov's Blues*, p. 261.

125. Vladimir Nabokov, *Lolita* (London: Penguin, 2000), p. 314.

126. Linda S. Kaufman, *Special Delivery: Epistolary Modes in Modern Fiction* (Chicago: University of Chicago Press, 1992), p. 58.

127. Johnson and Coates, *Nabokov's Blues*, p. 310.

128. David Rampton, *Vladimir Nabokov: A Critical Study of the Novels* (Cambridge: Cambridge University Press, 1984), p. 119.

129. Peggy Zeglin Brand, 'Disinterestedness and Political Art', in *Aesthetics: The Big Questions*, ed. Carolyn Korsmeyer (Oxford: Blackwell, 1998), pp. 155–71 (p. 159).

130. Nabokov, *Lolita*, p. 235.

131. Leland de la Durantaye, 'Eichmann, Empathy and Lolita', *Philosophy and Literature*, 30.2 (2006), 311–28 (p. 321).

132. Nabokov, *Lolita*, p. 107.

133. Nabokov, *Lolita*, pp. 40, 45.

134. Nabokov, *Lolita*, pp. 65, 62.

135. Elisabeth Bronfen, *Over Her Dead Body: Death, Femininity and the Aesthetic* (Manchester: Manchester University Press), pp. 374, 371.

136. Josipovici, *World and the Book*, pp. 215, 222.

137. Nabokov, *Lolita*, p. 134.

138. Jenefer Shute, '"So Nakedly Dressed": The Text of the Female Body in Nabokov's Novels', in *Vladimir Nabokov's Lolita: A Casebook*, ed. Elen Pifer (Oxford: Oxford University Press, 2003), pp. 111–20 (p. 114).

139. Kaufman, *Special Delivery*, p. 64.

140. Rebecca Solnit, 'Men Explain Lolita to Me', *Literary Hub*, 17 December 2015, https://lithub.com/men-explain-lolita-to-me/ (accessed 18 February 2019).

141. Shute, 'So Nakedly Dressed', p. 114.

142. Fetterley, cited in Kaufman, *Special Delivery*, pp. 61–2.

143. Nabokov, *Lolita*, pp. 26, 77.

144. Nabokov, *Lolita*, p. 175.

145. John, 'Empathy in Literature', para. 40.13

146. Nabokov, *Lolita*, p. 18.

147. Nabokov, *Lolita*, p. 98.

148. Durantaye, 'Eichmann, Empathy and Lolita', p. 323.

149. Page Stegner, *Escape into Aesthetics: The Art of Vladimir Nabokov* (London: Eyre and Spottiswoode, 1967), p. 114; Josipovici, *World and the Book*, p. 216.

150. Nabokov, *Lolita*, p. 148.

151. Nabokov, *Lolita*, pp. 5, 284.

152. Nabokov, *Lolita*, pp. 87, 174.

153. Kaufman, *Special Delivery*, p. 59.

154. Johnson and Coates, *Nabokov's Blues*, pp. 35-6, 305.

155. Nabokov, *Lolita*, pp. 16, 58.

156. Kaufman, *Special Delivery*, pp. 77, 64.

157. Matravers, *Empathy*, p. 144.

158. Johnson and Coates, *Nabokov's Blues*, p. 300.

159. Marren, *Rainbow Dust*, p. 69.

160. Vladimir Nabokov, *Strong Opinions* (London: Penguin, 2012), p. 20.

161. Johnson and Coates, *Nabokov's Blues*, p. 36.

162. Nabokov, *Lolita*, p. 174.

163. Amy Coplan, 'Empathetic Engagement with Narrative Fictions', *The Journal of Aesthetics and Art Criticism*, 62.2 (2004), 141–52 (p. 149).

164. Ron Broglio, *Surface Encounters: Thinking with Animals and Art* (Minneapolis: University of Minnesota Press, 2011), p. 23.

165. Bruno Latour, *Facing Gaia: Eight Lectures on the New Climatic Regime* (Cambridge: Polity, 2017), p. 34.

166. Kaufman, *Special Delivery*, p. 64.

167. Nabokov, *Lolita*, p. 165.

168. Nabokov, *Lolita*, p. 96.

169. Nabokov, *Lolita*, p. 308.

170. Aaltola, *Varieties of Empathy*, para. 15.3.

171. David Andrews, *Aestheticism, Nabokov and Lolita* (Lewiston, NY: Edwin Mellen Press, 1990), p. 130.

172. Nabokov, *Lolita*, p. 206.

5. Insect Ethics and Aesthetics: 'Their blood does not stain our hands'

The ultimate object of disgust is bare life itself, life deprived of the protective barrier. Life is a disgusting thing, a sleazy object moving out of itself, secreting humid warmth, crawling, stinking, growing.

Jela Krečič and Slavoj Žižek[1]

Richard Mabey contends that the most effective nature writing displays 'a willingness to admit both the kindredness and the otherness of the natural world', which informs 'a history of our views about ourselves as a species, part of the quest for the essential characteristics and boundaries of being human'.[2] Alert to the ethical limitations of a model of 'kindredness' which is predicated on sentience, individuality or anthropomorphic identification, Donna Haraway appeals for a broader definition. 'All earthlings', she contends, 'are kin in the deepest sense, and it is past time to practice better care of kinds-as-assemblages (not species one at a time). Kin is an assembling sort of word. All critters share a common "flesh," laterally, semiotically, and genealogically.'[3] Haraway has no particular interest in insects, over, for example, bacteria ('the greatest planetary terraformers'), yet her notion of kinship averts the sentience debate in a way which enables the emerging significance of insects, both as vectors of environmental change and as vulnerable subjects which trouble the figuration of the 'animal'.[4] The problem with Haraway's account, however, is its grounding in cognition rather than emotion. While intellectually we understand her claim of a shared 'flesh', her sense of kinship deviates from the affective immediacy of Mabey's 'kindredness'. This is not to deny the affective potency of insects. Indeed, human responses to insects reach affective extremes: from awe at the beauty of butterflies to fear, repulsion and disgust at beetles, flies and roaches' strange morphology, these insects being viewed as 'utterly alien', incomprehensible and apparently invulnerable.[5] However strongly one might side with Haraway intellectually, the latter, the striking velocity of disgust, poses a significant challenge to one's investment in such kinship.

In this chapter, the lepidoptera of Chapter 4 are superseded by those insects that we fear 'lurking in corners and under benches, flying into our hair and under our collars, crawling up our sleeves'.[6] We approach these differently; 'the killing of butterflies', Giovanni Aloi notes, 'aims at preserving the body in its perfect beauty, while the killing of flies aims at disintegrating the body as a source of disgust'.[7] Flies, cockroaches and beetles pose a particular affective and conceptual challenge. 'Insects', Maurice Maeterlinck observes, appear 'to come from another planet, more monstrous, more energetic, more insane, more atrocious, more infernal than our own.'[8] Their 'modes of feeding and fucking', Steven Shaviro notes of insects, 'are irretrievably different from ours'.[9] Their capacity for flight, collective intelligence, strength and apparent inscrutability stirs deep unease within us. They challenge what we think we know about the integration of the cognitive, affective and visceral, that 'in each individual the brain constitutes the controlling authority par excellence'.[10]

Insect strangeness is perceived as sufficient to exempt insects from ethics. As Elias Canetti observes:

> The destruction of these tiny creatures is the only act of violence which remains unpunished even *within* us. Their blood does not stain our hands, for it does not remind us of our own. We never look into their glazing eyes . . . They have never – at least not amongst us in the West – had the benefit of our growing, if not very effective, concern for life.[11]

Not only do insects appear non-sentient and therefore their deaths ethically insignificant, but their indifference to human structures and hierarchies affronts the human perception of itself as arbiter of universal standards. As such, insects are profoundly troubling; not only do they operate outside the ethical realm, their way of being appears to nullify it; 'they do not respond to acts of love or mercy or remorse', Hugo Raffles suggests. 'It is worse than indifference. It is a deep, dead space without reciprocity, recognition, or redemption.'[12] In this sense, while apparently excluding insects from ethical concern, insect difference continues to excite our interest, securing for insects an ongoing role in 'the quest for the essential characteristics and boundaries of being human'.

Insect imagery gains prominence at moments of historical disorder. The insect represents that which cannot be digested, incorporated or expressed. Cockroaches, Richard Schweid writes, signify the 'pools of darkness in our own selves'.[13] It is unsurprising, therefore, to see them 'creep into the supposedly intact but in fact crack-filled phantasm of the body of late modernity, revealing the distributed and assembled nature of any body taken to be natural'.[14] Kafka's 'Metamorphosis', the archetypal account of the manifestation of interior alienation in the form of an insect body, marks an historical juncture when, the association of entomology with imperialist triumph and financial success having waned, the strangeness of insects is once again foregrounded. As Charlotte Sleigh records, insects have generated complex anxieties about human identity:

> The early twentieth century is an identifiable transition period in the history of entomology, when insects were reconstructed as modernist bogeys. Their physiology and senses were reconsidered in the light of evolutionary theory; in particular, a reassessment of their psychology allied them to the savagery of the unconscious. Doubt and anxiety attended the question of where they should be posed on the evolutionary tree: at the topmost twig of an offshoot alternative to that of vertebrates, or lower down on the selfsame branch? In short, were insects protohuman or antihuman by nature?[15]

Thus, the perceived threat that insects pose is not simply external – buzzing, flying, jumping – but internal; insects reflect the strangeness and self-alienation which humans endeavour to repress. They reflect the presence of an inescapable inhuman force within the human, a force that undercuts human claims to sovereignty, independence and superiority. Often displaced, biopolitically, on to specific human or nonhuman groups, this fear of the inhuman is visible in the characterisation of immigrants as vermin. In a contemporary rewriting of Kafka's text, for example, Rawi Hage's novel *Cockroach* examines the manifestation of contemporary xenophobia, critiquing the framing of immigrants as vermin. Its unnamed protagonist's internalisation of negative social perceptions of immigrants leads to delusions of himself as a cockroach to be 'eradicated'.[16] Like *Maus*, however, the novel's concerns are solely human.

In their reading of J. M. G. Le Clézio's novel *Terra Amata*, Stephen Loo and Undine Sellbach note the challenge of engaging with insects in ways that recognise cross-species kinship without appropriating or homogenising insect difference. Describing a scene in which a small boy explores his own burgeoning power by killing insects, they explain: 'When a shared sense of animal vulnerability with insects is most palpably felt in the story, it is through the squashed bodies of the bugs in a way that effaces their distinctive physiology, instincts and distant perceptual worlds.'[17] The physiological dissimilarity between humans and insects severely stretches human imagination and thus hinders the development of empathy; as we have seen through Lori Gruen, '[e]mpathy does not appear to be the appropriate ethical response to the non-sentient world'.[18]

Yet we should not be deterred by the shortcomings of existing tools. As Loo and Sellbach insist, 'we can no longer afford to think about ethics in separation from insects, and the big and small edges of sentience they evoke'.[19] The perceptual and conceptual problems that insects raise, particularly those of scale, environmental boundaries and perceptibility, are revelatory of our Anthropocene condition. As '[t]iny miniatures', they explode our sense of anthropocentric scale and order, generating 'the same immense sense of estrangement as dinosaurs, dragons or other gigantic monsters'.[20] Similarly, their perceptual apparatus differs significantly from ours; in the case of the eye, for example, there is a 'continuous tension between the capacities of the insect that have formed the physiological eye and the environment as its needed partner for unraveling the perception event'.[21] Such a relation unsettles everything we assume about perception and cognition, revealing, Wendy Harding contends, 'that the center of consciousness does not hold'.[22] While 'they escape notice' or 'seem beyond or unworthy of perception',[23] our species' survival is dependent on attentiveness to insects, particularly 'indicator species', whose changing populations or habits are effective indexes of larger environmental change.[24] While we have long known that insects are crucial contributors to ecosystems, that they 'perform indispensable ecological services' and 'are the most important link between plants and animals that don't eat plants and have other important roles in virtually all terrestrial and freshwater ecosystems', insects are now perceived as signs of an environment, the Anthropocene, in which the micro and the macro are intertwined.[25] Premised on the unexpected arrival of an enormous swarm of Monarch butterflies in a small town in rural Tennessee, Barbara Kingsolver's novel *Flight Behaviour* invites us to perceive the butterflies' vulnerability alongside their increasing significance as barometers of environmental disturbance. The butterflies' presence, the scientist Dr Byron records, is 'evidence of a disordered system'; insects are 'writing on our wall'.[26] Thus, it is increasingly clear that '[s]tudying man's relation to insects can help us find a pathway through the maze of our representations' and facilitate new approaches to current environmental problems.[27]

This chapter will track the flying and scurrying of disparate unpinned insects, emphasising both their instrumental and intrinsic value and the necessity of supplementing empathetic with non-empathetic approaches when thinking and writing with them. It will examine three figures of the insect: the first, the insect as *other* other in Damien Hirst's work, exposes the limitations of empathetic responses to nonhuman life. The second, the queer insect, draws on Elizabeth Grosz's reading of Darwin, Roger Caillois's interpretation of mimicry and Lee Edelman's work in queer theory to argue that the insect provides a figure of the inhuman that counters logics of heteronormative futurity. The final figure, that of the disgusting insect, is generated through Braidotti's reading of Clarice Lispector's novel *The Passion of G.H.* and Derrida's reading of Kant's third critique. The chapter concludes by advancing disgust as a useful tool in the development of an inhuman ethics.

THE INSECT AS *OTHER* OTHER

In Chapter 4, we saw the depreciation of the 'heroic collector' to eccentric, even suspicious, recluse.[28] The superficial irony of collecting, a process of 'taking something out of the world and killing it to look at it', is dramatised in Damien Hirst's *Natural History* series, which interrogates the 'failure of trying so hard to do something that you destroy the thing that you're trying to preserve'.[29] While these works are mammal-focused, Hirst's interest in animal symbolism, and in the human impulses to collect and classify, extends to insects, most notably *In and Out of Love* (1991), which reportedly generated 9,000 butterfly deaths, *Black Sun* (2004) and *Doorways to the Kingdom of Heaven* (2007). For Hirst's detractors, his use of animal corpses and responsibility for animal deaths is unforgivable. With the tally standing at a startling 913,450 when counted in 2017,[30] Quentin Letts took great pleasure in declaring Hirst 'an entomological mass murderer'.[31] Although, at times, Hirst echoes the bombastic defence of collectors, asserting the need to 'kill things in order to look at them', rather than a mindless endorsement of killing in service of art, his work can be read more interestingly as an exploration of human violence and complicity, of the arbitrariness of the distinction between valuable and valueless life, as well as of the limits of representation of conceptuality.[32] Chris Townsend contends that '[w]hat Hirst would like to show us, I think, is Death *as itself* [. . .] What we get are forms of the index (cows' heads, sheep's heads, whole cows, whole sharks, butterflies...)'[33] His method is expressly and provocatively deconstructive: 'I always try to say something and deny it at the same time', he reveals.[34]

Acknowledging human complicity, both with animal suffering and environmental degradation, is central to contemporary ecological and animal thinking. Donna Haraway, for example, contends that we cannot avoid instrumentalising other living beings, and must address this honestly; 'in order to be *for* some ways of living and dying and not others', she discloses, 'I/we must kill'.[35] Similarly, Alexis Shotwell cautions against 'purity politics', contending that 'if we want a world with less suffering and more flourishing, it would be useful to perceive complexity and complicity as the constitutive situation of our lives, rather than as things we should avoid'.[36] The challenge faced by Hirst's critics is to distinguish between the exposure of complicity and the gratuitous perpetuation of animal death and suffering, a distinction that Hirst problematises. The *Natural History* series, for example, speaks the 'well-constructed language' of natural history only to pervert it, retaining its façade – the realistic poses and vitrines – while rendering absurd both the notion of a systematic and teleologically structured natural world and of an existentially distinct species, Man, whose task is the 'nomination of the visible'.[37] While natural history is ultimately specular – a complex tool which enables Man to see Man – despite the vulgar symbolism of the *Natural History* series, these works are irreducible to either the specular or the symbolic. Doubtless the disarming nature of these pieces follows from their exposure of 'the futility of preservation in the face of death – that whatever we do to protect bodies against entropy, inevitably, eventually they will disintegrate and die'.[38] However, the most affective works of the series (*Mother and Child (Divided)*, for example) ask us to linger on, and empathise with, individual subjects, the violence of their displacement from their natural environments, the impropriety of our own voyeurism and the limitations of our own symbolic narratives, even before we are confronted with the uncanny inescapability of our own deaths. These works capitalise on the empathy generated by shared, mammalian vulnerability.

Hirst's critique of both the ideologies and practices of natural history, however, problematically demands a near-identical reproduction of the latter, so much so that the critique implicit in his work often goes unnoticed. With reference to *The Physical Impossibility of Death in the Mind of Someone Living*, Giovanni Aloi contends that:

> the shark's body is stripped of its animality and allowed only to summon fears in humans. By animality, we here mean all the biological and behavioural traits along with the complex interconnectedness with other animals and environments that make the animal much more than a preserved dead body.[39]

Such an interpretation reads a complex work at face value. For Ron Broglio, Hirst's works require that we confront the limits of the knowability of the animal. Broglio writes: 'At the limit of our perception we encounter the friction and opacity of other ways of being that remain inaccessible to us [. . .] Hirst's works are a series of structures around the limits of access to this secret approached through the tradition of lifting nature's veil.'[40] Broglio leaves us wondering, however, whether the implications of this observation are aesthetic, ontological or even ethical.

While the affective potential (and controversy) of the *Natural History* series is dependent on empathetic identification (or dis-identification) with mammals, Hirst's insect pieces prompt other kinds of responses and challenge us to conceive of an ethics outside 'entangled empathy'. The earliest, *A Thousand Years* (1990), a rotting cow's head harbouring maggots which metamorphose into flies to be electrocuted, their corpses littering the space, has an 'air of maturity and finality' and remains widely perceived as a highpoint of Hirst's work.[41] For Townsend, this piece confronts 'the timid pieties of identification with the other', demonstrating that, when it comes to the ethical status of insects, different theoretical tools are needed.[42] Hirst's work demands that we consider how we might engage meaningfully with the insect as *other* other. Later works incorporate thousands of dead flies; the monochrome *Who's Afraid of the Dark?* (2002) and *Black Sun* (2004), for example, trade on our disgust towards flies, while opening increasingly pressing questions regarding perceptibility and scale. For Timothy Clark, the Anthropocene entails a shattering of existing conceptual frameworks, which means that we no longer know how to interpret or navigate our environments.[43] Unable either to focus on the sphere or the component parts of *Black Sun*, the viewer is similarly bewildered. It is no accident that, for Stephen Loo and Undine Sellbach, the insect is the archetypal index of that which is barely perceptible but maximally significant, a gauge of the epoch-shifting environmental change we are witnessing in the twenty-first century.

Exploiting the 'religious associations of resurrection' with butterflies (*psyche* for the Greeks, and a symbol of the immortality of the soul for Christianity), *Doorways to the Kingdom of Heaven* (2007), which consists of thousands of dead butterflies formed into kaleidoscopic stained-glass church window shapes, has been widely perceived as a celebration of the impermanence of life and beauty.[44] Hirst states that:

> It's about love and realism, dreams, ideals, symbols, life and death. I worked out many possible trajectories for these things, like the way the real butterfly can destroy the ideal (birthday-card) kind of love; the symbol exists apart from the real thing. Or the butterflies still being beautiful even when dead.[45]

It is easy to classify the work as an arrogant act of collecting which presupposes the superiority of the created object to that which has been destroyed, and of the human story to the lepidopterological stories that have been silenced. But, as Aloi asks:

> Wouldn't it be hypocritical to point the finger at Hirst for killing the insects when this is exactly what everyone, at some point, does, without thinking much of it? [...] In this case, the harming of a fly is used to indicate the

easiest and most commonplace sign of violence one could commit, at once irrelevant and normalised by cultural habits.[46]

For Hirst, symbolism is an extension of natural history, 'the possibility', Foucault advances, 'of seeing what one will be able to say, but what one could not say subsequently, or see at a distance, if things and words, distinct from one another, did not, from the very first, communicate in a representation'.[47] Here the butterfly, through and not aside from its own death, becomes a symbol of the disintegrating fragility of life. These monumental pieces are masterful displays of human dominance and creativity, harvesting and reconfiguring nature to challenge our assumptions about belief, beauty, freedom, art and transcendence. The butterflies, with their rich, jewel-like colours and complex symmetrical patterns, become signs within interlocking threads of human history – religious, aesthetic, entomological.

Hirst's work, however, invites an alternative reading. It is not simply that the butterflies remain 'beautiful even when dead'. It is rather that, for collectors, the butterflies are more beautiful when dead, when they, like Lolita, have transcended the exigencies of life and been transformed into aesthetic objects. Hirst acknowledges the seductiveness of aesthetic dematerialisation and reminds us that violence and destruction need to be rendered visible. Implicit here is a critique of the arrogant instrumentalisation of nonhuman life and a reminder that our vision is deficient or selective; in the processes of aesthetic disembodiment and rearrangement, the butterflies' own marked bodies, as stories and signs, are suppressed, subordinated to human signifiers. By juxtaposing butterflies and flies, Hirst's work also invites us to consider our moral investment in the distinction between the ugly and the beautiful: what can our flight from the insect as *other* other teach us about our fear of ourselves?

QUEER INSECTS

The perception that art is unique to the human has a long history. For Jacques Derrida, it is a question of framing: both the artwork and the artist are understood as distinct and unmistakable. While philosophy has often attempted to efface its frames, to naturalise them or attribute them to God, Derrida cautions against seduction by the impossible dream of removing the frame.[48] One task for deconstruction is exposure: uncovering the frame, and with it, the arbitrariness of its positioning. In *The Truth in Painting*, we find Derrida reading the *parerga* at the edges of Immanuel Kant's texts alongside the question of framing, or adornment, of visual art. Derrida's playful line of attack on Kant arrives via clothing, a sculpted figure wearing an entirely transparent veil; is the veil clearly separable from the 'representative essence' of the figure, Derrida asks, or from the artwork?[49] While Kant's analytic of aesthetic judgement presupposes a clear distinction between 'intrinsic beauty' and its ornamental, dispensable surrounds, such a distinction becomes blurred.[50] 'We think we know what properly belongs or does not belong to the human body', Derrida contends, 'what is detached or not detached from it – even though the parergon is precisely an ill-detachable detachment.'[51]

Within Derrida's destabilisation of Kantian 'beauty' is a broader challenge to Kant's humanism, rooted in the analogy between aesthetic and moral judgement that grounds the *Third Critique*, and to the oppositions – inside/outside, human/nonhuman, *physis/tekhne* – that underpin humanism more generally. Key to this challenge is the identification of an originary supplementarity that reveals the dependency of the superior term on the inferior. '[W]hat is it that is lacking in the representation of the body', Derrida asks, 'so that the garment should come and supplement it?'[52] The supplement reveals that the human is neither self-identical nor self-sufficient; it is constituted by prostheses. In the essay 'Economimesis' Derrida explicitly develops the implications of his critique of Kant for our understanding of the 'animal', taking aim at Kant's negative definition of art in the third critique: art is not a science; art is neither handicraft or remunerative art; art is human, not animal. 'By right', Kant argues:

> only production through freedom ie. through a capacity for choice that grounds its actions in reason, should be called art. For although people are fond of describing the product of the bees (the regularly constructed honeycombs) as a work of art, this is done only on account of the analogy with the latter; that is, as soon as we recall that they do not ground their work on any rational consideration of their own, we say that it is a product of their nature (of instinct), and as art it is ascribed only to their creator.[53]

Kant's framing of art permits only a disjunctive comparison between human and nonhuman animal. His scale, Derrida notes, is that of 'the body. Of man.'[54] Derrida glosses:

> What can be glimpsed in this inexhaustible reiteration of the humanist theme, of the ontology bound up with it as well, in this obscurantist buzzing that always treats animality in general [. . .] is that the concept of art is constructed with just such a guarantee in view. It is there to raise man up *[Eriger l'homme]*, that is, always, to erect a man-god, to avoid contamination from 'below', and to mark an incontrovertible limit of anthropological domesticity.[55]

For Derrida, Kant's definition of art proceeds from, and serves to reinforce, human exceptionalism; it leaves no space to interrogate its own terms.

The perceived danger of 'contamination from below' has been magnified by Charles Darwin's identification of a continuum of life in which the difference between human and nonhuman animals is 'one of degree and not of kind'.[56] Experiences and capacities are shared across species, Darwin contends; across the 'higher animals [. . .] all have the same senses, intuitions and sensations – similar passions, affections, and emotions, even the more complex ones'.[57] Darwin rejects mechanistic interpretations of nonhuman animal life in favour of those which acknowledge individual animals' agency. This is particularly clear in Darwin's account of Sexual Selection. Natural Selection describes the process by which certain variations, those which maximise the chance of a species' survival, are reproduced; it is the 'preservation of favourable variations and the rejection of injurious variations'.[58] The changes initiated by Natural Selection act in favour of the community and are therefore felt at species level. In contrast, Sexual Selection describes the process through which an individual animal chooses a mate; unlike Natural Selection, it is less explicitly a 'struggle for existence' than 'a struggle between the males for possession of the females'.[59] Building on Darwin's account of Sexual Selection, Elizabeth Grosz argues not only that it particularises each insect and reveals their capacities for choice, preferences and pleasure, but that in so doing, it grounds what we understand as the aesthetic.

Whereas Natural Selection is wholly 'biological', Sexual Selection is a kind of '*social* selection'.[60] Success in Sexual Selection depends on males' aesthetic 'special weapons',[61] which suggests the existence of 'powers of discrimination and taste' among nonhuman females.[62] Darwin puzzles:

> But when we behold male birds elaborately displaying their plumes and splendid colours before the females, whilst other birds not thus decorated make no such display, it is impossible to doubt that the females admire the beauty of their male partners [. . .] Why certain bright colours and certain sounds should excite pleasure, when in harmony, cannot, I presume, be explained any more than why certain flavours and scents are agreeable; but assuredly the same colours and the same sounds are admired by us and by many of the lower animals.[63]

While Sexual Selection occurs across a variety of species, Darwin is particularly startled by its implications for insects, of which it reveals an 'appreciation of the beautiful in sound, colour or form'.[64] As these characteristics are not directly related to the reproductive fitness of the individual, Sexual Selection 'is not about the production of a norm', but introduces taste and contingency into reproduction.[65] For Grosz, Sexual Selection has two interconnected consequences: first, it evidences excessive variation, 'lavish expenditure',[66] in life, the addition of 'something new to the world', which creates 'something that has no other purpose than to intensify, to experience itself'.[67] 'Like music, art, and language', this is an aesthetic excess, but its production is not restricted to the human.[68] Secondly, Sexual Selection is 'the queering of natural selection', the deviation of life away from predictable biological norms.[69]

For Grosz, therefore, Sexual Selection is the origin of the aesthetic. She argues:

> Art is engendered through the excess of matter that life utilizes for its own sake, and through that excess of life that directs it beyond itself and into the elaboration of materiality. This art cannot be identified with the creation of artworks, but rather it is a temporary, unstable, perhaps unsustainable union of the living and the nonliving, a co-becoming, like wave-surfing or gymnastics, in which unliving forces (an event) and living forces coalesce, impart to each other their impacts and resources, and create for a moment a hybrid, something nonliving which nonetheless lives a life of its own.[70]

While the origin of the aesthetic, as Grosz locates it, is distinct from human artwork, Grosz argues that the latter is simply the 'formal structuring or framing' of 'the power to appeal and enhance' via 'colors, sounds, and shapes' that we see in insects.[71] The capacity to produce art, therefore, does not underscore human exceptionalism, but reflects the evolutionary continuum of life. Grosz inverts Kant's assumption that art is a product of free will and therefore singularly human, by arguing that it is not 'of Man', but 'of the animal'.[72] At this juncture, Grosz and Kant diverge not only regarding their perceptions of species capacities, but also their definitions of ethics. Whereas, for Kant, ethics emerges from human free will, Grosz rejects the presupposition that ethics is restricted to human agents; rather, she argues that there is an 'ethics internal to life itself: to maximise action, to enable the proliferation of actions, movements'.[73] The specificity of human responsibility lies in not impeding this movement. Advancing a bottom-up, rather than top-down, perspective on animal capabilities, Frans de Waal argues that, when examining complex processes such as altruism, we should always begin by looking at similarities between basic processes rather than assuming the existence of novel processes; in this way, we can see the development of aesthetic sensibilities and capabilities across a variety of species.[74]

In Chapter 2, we saw how Anthropocene criticism, underpinned by apocalypticism, recuperates the teleological and anthropocentric narrative of the 'ends of man'. For such criticism, anthropogenic environmental degradation is read as a temporary deviation from, and an incitement to reinstate, a teleological trajectory that presupposes the fixed nature of 'Man' and his pre-determined role as steward of the natural world. Such approaches inevitably reinforce the anthropotheological thinking that has licensed destructive anthropocentrisms. Alternative modes of Anthropocene thinking must challenge this resurgent teleology. By reading Sexual Selection as queer, Grosz perceives in it a contestation of normative teleologies; the movement she observes is excessive rather than functional and futural. This definition of queerness corresponds with that of Lee Edelman, who contends:

> If the fate of the queer is to figure the fate that cuts the thread of futurity, if the jouissance, the corrosive enjoyment, intrinsic to queer (non)identity annihilates the fetishistic jouissance that works to *consolidate* identity by allowing reality to coagulate around its ritual reproduction, then the only oppositional status to which our queerness could ever lead would depend on our taking seriously the place of the death drive [. . .] And so what is queerest about us, queerest within us, and queerest despite us is this willingness to insist intransitively – to insist that the future stop here.[75]

The Anthropocene problematises existing temporal indexes by requiring us to think on a geological scale, and questions the notion of futurity, as a kind of archiving of the human, in an era after human extinction.[76] In fact, we might think of the Anthropocene as a fulfilment of this queering of futurity, in which, as Stefan Skrimshire, reading Derrida, suggests, 'the framing of the Anthropocene as an archive of the human in fact reflects a melancholic, auto-destructive impulse'.[77] It is problematic, therefore, that the prevailing Anthropocene narrative is insistently teleological. However, the combination of queer theory and deconstruction promises a critique of the anthropocentrism of Anthropocene theory, of, as Skrimshire writes, 'narratives of geological time that imagine only an extended *saeculum*, the "time of the human," that somehow outstrips human civilization as we know it'.[78] The absurd, impossible futurity which persists in Anthropocene thinking succumbs to Edelman's critique of the 'regulatory fantasy of reproductive futurism'.[79] For Edelman, '*sinthom*osexuality' is the alternative to such 'reproductive futurism', in which 'the sinthome refers to the mode of jouissance constitutive of the subject, which defines it no longer as subject of desire, but rather as subject of the drive'.[80]

Sinthomosexuality destabilises meaning itself, where reproductive heterosexuality is premised on the fantasy of the fulfilment of the future. Here the *sinthome* is not synonymous with the symptom (which follows the movement of the signifier) but follows Jacques Lacan's articulation of the *sinthome* in Seminar XXIII as pure jouissance. Sinthomosexuality, therefore, carries with it the disruptiveness of the death drive through which the futural normativity of heterosexuality is undermined. Thus, sinthomosexuality is 'a radically negative force', the undoing of meaning (in the sense of the explosion of the myth that futurity will eventually compensate for the 'primal loss') which demands a re-examination of the natural.[81] It is 'the gap opened up within nature by something inherently contra naturam', which reveals the constructedness of the associations between humanity, nature and meaning.[82] This is best understood through Edelman's framing of heterosexuality as 'the assurance of meaning itself' and his description of the politics that emerges from 'reproductive futurism' as one in which the myth of redemptive futurity (the 'fantasy of a social reality') – the very image that we perceive in Anthropocene criticism – is maintained through the figure of the child.[83] Edelman counters this with the notion of the inhuman, which is not something external to the human but, as I have been consistently emphasising, the otherness inherent to the human, which means that the human is 'always misrecognized catachresis'; in other words, not human after all.[84]

It is no accident that markers of the inhuman are found in other forms of life; for Edelman this is instantiated by Alfred Hitchcock's film *The Birds*, in which the birds themselves indicate 'a haunting, destructive excess bound up with its pious sentimentality, an overdetermination that betrays the place of the kernel of irony that futurism tries to allegorize as narrative, as history'.[85] See also Hugo Raffles's insistence that:

> we need better stories about queer insects too [. . .] It's so frustrating to have to deal with mechanistic models all these centuries after Descartes. We need to bring back pleasure and desire. Even deep, dark, complicated paraphilic praying mantis pleasure-desire. Especially deep, dark, paraphilic praying mantis pleasure-desire.[86]

Raffles, like Grosz, reminds us that nonhuman life is not always reproductively orientated; rather, it embodies queer, non-teleological forces. For Edelman and Colebrook, it is the task of theory to accommodate, rather than domesticate, 'the inhuman (that which exists beyond, beyond all givenness and imaging, and beyond all relations)', and to acknowledge its tension with our impulse to create and preserve order.[87] This tension, an originary disjunction, is suppressed by new materialist and posthumanist accounts which advocate the restoration of a lost relationship with the earth. Colebrook appeals instead to a theoretical response to the Anthropocene which does not postulate 'any preceding or ideal community'.[88] Such a response, a turn away from political projects rooted in the figure of the child, which 'are programmed to reify difference and thus to secure, in the form of the future, the order of the same', entails a relinquishing of human mastery and a reconfiguration of the ethico-political horizon.[89]

Psychoanalysis and deconstruction both acknowledge the recurrence of an infinite, inhuman force within human experience. For Alenka Zupančič, writing in response to Lacan's Seminar VII, this force provides 'the basis of ethics';[90] for Edelman, transcribing the same source in a different vernacular, queerness delivers the infinite task of 'embodying the remainder of the Real internal in the Symbolic order'.[91] For Derrida, the 'infinite ethical demand of deconstruction' renders ethics irretrievably excessive and irreducible to ethical prescriptions.[92] For these thinkers, the terms inhuman and infinite are interchangeable. As the embodiment of inhuman force, the insect is not exempt from ethical concern, but reveals the condition of human existence as a negotiation between the infinite and the finite. In its participation in Sexual Selection, which disrupts the collective species goals of Natural Selection, the insect both enacts a force that cannot be accommodated by teleological logics and reveals that art derives from this inhuman force, rather than from human freedom.

DISGUSTING INSECTS

In her critique of a 'poetics of desire' which has become associated with 'a general logic of inclusivity' to the point of meaninglessness, Sianne Ngai identifies a need to think beyond 'classical political passions'.[93] Accordingly, she turns to negative affects (envy, paranoia, irritation etc.), aiming to recuperate these 'for their *critical* productivity'.[94] Finally, she examines disgust, particularly the curious relationship between desire and disgust, 'paradoxically internal to Kantian disgust', in the *Critique of Judgment*.[95] Characteristic of a resurgence of interest in disgust since the 1990s,[96] Ngai's work proposes a shift from critical models based in proximity, such as empathy, to interruption, disgust being a clear 'operator of interruption'.[97] In this section, I shall argue that disgust, the affective response most frequently elicited by insects, can challenge our perceptions in three ways: first, by contesting an aesthetic system which, as we have seen, reinforces anthropological difference; secondly, by disrupting the boundary between subject and object, recalling the construction of the subject and emphasising the limitations of the symbolic; and finally, as we shall see in Clarice Lispector's novel *The Passion According to G.H.*, by reinforcing the relationship between the inhuman and the inassimilable, which, as we saw in Chapter 4, begins to ground an inhuman ethics.

Tracing the history of disgust through German aesthetics, Winfried Menninghaus offers a preliminary definition of disgust as having the following features: '(1) the violent repulsion vis-à-vis (2) a physical presence or some other phenomenon in our proximity, (3) which at the same time, in various degrees, can also exert a subconscious attraction or even an open fascination'.[98] As Menninghaus reminds us, the stakes of Kant's formulation of the faculty of taste and the identification of the beautiful are not restricted to the aesthetic; aesthetics and morality are often blurred, with taste functioning, for Kant, as 'the sole basis of the *sensus communis* and thus, in the end, of the informal coherence of society'.[99] While one type of disgust is opposed to the beautiful – disgust at that which is bad or rotten, functioning in terms of Freudian reaction formation[100] – the other, overindulgence, 'the disgusting satiation brought on by the merely sweet or purely beautiful', is intimately connected to it.[101] Whereas Menninghaus proficiently demonstrates the centrality of disgust to the German aesthetic tradition as a civilising force safeguarding morality, Derrida argues not only that disgust 'gives shape to the field of the aesthetic itself' but that it is ultimately disruptive and irrecuperable, overwhelming the faculty of taste.[102]

Kant suggests that 'only one kind of ugliness cannot be represented in a way adequate to nature without destroying all aesthetic satisfaction, hence beauty in art, namely that which arouses disgust (loathing)'.[103] The translated German, *Ekel*, both describes and simulates the viscerality of disgust, the gagging motion that it provokes. Accordingly, the mouth is the hinge between beauty and disgust; while being the locus of poetic expression, the pinnacle of the fine arts, it is also the portal of consumption, sensation and disgust, 'a kind of anus'.[104] As such, Derrida identifies 'a certain allergy in the mouth, between pure taste and actual tasting [*dégustation*]'.[105] Derrida maximises the viscerality of this conjunction: we are 'licking our chops [. . .] smacking our lips [. . .] whetting our palate'.[106] Disgust is so challenging because it yokes sensation and imagination more tightly than any other feeling; as John Macarthur notes, 'the idea of disgust is arguably more troubling and unpleasant than the sensation, as the mere idea of the disgusting can elicit the sensation, and collapse thought'.[107] Kant claims that poetry defies the mercantile economy; in having no determinate value, it has infinite value. Derrida's counter-claim is that disgust defies aesthetic economy through the irrecuperably material: vomit. Here, the disgusting becomes '"the true Kantian sublime" – more sublime than the sublime itself', as the sublime, like the ugly, is ultimately systematically recuperable.[108] Disgust is indigestible. It can be neither represented, reappropriated, nor replaced. It cannot take place within the aesthetic economy, yet it 'lends its form to this whole system'.[109] It is inseparable from the aesthetic, deriving from its imposition; 'as if', Kant writes, 'it were imposing the enjoyment which we are nevertheless forcibly resisting'.[110] It is too close to be either digested or effectively expelled; it is 'in-sensible and un-intelligible, irrepresentable and unnameable'.[111] In evading reappropriation by the aesthetic economy, vomit also evades logocentrism, where the living presence of the *logos*, through human mimesis of divine production (a mask or identification, not an imitation), takes its highest form in poetry; it is 'so extremely expressive that it fails to communicate'.[112] As that which disables the 'power of *identification*',[113] in other words, generates 'the collapse of the art–nature divide',[114] vomit, this disgusting supplement, must be 'absolutely repressed'.[115] In an article on David Lynch that takes Derrida's reading of Kant as a point of reference, Eugenie Brinkema counsels that 'vomit must neither be treated as a metaphor that rushes past its foul materiality nor reduced to narratives of provocation that bind it to the always-comforting logic of ordered causality'.[116] In this chapter, it is the insect, not vomit, whose inassimilability has ethical force.

For Kant, in being determined by 'purposiveness without an end', art generates an interiorising movement; 'since we never encounter it [the end of art] externally', he observes, 'we naturally seek within ourselves, and indeed in that which constitutes the ultimate end of our existence, namely the moral vocation'.[117] Disgust, however, challenges the distinction between interior and exterior. Whereas Ngai contends that disgust strengthens and polices the subject–object boundary, this is an incomplete account of the process.[118] Rather, disgust occurs when an external threat is exposed as internal; its practices of expulsion, therefore, are ineffectual. In so doing it demonstrates the porosity of subject boundaries. As Sara Ahmed writes, disgust 'shows us how the boundaries that allow the distinction between subjects and objects are undone in the moment of their making'.[119] Slavoj Žižek, too, notes that: 'Disgust arises when the border that separates the inside of our body from its outside is violated, when the inside penetrates out, as in the case of blood or shit.'[120]

The most detailed explanation of this experience of porosity is Julia Kristeva's discussion of abjection in *Powers of Horror*. Abjection, for Kristeva, is the identity-unsettling experience of enforced proximity to that which has been rejected or cast off; it is not an object *per se*, but a threat 'that seems to emanate from an exorbitant outside or inside, ejected beyond the scope of the possible, the tolerable, the thinkable'.[121]

Triggers of the experience of abjection are varied but connected: faeces, blood, vomit, corpses, even the skin on milk. While it is easy to perceive abjection, especially when it coincides with disgust, as related to 'cleanliness or health', this is misleading; abjection is, instead, 'what disturbs identity, system, order. What does not respect borders, positions, rules. The in-between, the ambiguous, the composite.'[122] It is intimately connected to subject formation. As a threat to the subject, like the *sinthome* for Lacan and Edelman, it threatens the Symbolic Order, drawing the subject 'toward the place where meaning collapses'.[123] This threat is affective, but it challenges the conceptual order that I have constructed; 'refuse and corpses', Kristeva observes, '*show me* what I permanently thrust aside in order to live'.[124] For Kristeva, abjection is inescapable and revelatory. 'I experience abjection', she explains, 'only if an Other has settled in place and stead of what will be "me" [. . .] An Other who precedes and possesses me, and through such possession causes me to be.'[125] The problem is not simply the intrusion of the other, but rather that my sense of an internal, distinct self is revealed to be merely an effect of the other; ultimately, it results in 'a "self-abjection"', necessarily denying its own origin in the mother's body.[126]

Ahmed is particularly interested in the political implications of disgust. Abjection entails 'the transformation of borders into objects' and in so doing, it creates separation and distance.[127] In his reading of Kant, Pierre Bourdieu politicises the faculty of taste by arguing that 'Kant's analysis of the judgment of taste finds its real basis in a set of aesthetic principles which are the universalization of the dispositions associated with a particular social and economic condition'.[128] In other words, the distinction between sensation and imagination that Derrida locates within taste maps seamlessly on to socio-economic, and ultimately species, lines, enjoyment being associated with a kind of 'reduction to animality'.[129] As Miller observes, 'hierarchies maintained by disgust cannot be benign'.[130] In a more positive reading, Ahmed perceives disgust not as an inherently conservative force, but as mobilising:

> Disgust, therefore, as an imperative not only to expel, but to make that very expulsion stick to some things and not others, does not always work simply to conserve that which is legitimated as a form of collective existence. Disgust can involve disgust at what disgust effects as a form of collective existence [. . .] The feeling of being disgusted may also be an element in a politics that seeks to challenge 'what is'. However, what the loop of disgust shows us is not simply the possibility of dissent within even the stickiest economies, but also how dissent cannot be exterior to its object. Dissent is always implicated in what is being dissented from. Furthermore, the limits of disgust as an affective response might be that disgust does not allow one the time to digest that which one designates as a 'bad thing'. I would argue

that critique requires more time for digestion. Disgust might not allow one to get close enough to an object before one is compelled to pull away.[131]

For Ahmed, disgust offers an enforced distancing that opens an internal space between oneself and one's context. While disgust, on its own, might generate too much distance, when accompanied by other affective and cognitive processes it has political purchase. Furthermore, as Kristeva and others demonstrate, disgust entails a negotiation with our animality, confronting us 'with those fragile states where man strays on the territory of *animal*'. While abjection entails an immediate, enforced separation on the level of the individual or the community, a distancing from 'the threatening world of animals or animalism', reflection on the process of abjection illuminates not only 'our personal archaeology', but our cultural history, and its destructive dependence on human exceptionalism.[132] Countering Martha Nussbaum's indictment of emotions such as envy and disgust as unethical, Ngai reads disgust, a block to 'sympathetic identification', as offering the potential for critical resistance.[133] She distinguishes it from desire which is now too pliable to be a useful tool, 'simply more concordant, ideologically as well as aesthetically, with the aesthetic, cultural, and political pluralisms that have come to define the postmodern than an emotional idiom defined by its vehement exclusion of the intolerable'.[134]

To illustrate the critical value of disgust, Ngai turns to Clarice Lispector's novel *The Passion According to G.H.*, an account of the mental turmoil and mystical crisis experienced by a wealthy female sculptor following an encounter with a cockroach. Fearfully slamming a wardrobe door on the cockroach, G.H. responds to her disgust with a failed attempt to consume 'the white paste' which emerges from its decapitated body:

> I dug my fingernails into the wall: now I tasted the bad taste [vomit] in my mouth, and then I began to spit, to spit out furiously that taste of nothing at all [the cockroach] [. . .] I spit myself out, never reaching the point of feeling that I had finally spit out my whole soul [. . .] I spat and spat and it kept on being me.[135]

G.H.'s experience is framed in terms of abjection; the paste of the roach is explicitly compared to maternal milk, with the text marking 'the confrontation with the maternal as an abject but unavoidable site of female identity'.[136] For G.H., the cockroach is literally inassimilable.

Ngai argues that the novel is 'an allegory of the failure of a reverent effort to absorb the intolerable from the perspective of the disgusted' which instantiates a mode of aesthetic resistance, art 'staging its refusal or inability to ingest what consumer culture proclaims all should want or desire to take in'.[137] In contrast, Rosi Braidotti views the novel as a dramatisation of the productivity of assimilation; for her, disgust is an obstacle to be overcome rather than an interruption to be exploited. Accordingly, G.H. is 'a living example of radical immanence' who 'plunges ever more deeply into the folds of her own materiality, becoming animal, insect, mineral'.[138] Braidotti's reading is expressly affirmative, grounded in the epiphanic final pages of the novel, in which G.H. observes:

> What I am feeling now is a joy. Through the living roach I am coming to understand that I too am whatever is alive. Being alive is a very high stage, it is something that I only reached now [. . .] Being alive is a coarse radiating indifference. Being alive is unattainable by the finest sensitivity. Being alive is inhuman.[139]

For Braidotti, G.H.'s liberating experience comprises an acknowledgement of the specificity of female embodiment with awareness of cross-species kinship, 'interconnectedness and empathy'.[140] This is a kind of prehistoric kinship; as G.H. says: 'I too had thousands of blinking cilia, and with my cilia I move forward, I protozoan, pure protein.'[141] In Braidotti's reading the cockroach is effaced in service of a greater force; G.H.'s encounter provokes a rebirth, inspiring 'alternative figurations for the new singularities being produced collectively at the moment'.[142]

It is concerning that both readings absent the cockroach itself; indeed, Irving Goh's observation that 'the ethical imperative to respect the limits when touch is in effect is almost absent in Lispector' might equally be applied to her interlocutors.[143] Neither is interested in addressing the violence of G.H. as she 'slammed the door on the half-emerged body of the cockroach', or the ethical implications of her professed 'solidarity'.[144] Although there are clear methodological and ideological differences between Ngai and Braidotti, both readings of the novel are ultimately recuperative. If disgust names the response to that which is literally inassimilable, then Ngai is too quick to engage the cockroach in aesthetic resistance via allegory. Indeed, to recall Derrida: 'what is absolutely foreclosed is not vomit, but the possibility of a vicariousness of vomit'; in other words that the materiality of disgust renders it non-exchangeable and unrepresentable; it cannot be critically recuperated.[145] This is only half the story, however, as disgust, 'a beyond of any thing', is only ever partially manifested.[146] These characteristics of disgust should serve as a guard-rail in the search for its 'critical productivity': how can we meaningfully engage with that towards which disgust can only gesture? How can we escape representation? Brinkema shapes a comparable question through a reformulation of the classic Lacanian dictum 'do not give up on your desire'. 'A practice', she says, 'textual, or let us say, any – of not giving up on one's *Ekel* designates the unassimilable without attempting to return it to the realm of the assimilable through what is always a form of violence.'[147]

The tenor of Brinkema's pronouncement shifts when we address the unassimilable insect. G.H.'s violence, neutralised by both Ngai and Braidotti, enacts '*carno-phallogocentrism*' in the form of the literal, at least attempted, consumption of the cockroach.[148] This is not aberrant or pathological violence, but deeply humanistic violence. It is illegible outside the economy of subject formation through which 'the subject does not want just to master and possess nature actively. In our cultures, he accepts sacrifice and eats flesh.'[149] As Hirst's work suggests, the insect other lays bare the 'conception-appropriation-assimilation of the other', which continues to underpin humanism by presenting an otherness that is genuinely indigestible.[150] As such, it can neither be ethically codified nor effectively expelled. Indeed, the cockroach, as abject, designates a disavowed relationship; 'abjection', Kristeva prompts, 'is elaborated through a failure to recognize its kin'.[151] The insect presents the inhuman origins of the human, reconnecting with 'drives and desires that are alien to the civilized human being'.[152] For Steven Shaviro, this proves that we cannot 'extricate ourselves from the insect continuum that marks life on this planet. The sensational forces that modulate insect bodies and behaviors are also restlessly at work in our own brains, shaping our neurons and even our thoughts.' In a turn against futurity that parallels that of Edelman, Shaviro reads in this a call 'to cultivate your inner housefly or cockroach, instead of your inner child'.[153]

Empathy and disgust share unexpected similarities: while perceived as humanising or even civilising, they both draw upon 'the common animality' shared by humans and other species.[154] They move, however, in different directions. Cross-species empathy begins proximately, often from anthropomorphism: the appreciation of a human quality, even that of vulnerability, exhibited by a nonhuman animal. Only at its peripheries does it begin to destabilise our conceptions of the human. In contrast, the starting point for disgust is distance, shockingly violated by an undesirable proximity, which, at first perceived as an accidental violation, inevitably reveals an originary, disavowed proximity: abjection. As Miller observes, 'disgust admits our own vulnerability and compromise even as it constitutes an assertion of superiority'. It entails 'an admission that we did not escape contamination'.[155] Whereas empathy is something that we can and, arguably, should cultivate, disgust needs no cultivation; rather *Ekel* overtakes us. Nevertheless, we can consider our responses to disgust – most often flight from the perceived contaminant – and heed both its call for the centrality of the sensation and its exposure of the absurdity of our pretensions to mastery. Disgust, Menninghaus notes, operates 'on physical, aesthetic, and moral levels'; however, it does not unite 'all faculties' as Kant's presentation suggests. Rather, it leaves the faculties, and Kant's aesthetic system, in total disarray.[156] To pause with, rather than flee from, one's disgust entails two things. First, an unflinching gaze at what disgust reveals about the disgusted; here the language of lack (that 'disgust fills in and substitutes for a lack')[157] is almost interchangeable with plenitude (the infinite, inhuman force that upends human mastery). And secondly, the material as well as conceptual accommodation of the inassimilable: the acknowledgement of tactile boundaries, even when they are transgressed, between human and nonhuman subjects.

NOTES

1. Jela Krečič and Slavoj Žižek, 'Ugly, Creepy, Disgusting, and Other Modes of Abjection', *Critical Inquiry*, 43.1 (2016), 60–83 (p. 66).
2. Richard Mabey, *The Oxford Book of Nature Writing* (Oxford: Oxford University Press, 1995), p. vii.
3. Haraway, 'Anthropocene', p. 162.
4. Haraway, 'Anthropocene', p. 159.
5. Clark, *Bugs and the Victorians*, p. 77.
6. Raffles, *Insectopedia*, p. 44.
7. Giovanni Aloi, *Art and Animals* (London: I.B. Tauris, 2012), p. 117.
8. Maurice Maeterlinck, cited in Jean-Henri Fabre, *The Life of the Spider* (New York: Dodd, Mead and Co., 1913), pp. 9–10.
9. Steven Shaviro, 'Two Lessons from Burroughs', in *Posthuman Bodies*, ed. Judith Halberstam and Ira Livingston (Bloomington: Indiana University Press, 1995), pp. 38–54 (p. 46).
10. Catherine Malabou, *What Should We Do With Our Brain?* (New York: Fordham University Press, 2008), p. 32.
11. Elias Canetti, cited in Raffles, *Insectopedia*, p. 121.
12. Raffles, *Insectopedia*, p. 44.
13. Schweid, *Cockroach Papers*, p. xiv.
14. Jussi Parikka, *Insect Media: An Archaeology of Animals and Technology* (Minneapolis: University of Minnesota Press, 2010), p. xxiii.
15. Sleigh, 'Inside Out', p. 281.
16. Ravi Hage, *Cockroach* (Toronto: Anansi, 2008), p. 53.
17. Loo and Sellbach, 'Insect Affects', p. 83.
18. Gruen, *Entangled Empathy*, p. 68.
19. Loo and Sellbach, 'Insect Affects', p. 80.
20. Braidotti, *Metamorphoses*, p. 149.
21. Parikka, *Insect Media*, p. 69.

22. Wendy Harding, 'Insects and Texts: Worlds Apart', in *Insects in Literature and the Arts*, ed. Laurence Talairach-Vielmas and Marie Bouchet (Brussels: P.I.E. Peter Lang, 2014), pp. 219–34 (p. 230).

23. Harding, 'Insects and Texts', p. 221.

24. This notion has passed into popular discourse. See, for example, http://www.nhm.ac.uk/discover/butterflies-unlocking-climate-secrets.ht ml?utm_source=tw-image-post-20180128-lb&utm_medium=social&ut m_campaign=content (accessed 19 February 2019).

25. Gilbert Waldbauer, *How Not To Be Eaten: The Insects Fight Back* (Berkeley: University of California Press, 2012), p. 9.

26. Barbara Kingsolver, *Flight Behaviour* (London: Faber and Faber, 2012), pp. 503, 442.

27. Harding, 'Insects and Texts', p. 232.

28. Benjamin, 'To Have and to Hold', p. 16.

29. Damien Hirst and Gordon Burn, *On the Way to Work* (London: Faber and Faber, 2001), p. 219.

30. https://news.artnet.com/art-world/damien-whats-your-beef-916097 (accessed 19 February 2019).

31. http://www.dailymail.co.uk/news/article-2125359/Moral-vacuity-ran cid-opportunism-Sorry-Damien-youre-fraud.html (accessed 19 February 2019).

32. https://news.artnet.com/art-world/damien-whats-your-beef-916097 (accessed 19 February 2019).

33. Chris Townsend, *Art and Death* (London: I.B. Tauris, 2008), p. 38.

34. Damien Hirst in 'Damien Hirst, 4 April–9 September 2012', exhibition booklet, Tate Modern, n.p.

35. Haraway, *Manifestly Haraway*, p. 236.

36. Shotwell, *Against Purity*, pp. 7, 8.

37. Foucault, *Order of Things*, pp. 151, 144.

38. http://www.tate.org.uk/art/artworks/hirst-mother-and-child-divided-t12751 (accessed 19 February 2019).

39. Aloi, *Art and Animals*, p. 4.

40. Broglio, *Surface Encounters*, p. 23.

41. https://www.theguardian.com/artanddesign/2012/apr/02/damien-hirst-tate-review (accessed 19 February 2019).

42. Townsend, *Art and Death*, p. 49.

43. Clark, *Ecocriticism on the Edge*, p. 9

44. Damien Hirst in 'Damien Hirst, 4 April–9 September 2012', exhibition booklet, Tate Modern.

45. http://www.damienhirst.com/in-and-out-of-love-white-pain (accessed 19 February 2019).

46. Aloi, *Art and Animals*, p. 116

47. Foucault, *Order of Things*, pp. 141–2.

48. Jacques Derrida, *The Truth in Painting*, trans. Geoffrey Bennington and Ian McLeod (Chicago: University of Chicago Press, 1987), p. 73.

49. Derrida, *The Truth in Painting*, p. 57.
50. Derrida, *The Truth in Painting*, p. 63.
51. Derrida, *The Truth in Painting*, p. 59.
52. Derrida, *The Truth in Painting*, pp. 57–8.
53. Immanuel Kant, *Critique of the Power of Judgment*, trans. Paul Guyer (Cambridge: Cambridge University Press, 2000), S43, p. 182.
54. Derrida, *The Truth in Painting*, p. 140
55. Derrida, 'Economimesis', p. 5.
56. Charles Darwin, *The Descent of Man* (London: Wordsworth Editions, 2013 [1871]), p. 80.
57. Darwin, *The Descent of Man* p. 39.
58. Darwin, *On the Origin of Species*, p. 63.
59. Darwin, *On the Origin of Species*, p. 68.
60. Gillian Beer, 'Introduction', in Darwin, *On the Origin of Species*, p. xxiii.
61. Darwin, *On the Origin of Species*, p. 69.
62. Darwin, *The Descent of Man*, p. 201.
63. Darwin, *The Descent of Man*, p. 49.
64. Darwin, *The Descent of Man*, p. 645.
65. Elizabeth Grosz, *Becoming Undone: Darwinian Reflections on Life, Politics and Art* (Durham, NC: Duke University Press, 2011), p. 130.
66. Shaviro, 'Two Lessons from Burroughs', p. 48.
67. Elizabeth Grosz, *Chaos, Territory, Art: Deleuze and the Framing of the Earth* (New York: Columbia University Press, 2008), p. 39.
68. Grosz, *Becoming Undone*, p. 131.
69. Grosz, *Becoming Undone*, p. 132.
70. Grosz, *Becoming Undone*, p. 39.
71. Grosz, *Becoming Undone*, p. 135.
72. Grosz, *Chaos, Territory, Art*, p. 63. On this point, Jeffrey Jerome Cohen accuses Grosz of 'organic bias' and suggests that we might also be able to identify 'a lithic sexuality'. Cohen, *Stone*, p. 238.
73. Grosz, *Becoming Undone*, p. 22.
74. Frans de Waal, 'Towards a Bottom-up Perspective on Human and Animal Cognition', *Trends in Cognitive Sciences*, 14.5 (2000), 201–7.
75. Lee Edelman, *No Future: Queer Theory and the Death Drive* (Durham, NC: Duke University Press, 2004), p. 30.
76. See Stefan Skrimshire's discussion of Claire Colebrook's engagement with the notion of the readability of the human after the human. Stefan Skrimshire, 'Anthropocene Fever: Memory and the Planetary Archive', in *Religion in the Anthropocene*, ed. Celia Deane-Drummond (Eugene, OR: Cascade, 2017), pp. 138–54 (pp. 142–3).
77. Skrimshire, 'Anthropocene Fever', p. 147.
78. Skrimshire, 'Anthropocene Fever', p. 148.
79. Edelman, *No Future*, p. 117.
80. Edelman, *No Future*, pp. 114, 113.
81. Edelman, *No Future*, pp. 117, 134.

82. Edelman, *No Future*, p. 119.
83. Edelman, *No Future*, pp. 127, 135.
84. Edelman, *No Future*, p. 152.
85. Edelman, *No Future*, p. 153.
86. Raffles, *Insectopedia*, p. 262.
87. Colebrook, *Death of the PostHuman*, p. 31.
88. Colebrook, *Death of the PostHuman*, pp. 44–5.
89. Edelman, *No Future*, p. 151.
90. Alenka Zupančič, *Ethics of the Real: Kant and Lacan* (London: Verso, 2000), p. 249.
91. Edelman, *No Future*, p. 25.
92. Simon Critchley, *Ethics, Politics, Subjectivity: Essays on Derrida, Levinas and Contemporary French Thought* (London: Verso, 1999), p. 283.
93. Sianne Ngai, *Ugly Feelings* (Cambridge, MA: Harvard University Press, 2007), pp. 344, 5.
94. Ngai, *Ugly Feelings*, p. 3.
95. Ngai, *Ugly Feelings*, p. 335.
96. Paul Rozin, Jonathan Haidt and Clark R. McCauley, 'Disgust', in *Handbook of Emotions*, ed. M. Lewis, J. M. Haviland-Jones and L. F. Barrett (New York: Guildford Press, 2008), pp. 757–76 (p. 758).
97. Winfred Menninghaus, *Disgust: Theory and History of a Strong Sensation*, trans. Howard Eiland and Joel Golb (Albany, NY: SUNY Press, 2003), p. 386.
98. Menninghaus. *Disgust*, p. 6.
99. Menninghaus, *Disgust*, p. 4.
100. On the former, see William Ian Miller, *The Anatomy of Disgust* (Cambridge, MA: Harvard University Press, 1997), p. 109.
101. Menninghaus, *Disgust*, p. 7.
102. Eugenie Brinkema, 'Laura Dern's Vomit, or, Kant and Derrida in Oz', *Film-Philosophy*, 15.2 (2011), 51–69 (p. 58). It is worth noting Menninghaus's contention that both Bourdieu and Derrida lack familiarity with the centrality of disgust to aesthetic discussions in the 1750s and 1760s. Menninghaus, *Disgust*, p. 103.
103. Kant, *Critique of the Power of Judgment*, S48, p. 190.
104. John Macarthur, *The Picturesque: Architecture, Disgust and other Irregularities* (London: Routledge, 2007), p. 58.
105. Derrida, 'Economimesis', p. 16.
106. Derrida, 'Economimesis', p. 14.
107. Macarthur, *The Picturesque*, p. 58.
108. Ngai, *Ugly Feelings*, p. 334.
109. Derrida, 'Economimesis', p. 21.
110. Kant, *Critique of the Power of Judgment*, S48, p. 190.
111. Derrida, 'Economimesis', p. 22.
112. Macarthur, *The Picturesque*, p. 61.
113. Derrida, 'Economimesis', p. 25.

114. Macarthur, *The Picturesque*, p. 69.
115. Derrida, 'Economimesis', p. 25.
116. Brinkema, 'Laura Dern's Vomit', p. 52.
117. Kant, *Critique of the Power of Judgment*, S43, p. 181.
118. Ngai, *Ugly Feelings*, p. 335.
119. Ahmed, *Cultural Politics of Emotion*, p. 83.
120. Krečič and Žižek, 'Ugly, Creepy, Disgusting', p. 64.
121. Julia Kristeva, *Powers of Horror: An Essay on Abjection*, trans. Leon S. Roudiez (New York: Columbia University Press, 1982), p. 1.
122. Kristeva, *Powers of Horror*, p. 4.
123. Kristeva, *Powers of Horror*, p. 2.
124. Kristeva, *Powers of Horror*, p. 3.
125. Kristeva, *Powers of Horror*, p. 10.
126. Menninghaus, *Disgust*, p. 375.
127. Ahmed, *Cultural Politics of Emotion*, p. 87.
128. Pierre Bourdieu, *Distinction: A Social Critique of the Judgement of Taste*, trans. Richard Nice (London: Routledge, 1984), p. 495.
129. Bourdieu, *Distinction*, p. 490.
130. Miller, *Anatomy of Disgust*, p. 251.
131. Ahmed, *Cultural Politics of Emotion*, p. 99.
132. Kristeva, *Powers of Horror*, p. 13.
133. Ngai, *Ugly Feelings*, p. 340.
134. Ngai, *Ugly Feelings*, p. 344.
135. Clarice Lispector, *The Passion According to G.H.*, trans. Idra Novey (New York: New Directions, 2012 [1964]), p. 188.
136. Braidotti, *Metamorphoses*, p. 163.
137. Ngai, *Ugly Feelings*, pp. 348, 353.
138. Braidotti, *Metamorphoses*, p. 161.
139. Lispector, *Passion According to G.H.*, p. 181.
140. Braidotti, *Metamorphoses*, pp. 162, 165.
141. Lispector, *Passion According to G.H.*, p. 54.
142. Braidotti, *Metamorphoses*, p. 169.
143. Irving Goh, '*Le Toucher, le cafard*, or, On Touching – the Cockroach in Clarice Lispector's *The Passion According to G.H.*', *MLN*, 131 (2016), 461–80 (p. 462).
144. Lispector, *Passion According to G.H.*, pp. 46, 52.
145. Derrida, 'Economimesis', p. 25.
146. Brinkema, *Forms of the Affects*, p. 66.
147. Brinkema, *Forms of the Affects*, p. 67.
148. Derrida, 'Eating Well', p. 280.
149. Derrida, 'Eating Well', p. 281.
150. Derrida, 'Eating Well', p. 281.
151. Kristeva, *Powers of Horror*, p. 5.
152. Braidotti, *Metamorphoses*, p. 163.
153. Shaviro, 'Two Lessons from Burroughs', p. 53.

154. Bourdieu, *Distinction*, p. 491.
155. Miller, *Anatomy of Disgust*, p. 204.
156. Menninghaus, *Disgust*, p. 114.
157. Menninghaus, *Disgust*, p. 115.

Conclusion

What if what is 'proper' to humankind were to be inhabited by the inhuman?

Jean-François Lyotard[1]

Implicit in the conversations raised by this book is a sense of concern. Not only has our abuse of nonhuman animals reached unprecedented levels but we have also, it seems, entered a period of anthropogenic geological change, the Anthropocene, which 'blurs and even scrambles some crucial categories by which people have made sense of the world, and their lives'.[2] What is to be done? Is this crisis qualitatively different from previous crises, and if so, how? This book has been cautious about apocalyptic rhetoric and the redemptive oaths that tend to follow it, both in the Anthropocene context and more broadly, in relation to new materialist and posthumanist inclinations to downplay destructive, atavistic human tendencies. To identify such tendencies is not to insist that they pre-exist material conditions or reflect a transcendent human nature, but to pre-emptively recognise potential challenges to our crisis-response strategies. 'What is to be done?' is a question that this book is ill-equipped to answer; consequently, the book has focused on other, related questions: how should we structure our thinking in the context of crisis? Why should we continue to theorise and how? What model or models of humanity should we cultivate? While material conditions determine the reach of our actions, it matters how we think about ourselves; practical applications of human mastery enact and stabilise belief in human mastery.

Presupposing the ongoing value of theoretical approaches to these questions, this book has questioned and qualified the predominance of empathy-led responses to animal studies issues. Casting empathy as a mode of imaginative identification, it has stressed the necessity of retaining clear subjective boundaries for effective empathetic engagement. While exposing the consequences of empathetic deficits, particularly their role in reinforcing ethical hierarchies, it has addressed the tendency of empathetic responses to strengthen existing ethical ties, rather than generating new ones, and noted the risk of empathy creating 'a self-righteous monster instead of a good human being'.[3] It has examined literature as a privileged space for developing and extending empathy. Rebecca Solnit's description of empathy as an act of 'paying attention [. . .] of listening, of seeing, of imagining experiences other than one's own, of getting out of the boundaries of one's own experience' is also a description of close, careful reading.[4] Rather than perceiving literature as a protected space, distinct from politics, this book has repeatedly demonstrated that the text is a world-making space and that the tools we use within it – metaphor, trope, allegory – should be evaluated as better or worse tools of being-with, rather than assessed merely in terms of their representational value.

The argument that theory is of continuing, even increasing, value resonates in different registers. In a very rudimentary sense, as Andreas Malm notes, 'some theories can make the situation clearer while others might muddy it'.[5] His insistence on the employment of theory runs counter to the reductive suggestion that a material problem calls for a solely material solution. To some extent, new materialism is in thrall to such a suggestion, disavowing 'the deep attention required for interminable difficult reading' in the name of a, largely unmediated, relationship with matter.[6] For Malm, the claim of post-anthropocentrism which arrives with new materialism and posthumanism is not merely absurd, but dangerous, licensing a totalising repudiation of the distinctively human power that has generated our Anthropocene condition. He takes particular issue with Braidotti's contention that 'the concept of the human has exploded', a 'theoretical proposition' for which he cannot imagine 'worse historical timing'.[7]

Malm's critique uncovers the complexity of this historical moment, which problematically combines an awareness of the unprecedented scope of human power with increasing scientific and philosophical insight into our complex embeddedness within biological and technological networks. Malm is mistaken to assume that a declaration of the specificity of human responsibility requires a wholesale denial of such embeddedness, particularly in its manifestation in 'contemporary hybridism'.[8] Braidotti's statement gestures towards the problem of 'we', that of affirming species identity when responsibility for anthropogenic environmental destruction is so unevenly spread.[9] Astute in his criticisms of new materialism and of the dangers of unchecked constructionism, Malm responds to the problem of 'we' by endorsing the sedimentation of species identity in service of collective resistance alongside '*more radical polarisation*' in our approach to human communities.[10] The problem with Malm's response, however, is its inconsistent view of the theoretical; if scholars are unproductively 'hypnotised by the rigidities of language' and thus distracted from the genuinely political, then why is he so incensed by Braidotti's theoretical intervention?[11]

Unlike Malm, I am convinced, like Joanna Zylinska, that 'thinking is the most political thing we can do with regard to the Anthropocene'.[12] I am also convinced that Braidotti's assertion is neither banal, counter-productive, nor irrelevant. Rather, while I agree with Malm's deeply unfashionable proposal that '*a resistance can be conceived solely by affirmation of the most singularly human forms of agency*', I am persuaded that, rather than shoring up or rebirthing the figure of Man, a spectre insufficiently addressed by Malm's account, the 'explosion' or deconstruction of the human is compatible with resistance.[13] Such a deconstructive approach would hamper the unimpeded development of the figure of Man, now so ably assisted by the Anthropocene narrative; effective resistance is incompatible with Man. Here the Anthropocene narrative might be usefully repurposed. The Anthropocene exposes the duality of the human: on the one hand, its power, and on the other, its insufficiency. Power and mastery are not synonymous; we remain ultimately subjected to more than human economies, to 'a world that is not ourselves and a force that cannot be returned to the human'.[14]

While the possibility of collective human action is predicated on an understanding of the specificity of human agency and responsibility, as Malm recognises, the effectiveness of such action is dependent on a desire and perspective which transcends anthropocentrism to clearly see value and order beyond the human. This double movement has been in place throughout this book, which has advanced a reframing of the human in relation to that which it most strongly disavows, the inhuman, in tandem with a sustained attentiveness to living and non-living beings.

While it is perhaps a truism to note, as Judith Butler does, that 'where there is the human, there is the inhuman', the centrality of this truth to the development of philosophical and political structures cannot be overstated in a world where the anthropo-theological continues to serve as an organising force.[15] As the theological tone of so much Anthropocene scholarship demonstrates, the human has not adjusted to its own radical contingency. This is the lesson of disgust, best regarded as illuminating an evolutionary history whose implications we have largely disavowed. As Jeffrey Jerome Cohen observes, in the inhuman, this is doubly figured, emphasising 'both difference ("in-" as negative prefix) and intimacy ("in-" as indicator of estranged interiority)'.[16] In this sense, we might put empathy and disgust to work on the same task: that of familiarising oneself with this 'estranged interiority' as it emerges in nonhuman others and minimising its expression in conceptual and material violence, for as *carno-phallogocentrism* demonstrates, the anthropological difference always emerges violently. Rather than denying or looking to eradicate this impulse, in, for example, the temptation to treat the inhuman as a reservoir for the development of 'a posthuman and post-anthropocentric set of practices', we must accept and acknowledge it.[17] This demands a mode of 'noninnocent thinking', both in the sense of acknowledging the 'entanglement between the critical and speculative stance',[18] and, following Derrida, in the ethical injunction to cultivate the least worst violence, its eradication being impossible.[19]

NOTES

1. Jean-François Lyotard, *The Inhuman: Reflections on Time*, trans. Geoffrey Bennington and Rachel Bowlby (Cambridge: Polity, 1991), p. 2.
2. Clark, *Ecocriticism*, p. 9.
3. Koehn, *Rethinking Feminist Ethics*, p. 75.
4. Solnit, 'Men Explain Lolita to Me'.
5. Andreas Malm, *The Progress of this Storm: Nature and Society in a Warming World* (London: Verso, 2018), p. 16.
6. Brinkema, *Forms of the Affects*, p. xiv.
7. Malm, *Progress of this Storm*, p. 115.
8. Malm, *Progress of this Storm*, p. 149.
9. On this, see Zylinska, *Minimal Ethics*, p. 13.
10. Malm, *Progress of this Storm*, p. 189.
11. Malm, *Progress of this Storm*, p. 188.
12. Zylinska, *Minimal Ethics*, p. 125.
13. Malm, *Progress of this Storm*, p. 108.
14. Colebrook, *Death of the PostHuman*, p. 37.
15. Butler, *Frames of War*, p. 76
16. Cohen, *Stone*, p. 10.
17. Braidotti, *The Posthuman*, p. 109.
18. Bellacasa, *Matters of Care*, p. 204.
19. Jacques Derrida, 'Violence and Metaphysics: An Essay on the Thought of Emmanuel Levinas', in *Writing and Difference*, trans. Alan Bass (London: Routledge, 2005), pp. 97–192.

Bibliography

Aaltola, Elisa, *Varieties of Empathy: Moral Psychology and Animal Ethics* (New York: Rowman and Littlefield, 2018).

Adams, Carol, *The Sexual Politics of Meat: A Feminist-Vegetarian Critical Theory* (New York: Continuum, 1999).

Adams, Jenni, *Magic Realism in Holocaust Literature* (London: Palgrave Macmillan, 2011).

Adorno, Theodor W., 'Commitment', in *Notes to Literature Volume II*, ed. Rolf Tiedemann, trans. Shierry Weber Nicholsen (New York: Columbia University Press, 1992), pp. 76–94.

Adorno, Theodor W., *Negative Dialectics*, trans. E. B. Ashton (London: Routledge, 1973).

Adorno Theodor W., 'Trying to Understand *Endgame*', in *Notes to Literature Volume I*, ed. Rolf Tiedemann, trans. Shierry Weber Nicholsen (New York: Columbia University Press, 1991), pp. 241–76.

Adorno, Theodor W., and Max Horkheimer, *Dialectic of Enlightenment*, trans. John Cumming (London: Verso, 2010).

Agamben, Giorgio, *Homo Sacer: Sovereign Power and Bare Life*, trans. Daniel Heller-Roazen (Stanford: Stanford University Press, 1998).

Agamben, Giorgio, *The Open: Man and Animal*, trans. Kevin Attell (Stanford: Stanford University Press, 2004).

Agosta, Lou, *Empathy in the Context of Philosophy* (New York: Palgrave Macmillan, 2010).

Ahmed, Sara, *The Cultural Politics of Emotion* (Edinburgh: Edinburgh University Press, 2014).

Alaimo, Stacy, *Exposed: Environmental Politics and Pleasures in Posthuman Times* (Minneapolis: University of Minnesota Press, 2016).

Aloi, Giovanni, *Art and Animals* (London: I.B. Tauris, 2012).

Anderson, Mark M., 'Sliding Down the Evolutionary Ladder? Aesthetic Autonomy in *The Metamorphosis*', in Harold Bloom (ed.), *Franz Kafka's The Metamorphosis* (New York: Chelsea House, 2008), pp. 79–94.

Andrews, David, *Aestheticism, Nabokov and Lolita* (Lewiston, NY: Edwin Mellen Press, 1990).

Andrews, Kristin, and Lori Gruen, 'Empathy in Other Apes', in Heidi L.

Maibom (ed.), *Empathy and Morality* (Oxford: Oxford University Press, 2014), pp. 193–209.

Angelis, Richard de, 'Of Mice and Vermin: Animals as Absent Referent in Art Spiegelman's *Maus*', *IJOCA*, 7.1 (2005), 230–49.

Arendt, Hannah, *Origins of Totalitarianism* (New York: Meridian, 1958).

Armstrong, Philip, *What Animals Mean in the Fiction of Modernity* (Abingdon: Routledge, 2008).

Bailey, Cathryn, 'On the Backs of Animals: The Valorization of Reason in Contemporary Animal Ethics', *Ethics and the Environment*, 10.1 (2005), 1–17.

Barad, Karen, *Meeting the Universe Halfway: Quantum Physics and the Entanglement of Matter and Meaning* (Durham, NC: Duke University Press, 2007).

Barkham, Patrick, *The Butterfly Isles: A Summer in Search of Our Emperors and Admirals* (London: Granta, 2010).

Batson, Dan, 'Empathy, Altruism and Helping: Conceptual Distinctions, Empirical Relations', in Neil Roughley and Thomas Schramme (eds), *Forms of Fellow Feeling: Empathy, Sympathy, Concern and Moral Agency* (Cambridge: Cambridge University Press, 2018), pp. 59–77.

Beer, Gillian, 'Introduction', in Charles Darwin, *On the Origin of Species* (Oxford: Oxford University Press, 2008).

Bekoff, Marc, *Minding Animals: Awareness, Emotions and Heart* (Oxford: Oxford University Press, 2002).

Bellacasa, Maria Puig de la, *Matters of Care: Speculative Ethics in More Than Human Worlds* (Minneapolis: University of Minnesota Press, 2017).

Benjamin, Marina, 'To Have and to Hold', in Kate Salway (ed.), *Collectors' Items* (London: Pale Green Press, 1996), pp. 10–31.

Benjamin, Walter, *Illuminations*, trans. Harry Zohn, ed. Hannah Arendt (New York: Schocken Books, 1969).

Bennett, Jane, 'Systems and Things: A Response to Graham Harman and Timothy Morton', *New Literary History*, 43 (2012), 225–33.

Bennett, Jane, *Vibrant Matter: A Political Ecology of Things* (Durham, NC: Duke University Press, 2010).

Berger, Anne Emanuelle, and Marta Segarra, 'Thoughtprints', in Anne Emanuelle Berger and Marta Segarra (eds), *Demenageries: Thinking (of) Animals after Derrida*, special issue of *Critical Studies*, 35 (2011), 3–22.

Berger, John, *Ways of Seeing* (London: Penguin, 2008 [1972]).

Berger, John, *Why Look at Animals?* (London: Penguin, 2009).

Berlatsky, Eric L., *The Real, the True and the Told: Postmodern Historical Narrative and the Ethics of Representation* (Columbus: Ohio State University Press, 2011).

Bernasconi, Robert, 'The Trace of Levinas in Derrida', in David Wood and Robert Bernasconi (eds), *Derrida and Différance* (Evanston: Northwestern University Press, 1988), pp. 13–29.

Birkeland, Janis, 'Ecofeminism: Linking Theory and Practice', in Greta Gaard (ed.), *Ecofeminism: Women, Animals, Nature* (Philadelphia: Temple University Press, 1993), pp. 13–59.

Blackman, Lisa, *Immaterial Bodies: Affect, Embodiment, Mediation* (London: Sage, 2012).

Bloom, Paul, *Against Empathy: The Case for Radical Compassion* (London: Vintage, 2017).

Bogost, Ian, *Alien Phenomenology or What It's Like to Be a Thing* (Minneapolis: University of Minnesota Press, 2012).

Bouchet, Marie, 'Nabokov's Text Under the Microscope: Textual Practices of Detail in his Lepidopterological and Fictional Writings', in Laurence Talairach-Vielmas and Marie Bouchet (eds), *Insects in Literature and the Arts* (Brussels: P.I.E. Peter Lang, 2014), pp. 81–97.

Bourdieu, Pierre, *Distinction: A Social Critique of the Judgement of Taste*, trans. Richard Nice (London: Routledge, 1984).

Braidotti, Rosi, *Metamorphoses: Towards a Materialist Theory of Becoming* (Cambridge: Polity, 2002).

Braidotti, Rosi, *The Posthuman* (Cambridge: Polity, 2013).

Brennan, Teresa, *The Transmission of Affect* (Ithaca, NY: Cornell University Press, 2004).

Brinkema, Eugenie, *The Forms of the Affects* (Durham, NC: Duke University Press, 2015).

Brinkema, Eugenie, 'Laura Dern's Vomit, or, Kant and Derrida in Oz', *Film-Philosophy*, 15.2 (2011), 51–69.

Broglio, Ron, *Surface Encounters: Thinking with Animals and Art* (Minneapolis: University of Minnesota Press, 2011).

Bronfen, Elisabeth, *Over Her Dead Body: Death, Femininity and the Aesthetic* (Manchester: Manchester University Press, 1992).

Brown, Nathan, 'The Nadir of OOO from Graham Harman's *Tool-Being* to Timothy Morton's *Realist Magic: Objects, Ontology, Causality* (Open Humanities Press, 2013)', *Parrhesia*, 17 (2013), 62–71.

Burghardt, Gordon, 'Animal Awareness: Current Perceptions and Historical Perspectives', *American Psychologist*, 40 (1985), 905–19.

Butler, Judith, *Frames of War: When is Life Grievable?* (London: Verso, 2016).

Butler, Judith, *Precarious Life: The Powers of Mourning and Violence* (London: Verso, 2004).

Butler, Judith, *Senses of the Subject* (New York: Fordham University Press, 2015).

Caillois, Roger, *The Edge of Surrealism: A Roger Caillois Reader*, ed. Claudine Frank (Durham, NC: Duke University Press, 2003).

Calarco, Matthew, 'Boundary Issues: Human–Animal Relationships in Karen Joy Fowler's *We Are All Completely Beside Ourselves*', *Modern Fiction Studies*, 60.3 (2014), 616–35.

Chakrabarty, Dipesh, 'The Climate of History: Four Theses', *Critical Inquiry*, 35.2 (2009), 197–222.

Churchwell, Sarah, '*Beatrice and Virgil* by Yann Martel', *The Observer*, 30

May 2010, https://www.theguardian.com/books/2010/may/30/yann-mart ell-beatrice-and-virgil (accessed 20 March 2019).

Clark, J. F. M., *Bugs and the Victorians* (New Haven, CT: Yale University Press, 2009).

Clark, Timothy, *Ecocriticism on the Edge: The Anthropocene as a Threshold Concept* (London: Bloomsbury, 2015).

Clough, Patricia Ticineto, 'Introduction', in Patricia Ticineto Clough with Jean Halley (eds), *The Affective Turn: Theorizing the Social* (Durham, NC: Duke University Press, 2007), pp. 1–33.

Coetzee, J. M., *The Lives of Animals*, The Tanner Lectures on Human Values, Princeton University, 15 and 16 October 1997, https://tannerlectures.utah. edu/_documents/a-to-z/c/Coetzee99.pdf (accessed 18 February 2019).

Cohen, Jeffrey Jerome, *Stone: An Ecology of the Inhuman* (Minneapolis: University of Minnesota Press, 2015).

Cohen, Tom, and Claire Colebrook, 'Preface', in Tom Cohen, Claire Colebrook and J. Hillis Miller (eds), *The Twilight of the Anthropocene Idols* (London: Open Humanities Press, 2016), pp. 7–19.

Cole, Stewart, 'Believing in Tigers: Anthropomorphism and Incredulity in Yann Martel's *Life of Pi*', *Studies in Canadian Literature*, 29.2 (2004), 22–36.

Colebrook, Claire, 'The Calculus of Individual Worth', in Tom Cohen, Claire Colebrook and J. Hillis Miller, *Theory and the Disappearing Future: On De Man, on Benjamin* (London: Routledge, 2012), pp. 130–52.

Colebrook, Claire, *Death of the PostHuman: Essays on Extinction, Vol. 1* (London: Open Humanities Press, 2014).

Colebrook, Claire, 'Not Symbiosis, Not Now: Why Anthropogenic Change is Not Really Human', *Oxford Literary Review*, 34.2 (2012), 185–209.

Colebrook, Claire, *Sex After Life: Essays on Extinction, Vol. 2* (London: Open Humanities Press, 2014).

Colebrook, Claire, 'What is the Anthropo-Political?', in Tom Cohen, Claire Colebrook and J. Hillis Miller (eds), *The Twilight of the Anthropocene Idols* (London: Open Humanities Press, 2016), pp. 81–125.

Conradi, Peter, *John Fowles* (London: Methuen, 1982).

Coplan, Amy, 'Empathetic Engagement with Narrative Fictions', *The Journal of Aesthetics and Art Criticism*, 62.2 (2004), 141–52.

Coplan, Amy, 'Understanding Empathy: Its Features and Effects', in Amy Coplan and Peter Goldie (eds), *Empathy: Philosophical and Psychological Perspectives* (Oxford: Oxford University Press, 2011), pp. 3–18.

Coplan, Amy, and Peter Goldie, 'Introduction', in Amy Coplan and Peter Goldie (eds), *Empathy: Philosophical and Psychological Perspectives* (Oxford: Oxford University Press, 2011), pp. ix–xlvii.

Coupland, Douglas, *Generation A* (London: Windmill Books, 2009).

Crace, Jim, *The Gift of Stones* (London: Vintage, 1997).

Crace, Jim, *Harvest* (London: Picador, 2013).

Crace, Jim, *Quarantine* (London: Picador, 2010).

Crace, Jim, *Signals of Distress* (London: Picador, 2008).

Crist, Eileen, *Images of Animals: Anthropomorphism and Animal Mind* (Philadelphia: Temple University Press, 1999).

Crist, Eileen, and H. Bruce Rinke, 'One Grand Organic Whole', in Eileen Crist and H. Bruce Rinke (eds), *Gaia in Turmoil: Climate Change, Biodepletion, and Earth Ethics in an Age of Crisis* (Cambridge, MA: MIT Press, 2010), pp. 315–34.

Critchley, Simon, *Ethics, Politics, Subjectivity: Essays on Derrida, Levinas and Contemporary French Thought* (London: Verso, 1999).

Darwin, Charles, *The Descent of Man* (London: Wordsworth Editions, 2013 [1871]).

Darwin, Charles, *On the Origin of Species*, ed. Gillian Beer (Oxford: Oxford University Press, 2008).

Daston, Lorraine, 'Intelligences: Angelic, Animal, Human', in Lorraine Daston and Gregg Mitman (eds), *Thinking with Animals: New Perspectives on Anthropomorphism* (New York: Columbia University Press, 2005), pp. 37–58.

Daston, Lorraine, and Gregg Mitman, 'The How and Why of Thinking with Animals', in Lorraine Daston and Gregg Mitman (eds), *Thinking with Animals: New Perspectives on Anthropomorphism* (New York: Columbia University Press, 2005), pp. 1–14.

Davidson, Tonya K., Ondine Part and Rob Shields, 'Introduction', in Tonya K. Davidson, Ondine Part and Rob Shields (eds), *Ecologies of Affect: Placing Nostalgia, Desire and Hope* (Waterloo, Ont.: Wilfrid Laurier University Press, 2011), pp. 1–15.

Davis, Karen, *The Holocaust and the Henmaid's Tale: A Case for Comparing Atrocities* (New York: Lantern Books, 2005).

De Boever, Arne, *States of Exception in the Contemporary Novel: Martel, Eugenides, Coetzee, Sebald* (London: Continuum, 2012).

de Waal, Frans, *The Age of Empathy: Nature's Lessons for a Kinder Society* (London: Souvenir Press, 2010).

de Waal, Frans, *The Bonobo and the Atheist* (New York: W.W. Norton, 2013).

de Waal, Frans, *Chimpanzee Politics: Power and Sex Amongst Apes* (Baltimore: Johns Hopkins University Press, 2007).

de Waal, Frans, *Good Natured: The Origins of Right and Wrong in Humans and Other Animals* (Cambridge, MA: Harvard University Press, 1996).

de Waal, Frans, 'Towards a Bottom-up Perspective on Human and Animal Cognition', *Trends in Cognitive Sciences*, 14.5 (2000), 201–7.

Dee, Tim, *The Running Sky* (London: Vintage, 2009).

Derrida, Jacques, *The Animal That Therefore I Am*, trans. David Wills (Ashland, OH: Fordham University Press, 2008).

Derrida, Jacques, *The Beast and the Sovereign: Volume I*, trans. Geoffrey Bennington (Chicago: University of Chicago Press, 2009).

Derrida, Jacques, 'Deconstruction and the Other', in Richard Kearney (ed.), *States of Mind: Dialogues with Contemporary Thinkers on the European Mind* (Manchester: Manchester University Press, 1995), pp. 156–76.

Derrida, Jacques, '"Eating Well," or the Calculation of the Subject', in *Points… Interviews 1974–1994*, ed. Elisabeth Weber, trans. Peter Connor and Avital Ronell (Stanford: Stanford University Press, 1995), pp. 255–87.

Derrida, Jacques, 'Economimesis', trans. R. Klein, *Diacritics*, 11.2 (1981), 2–25.

Derrida, Jacques, 'The Ends of Man', in *Margins of Philosophy*, trans. Alan Bass (Chicago: University of Chicago Press, 1972), pp. 111–36.

Derrida, Jacques, *Learning to Live Finally: An Interview with Jean Birnbaum* (Hoboken, NJ: Melville House Publishing, 2007).

Derrida, Jacques, *Limited Inc.*, ed. Gerald Graff, trans. Samuel Weber and Jeffrey Mehlman (Evanston: Northwestern University Press, 1988).

Derrida, Jacques, *Of Grammatology*, trans. Gayatri Spivak (Baltimore: Johns Hopkins University Press, 1976).

Derrida, Jacques, *Rogues: Two Essays on Reason*, trans. Pascale-Anne Brault and Michael Naas (Stanford: Stanford University Press, 2005).

Derrida, Jacques, '"This Strange Institution Called Literature": An Interview with Jacques Derrida', trans. and ed. Rachel Bowlby, in *Acts of Literature*, ed. Derek Attridge (London: Routledge, 1992), pp. 33–75.

Derrida, Jacques, *The Truth in Painting*, trans. Geoffrey Bennington and Ian McLeod (Chicago: University of Chicago Press, 1987).

Derrida, Jacques, 'Violence and Metaphysics: An Essay on the Thought of Emmanuel Levinas', in *Writing and Difference*, trans. Alan Bass (London: Routledge, 2005), pp. 97–192.

Diamond, Cora, 'The Difficulty of Reality and the Difficulty of Philosophy', *Partial Answers: Journal of Literature and the History of Ideas*, 1.2 (2003), 1–26.

Diamond, Cora, 'Injustice and Animals', in Carl Elliott (ed.), *Slow Cures and Bad Philosophers: Essays on Wittgenstein, Medicine and Bioethics* (Durham, NC: Duke University Press, 2001), pp. 118–48.

Dundar, Robin, 'The Apes as We Want to See Them', *The New York Times*, 7 January 1990, https://www.nytimes.com/1990/01/07/books/the-apes-as-we-want-to-see-them.html (accessed 18 February 2019).

Durantaye, Leland de la, 'Eichmann, Empathy and Lolita', *Philosophy and Literature*, 30.2 (2006), 311–28.

Eaglestone, Robert, *The Holocaust and the Postmodern* (Oxford: Oxford University Press, 2004).

Edelman, Lee, *No Future: Queer Theory and the Death Drive* (Durham, NC: Duke University Press, 2004).

Eisenberg, Nancy, 'Empathy and Sympathy', in Michael Lewis and Jeannette M. Haviland Jones (eds), *Handbook of Emotions* (New York: The Guildford Press, 2000), pp. 677–92.

Eisenberg, Nancy, 'Empathy-related Responding and Prosocial Behaviour', in *Empathy and Fairness: Novartis Foundation Symposium 278* (Chichester: Wiley, 2007), pp. 71–88.

Elmarsafy, Ziad, 'Aping the Ape: Kafka's "Report to an Academy"', *Studies in Twentieth Century Literature*, 2 (1995), 159–70.

Fabre, Jean-Henri, *The Life of the Spider* (New York: Dodd, Mead and Co., 1913).

Fabre, Jean Henri, 'The Song of the Cigal', in Charles Neider (ed.), *The Fabulous Insects* (New York: Harper and Brothers, 1954), pp. 116–27.

Finkelstein, Norman G., *The Holocaust Industry: Reflections on the Exploitation of Jewish Suffering* (London: Verso, 2000).

Fisher, John Andrew, 'The Myth of Anthropomorphism', in Marc Bekoff and Dale Jamieson (eds), *Readings in Animal Cognition* (Cambridge, MA: MIT Press, 1995), pp. 3–15.

Foucault, Michel, *The Order of Things: An Archaeology of the Human Sciences* (London: Routledge, 2002 [1966]).

Fowler, Karen Joy, *The Science of Herself* (Oakland: PM Press, 2013).

Fowler, Karen Joy, *We Are All Completely Beside Ourselves* (London: Serpent's Tail, 2013).

Fowles, John, *The Collector* (London: Vintage, 2004 [1963]).

Fowles, John, 'Introduction', in Kate Salway (ed.), *Collectors' Items* (London: The Pale Green Press, 1996), pp. 8–9.

French, Marilyn, *Beyond Power: Women, Men and Morals* (London: Abacus, 1985).

Gaard, Greta, 'Living Interconnections with Animals and Nature', in Greta Gaard (ed.), *Ecofeminism: Women, Animals, Nature* (Philadelphia: Temple University Press, 1993), pp. 1–12.

Gallese, Vittorio, 'Embodied Simulation: From Mirror Neuron Systems to Interpersonal Relations', in *Empathy and Fairness: Novartis Foundation Symposium 278* (Chichester: Wiley, 2007), pp. 3–19.

Geary, James, *I Is An Other: The Secret Life of Metaphor and How it Shapes the Way we See the World* (New York: Harper Collins, 2011).

Geis, Deborah, R., 'Introduction', in Deborah R. Geis (ed.), *Considering Maus: Approaches to Art Spiegelman's 'Survivor's Tale'* (Tuscaloosa: University of Alabama Press, 2003), pp. 1–14.

Gifford, Terry, 'Afterword: New Senses of Environment', in David James and Philip Tew (eds), *New Versions of Pastoral: Post-Romantic, Modern and Contemporary Responses to the Tradition* (Madison, WI: Fairleigh Dickinson University Press, 2009), pp. 245–57.

Goh, Irving, 'Le Toucher, le cafard, or, On Touching – the Cockroach in Clarice Lispector's *The Passion According to G.H.*', MLN, 131 (2016), 461–80.

Goldie, Peter, 'How We Think of Others' Emotions', *Mind and Language*, 14.4 (1999), 394–423.

Gottschall, Jonathan, *The Storytelling Animal: How Stories Make Us Human* (Wilmington, MA: Mariner Books, 2013).

Gould, Stephen Jay, 'A Lover's Quarrel', in Marc Bekoff (ed.), *The Smile of a Dolphin: Remarkable Accounts of Animal Emotions* (London: Discovery, 2000), pp. 13–17.

Gregg, Melissa, and Gregory J. Seigworth, 'An Inventory of Shimmers', in

Melissa Gregg and Gregory J. Seigworth (eds), *The Affect Theory Reader* (Durham, NC: Duke University Press, 2010), pp. 1–28.

Grosz, Elizabeth, 'Animal Sex: Libido as Desire and Death', in Elizabeth Grosz and Elspeth Probyn (eds), *Sexy Bodies: The Strange Carnalities of Feminism* (London: Routledge, 1995), pp. 278–99.

Grosz, Elizabeth, *Becoming Undone: Darwinian Reflections on Life, Politics and Art* (Durham, NC: Duke University Press, 2011).

Grosz, Elizabeth, *Chaos, Territory, Art: Deleuze and the Framing of the Earth* (New York: Columbia University Press, 2008).

Grosz, Elizabeth, 'The Creative Impulse', interview, 14 August 2005, http://www.abc.net.au/rn/legacy/programs/sunmorn/stories/s1435592.htm (accessed 18 February 2019).

Gruen, Lori, 'Dismantling Oppression: An Analysis of the Connection Between Women and Animals', in Greta Gaard (ed.), *Ecofeminism: Women, Animals, Nature* (Philadelphia: Temple University Press, 1993), pp. 60–90.

Gruen, Lori, *Entangled Empathy: An Alternative Ethic for our Relationships with Animals* (New York: Lantern Books, 2015).

Hage, Ravi, *Cockroach* (Toronto: Anansi, 2008).

Harel, Naama, 'Deallegorizing Kafka's Ape: Two Animalistic Contexts', in Marc Lucht and Donna Yarri (eds), *Kafka's Creatures: Animals, Hybrids, and Other Fantastic Beings* (Lanham, MD: Rowman and Littlefield, 2010), pp. 53–66.

Haraway, Donna, 'Anthropocene, Capitalocene, Plantationocene, Chthulucene: Making Kin', *Environmental Humanities*, 6 (2015), 159–65.

Haraway, Donna, *The Companion Species Manifesto: Dogs, People and Significant Otherness* (Chicago: Prickly Paradigm Press, 2003).

Haraway, Donna, 'In the Beginning was the Word: The Genesis of Biological Theory', *Signs*, 6.3 (1981), 469–81.

Haraway, Donna, *Manifestly Haraway* (Minneapolis: University of Minnesota Press, 2016).

Haraway, Donna, *Primate Visions: Gender, Race and Nature in the World of Modern Science* (London: Verso, 1989).

Haraway, Donna, *Simians, Cyborgs and Women: The Reinvention of Nature* (New York: Routledge, 1991).

Haraway, Donna, 'Situated Knowledges: The Science Question in Feminism and the Privilege of the Partial Perspective', *Feminist Studies*, 14.3 (1988), 575–99.

Haraway, Donna, *Staying with the Trouble: Making Kin in the Chthulucene* (Durham, NC: Duke University Press, 2016).

Haraway, Donna, *When Species Meet* (Minneapolis: University of Minnesota Press, 2008).

Haraway, Donna, 'When We Have Never Been Human, What Is To Be Done?', *Theory, Culture and Society*, 23.7–8 (2006), 135–58.

Harding, Wendy, 'Insects and Texts: Worlds Apart', in Laurence Talairach-

Vielmas and Marie Bouchet (eds), *Insects in Literature and the Arts* (Brussels: P.I.E. Peter Lang, 2014), pp. 219–34.

Harman, Graham, 'Aesthetics as First Philosophy: Levinas and the Non-Human', *Naked Punch* (2012), http://www.nakedpunch.com/articles/147 (accessed 14 July 2016).

Harman, Graham, 'Art Without Relations', *ArtReview*, September 2014, http://artreview.com/features/september_2014_graham_harman_relations/ (accessed 14 July 2016).

Harman, Graham, *Guerrilla Metaphysics* (Chicago: Open Court, 2004).

Harman, Graham, *Immaterialism: Objects and Social Theory* (Cambridge: Polity, 2016).

Harman, Graham, 'Materialism is Not the Solution: On Matter, Form and Mimesis', *The Nordic Journal of Aesthetics*, 47 (2014), 94–100.

Harman, Graham, 'On Vicarious Causation', *Collapse*, II, (2007), 171–205.

Harman, Graham, *Prince of Networks: Bruno Latour and Metaphysics* (Melbourne: re.press, 2009).

Harman, Graham, *Towards Speculative Realism: Essays and Lectures* (Winchester: Zero Books, 2010).

Harrison, Peter, 'Linnaeus as a Second Adam? Taxonomy as a Religious Vocation', *Zygon*, 44 (2009), 879–93.

Heidegger, Martin, 'The Origin of the Work of Art', in *Off the Beaten Track*, ed. and trans. Julian Young and Kenneth Haynes (Cambridge: Cambridge University Press, 2002), pp. 1–56.

Heller, Chaia, 'For the Love of Nature: Ecology and the Cult of the Romantic', in Greta Gaard (ed.), *Ecofeminism: Women, Animals, Nature* (Philadelphia: Temple University Press, 1993), pp. 219–42.

Herman, David, 'Storyworld/Umwelt: Nonhuman Experiences in Graphic Narratives', *SubStance*, 40.1 (2011), 156–81.

Hird, Myra J., 'Waste, Landfills, and an Environmental Ethic of Vulnerability', *Ethics and the Environment*, 18.1 (2013), 105–24.

Hirsch, Marianne, *The Generation of Postmemory: Writing and Visual Culture after the Holocaust* (New York: Columbia University Press, 2012).

Hirst, Damien, 'Damien Hirst, 4 April–9 September 2012', exhibition booklet, Tate Modern, 2012.

Hirst, Damien, and Gordon Burn, *On the Way to Work* (London: Faber and Faber, 2001).

Hodder, Ian, *Entangled: An Archaeology of the Relationships between Humans and Things* (Malden, MA: Wiley-Blackwell, 2012).

Holton, Richard, and Rae Langton, 'Empathy and Animal Ethics', in Dale Jamieson (ed.), *Singer and his Critics* (Oxford: Blackwell, 1999), pp. 209–32.

Hoffman, Martin L., 'Empathy, Justice, and Social Change', in Heide L. Maibom (ed.), *Empathy and Morality* (New York: Oxford University Press, 2014), pp. 1–40.

Hoffman, Martin L., *Empathy and Moral Development: Implications for Caring and Justice* (Cambridge: Cambridge University Press, 2000).

Huffaker, Robert, *John Fowles* (Boston: G. K. Hall, 1980).

Jensen, Liz, '*We Are All Completely Beside Ourselves* review – "A Provocative Take on Family Love"', *The Guardian*, 20 March 2014, https://www.the-guardian.com/books/2014/mar/20/completely-beside-ourselves-family-love-review (accessed 18 February 2019).

John, Eileen, 'Empathy in Literature', in Heidi L. Maibom (ed.), *The Routledge Handbook of Philosophy of Empathy* (London: Routledge, 2017).

Johnson, Kurt, and Steve Coates, *Nabokov's Blues: The Scientific Odyssey of a Literary Genius* (New York: McGraw-Hill, 1999).

Josipovici, Gabriel, *The World and the Book* (St Albans: Paladin, 1973).

Kakutani, Michiko, 'From "Life of Pi" Author: Stuffed-Animal Allegory about Holocaust', *The New York Times*, 12 April 2010, https://www.nytimes.com/2010/04/13/books/13book.html (accessed 20 March 2019).

Kant, Immanuel, *Critique of the Power of Judgment*, trans. Paul Guyer (Cambridge: Cambridge University Press, 2000).

Kaufman, Linda S., *Special Delivery: Epistolary Modes in Modern Fiction* (Chicago: University of Chicago Press, 1992).

Kearney, Richard, *Anatheism: Returning to God after God* (New York: Columbia University Press, 2010).

Keen, Suzanne, *Empathy and the Novel* (Oxford: Oxford University Press, 2007).

Kim, Claire Jean, *Dangerous Crossings: Race, Species, and Nature in a Multicultural Age* (Cambridge: Cambridge University Press, 2015).

Kingsolver, Barbara, *Flight Behaviour* (London: Faber and Faber, 2012).

Kingsolver, Barbara, 'The Other Sister: Karen Joy Fowler's *We Are All Completely Beside Ourselves*', *New York Times*, 6 June 2013, http://www.nytimes.com/2013/06/09/books/review/karen-joy-fowlers-we-are-all-completely-beside-ourselves.html (accessed 18 February 2019).

Koehn, Daryl, *Rethinking Feminist Ethics: Care, Trust and Empathy* (London: Routledge, 1998).

Kolodny, Annette, *The Lay of the Land: Metaphor as Experience and History in American Life and Letters* (Chapel Hill: University of North Carolina Press, 1975).

Krečič, Jela, and Slavoj Žižek, 'Ugly, Creepy, Disgusting, and Other Modes of Abjection', *Critical Inquiry*, 43.1 (2016), 60–83.

Kristeva, Julia, *Powers of Horror: An Essay on Abjection*, trans. Leon S. Roudiez (New York: Columbia University Press, 1982).

Langer, Lawrence L., *Using and Abusing the Holocaust* (Bloomington: Indiana University Press, 2006).

Latour, Bruno, *Facing Gaia: Eight Lectures on the New Climatic Regime* (Cambridge: Polity, 2017).

Latour, Bruno, 'On Interobjectivity', *Mind, Culture, Activity*, 3.4 (1996), 228–45.

Latour, Bruno, 'Waiting for Gaia. Composing the Common World through Arts and Politics', a lecture at the French Institute, London, November

2011, http://www.bruno-latour.fr/sites/default/files/124-GAIA-LONDON-SPEAP_0.pdf (accessed 18 February 2019).

Latour, Bruno, *We Have Never Been Modern*, trans. Catherine Porter (London: Harvester Wheatsheaf, 1993).

Latour, Bruno, 'Where Are the Missing Masses? The Sociology of a Few Mundane Artifacts', in Wiebe Bijker and John Law (eds), *Shaping Technology – Building Society* (Cambridge, MA: MIT Press, 1992), pp. 151–80.

Latour, Bruno, 'Why Has Critique Run Out of Steam? From Matters of Fact to Matters of Concern', *Critical Inquiry*, 30.2 (2004), 225–48.

Lispector, Clarice, *The Passion According to G.H.*, trans. Idra Novey (New York: New Directions, 2012 [1964]).

Llewelyn, John, 'Thresholds', in David Wood and Robert Bernasconi (eds), *Derrida and Différance* (Evanston: Northwestern University Press, 1988), pp. 51–62.

Lo Dico, Joy, 'Beatrice and Virgil, by Yann Martel', *The Independent*, 30 May 2010, https://www.independent.co.uk/arts-entertainment/books/reviews/beatrice-and-virgil-by-yann-martel-1984399.html (accessed 20 March 2019).

Loo, Stephen, and Undine Sellbach, 'Insect Affects', *Angelaki*, 20.3 (2015), 79–88.

Lovelock, James, *The Revenge of Gaia: Why the Earth is Fighting Back – And How We Can Still Save Humanity* (London: Allen Lane, 2006).

Mabey, Richard, *The Oxford Book of Nature Writing* (Oxford: Oxford University Press, 1995).

Macarthur, John, *The Picturesque: Architecture, Disgust and Other Irregularities* (London: Routledge, 2007).

Maibom, Heide L., 'Introduction: (Almost) Everything You Ever Wanted to Know about Empathy', in Heide L. Maibom (ed.), *Empathy and Morality* (New York: Oxford University Press, 2014), pp. 1–40.

Malabou, Catherine, *What Should We Do With Our Brain?* (New York: Fordham University Press, 2008).

Malm, Andreas, *The Progress of this Storm: Nature and Society in a Warming World* (London: Verso, 2018).

Marren, Peter, *Rainbow Dust: Three Centuries of Delight in British Butterflies* (London: Vintage, 2015).

Marsh, Abigail A., 'Empathy and Moral Deficits in Psychopathy', in Heide L. Maibom (ed.), *Empathy and Morality* (New York: Oxford University Press, 2014), pp. 138–54.

Martel, Yann, *Beatrice and Virgil* (Edinburgh: Canongate, 2010).

Martel, Yann, *The Facts behind the Helsinki Roccamatios and Other Stories* (Edinburgh: Canongate, 2005).

Martel, Yann, *The High Mountains of Portugal* (Edinburgh: Canongate, 2016).

Martel, Yann, *Life of Pi* (Edinburgh: Canongate, 2009).

Massumi, Brian, *Politics of Affect* (Cambridge: Polity, 2015).

Matravers, Derek, *Empathy* (Cambridge: Polity, 2017).

May, Joshua, 'Empathy and Intersubjectivity', in Heide L. Maibom (ed.), *The Routledge Handbook of Philosophy of Empathy* (London: Routledge, 2017).

McCarthy, Michael, *The Moth Snowstorm: Nature and Joy* (London: John Murray, 2015).

McFarland, Sarah E., 'Animal Studies, Literary Animals, and Yann Martel's *Life of Pi*', in Louise Westling (ed.), *The Cambridge Companion to Literature and the Environment* (Cambridge: Cambridge University Press, 2014), pp. 152–68.

McHugh, Susan, *Animal Stories: Narrating Across Species Lines* (Minneapolis: University of Minnesota Press, 2011).

Meillassoux, Quentin, *After Finitude: An Essay on the Necessity of Contingency*, trans. Ray Brassier (London: Continuum, 2008).

Menninghaus, Winfried, *Disgust: Theory and History of a Strong Sensation*, trans. Howard Eiland and Joel Golb (Albany, NY: SUNY Press, 2003).

Mensch, James, 'Empathy and Rationality', in Barbara Weber, Eva Marsal and Takara Dobashi (eds), *The Politics of Empathy: New Interdisciplinary Perspectives on an Ancient Phenomenon* (Berlin: Lit, 2011), pp. 17–24.

Mensch, James, 'The Intertwining of Incommensurables: Yann Martel's *Life of Pi*', in Corinne Painter and Christian Lotz (eds), *Phenomenology and the Non-Human Animals: At the Limits of Experience* (Dordrecht: Springer, 2007), pp. 135–47.

Merchant, Carolyn, *The Death of Nature: Women, Ecology and the Scientific Revolution* (San Francisco: Harper, 1980).

Mikics, David, 'Underground Comics and Survival Tales: *Maus* in Context', in Deborah R. Geis (ed.), *Considering Maus: Approaches to Art Spiegelman's 'Survivor's Tale'* (Tuscaloosa: University of Alabama Press, 2003), pp. 15–25.

Miller, Andrew, *Pure* (London: Sceptre, 2011).

Miller, William Ian, *The Anatomy of Disgust* (Cambridge, MA: Harvard University Press, 1997).

Milton, Kay, 'Anthropomorphism or Egomorphism? The Perception of Nonhuman Persons by Human Ones', in John Knight (ed.), *Animals in Person: Cultural Perspectives on Human–Animal Intimacies* (London: Berg, 2005), pp. 255–71.

Moore, Bryan L., *Ecology and Literature: Ecocentric Personification from Antiquity to the Twenty-First Century* (New York: Palgrave Macmillan, 2008).

Morton, Timothy, *Ecology Without Nature: Rethinking Environmental Aesthetics* (Cambridge, MA: Harvard University Press, 2007).

Morton, Timothy, *Humankind: Solidarity with Nonhuman People* (London: Verso, 2017).

Mulvey, Laura, 'Visual Pleasure and Narrative Cinema', in Patricia Erens (ed.), *Issues in Feminist Film Criticism* (Bloomington: Indiana University Press, 1990), pp. 28–40.

Nabokov, Vladimir, *Lolita* (London: Penguin, 2000).

Nabokov, Vladimir, 'On Discovering a Butterfly', *The New Yorker*, 15 May 1943, p. 26.

Nabokov, Vladimir, *Strong Opinions* (London: Penguin, 2012).

Ngai, Sianne, *Ugly Feelings* (Cambridge, MA: Harvard University Press, 2007).

Norris, Margot, *Beasts of the Modern Imagination: Darwin, Nietzsche, Kafka, Ernst, and Lawrence* (Baltimore: Johns Hopkins University Press, 1985).

Norris, Margot, 'Darwin, Nietzsche, Kafka and the Problem of Mimesis', *MLN*, 95.5 (1980), 1232–53.

Nussbaum, Martha, 'Compassion: Human and Animal', in Marianne DeKoven and Michal Lundblad (eds), *Species Matters: Humane Advocacy and Cultural Theory* (New York: Columbia University Press, 2012), pp. 139–72.

Nussbaum, Martha, *Love's Knowledge: Essays on Philosophy* (Oxford: Oxford University Press, 1990).

Nussbaum, Martha, *Upheavals of Thought: The Intelligence of Emotions* (Cambridge: Cambridge University Press, 2001).

Oates, Matthew, *In Pursuit of Butterflies: A Fifty Year Affair* (London: Bloomsbury, 2015).

Olson, Gary, *Empathy Imperiled: Capitalism, Culture and the Brain* (New York: Springer, 2013).

Ortiz Robles, Mario, *Literature and Animal Studies* (London: Routledge, 2016).

Oxley, Julinna C., *The Moral Dimensions of Empathy: Limits and Applications in Ethical Theory and Practice* (New York: Palgrave Macmillan, 2011).

Packman, David, *Vladimir Nabokov: The Structure of Literary Desire* (Columbia: University of Missouri Press, 1982).

Parikka, Jussi, *Insect Media: An Archaeology of Animals and Technology* (Minneapolis: University of Minnesota Press, 2010).

Peterson, Laura, '"We Are Story Animals": Aesopics in Holocaust Literature by Art Spiegelman and Yann Martel', in Gert Reifarth and Philip Morrisey (eds), *Aesopic Voices: Re-framing Truth through Concealed Ways of Presentation in the 20th and 21st Centuries* (Newcastle-upon-Tyne: Cambridge Scholars, 2011), pp. 174–207.

Pick, Anat, *Creaturely Poetics: Animality and Vulnerability in Literature and Film* (New York: Columbia University Press, 2011).

Pifer, Ellen (ed.), *Vladimir Nabokov's Lolita: A Casebook* (Oxford: Oxford University Press, 2003).

Plato, *The Republic*, trans. Melissa Lane (London: Penguin, 2007).

Plumwood, Val, *Feminism and the Mastery of Nature* (London: Routledge, 1993).

Prinz, Jesse J., 'Is Empathy Necessary for Morality?', in Amy Coplan and Peter Goldie (eds), *Empathy: Philosophical and Psychological Perspectives* (Oxford: Oxford University Press, 2011), pp. 211–29.

Punter, David, 'Gothic and Neo-Gothic in Fowles's *The Collector*', in James

Acheson (ed.), *John Fowles* (Basingstoke: Palgrave Macmillan, 2013), pp. 62–75.

Raffles, Hugo, *Insectopedia* (New York: Pantheon Books, 2010).

Rampton, David, *Vladimir Nabokov: A Critical Study of the Novels* (Cambridge: Cambridge University Press, 1984).

Rawles, Kate, 'Love a Duck! Emotions, Animals and Environmental Ethics', in H. Li and A. Yeung (eds), *New Essays in Applied Ethics: Animal Rights, Personhood and the Ethics of Killing* (Basingstoke: Palgrave Macmillan, 2007), pp. 91–103.

Regan, Tom, *The Case for Animal Rights* (Berkeley: University of California Press, 1983).

Regan, Tom, *Defending Animal Rights* (Urbana: University of Illinois Press, 2001).

Roach, Catherine, 'Loving Your Mother: On the Woman–Nature Relation', *Hypatia*, 6.1 (1991), 46–59.

Rothberg, Michael, *Traumatic Realism* (Minneapolis: University of Minnesota Press, 2000).

Roughley, Neil, and Thomas Schramme, 'Forms of Fellow Feeling: Empathy, Sympathy, Concern and Moral Agency', in Neil Roughley and Thomas Schramme (eds), *Forms of Fellow Feeling: Empathy, Sympathy, Concern and Moral Agency* (Cambridge: Cambridge University Press, 2018), pp. 3–55.

Rozin, Paul, Jonathan Haidt and Clark R. McCauley, 'Disgust', in M. Lewis, J. M. Haviland-Jones and L. F. Barrett (eds), *Handbook of Emotions* (New York: Guildford Press, 2008), pp. 757–76.

Ryan, Derek, *Animal Theory: A Critical Introduction* (Edinburgh: Edinburgh University Press, 2015).

Sax, Boria, *Animals in the Third Reich: Pets, Scapegoats, and the Holocaust* (London: Continuum, 2000).

Scarry, Elaine, *The Body in Pain: The Making and Unmaking of the World* (Oxford: Oxford University Press, 1985).

Schmitt, Carl, *Political Theology: Four New Chapters on the Concept of Sovereignty*, trans. Paul Kahn (New York: Columbia University Press, 2011).

Schneider, Joseph, *Donna Haraway: Live Theory* (London: Continuum, 2005).

Schweid, Richard, *The Cockroach Papers: A Compendium of History and Lore* (Chicago: University of Chicago Press, 1999).

Seshadri, Kalpana Rahita, *HumAnimal: Race, Law, Language* (Minneapolis: University of Minnesota Press, 2012).

Shaviro, Steven, 'Object Oriented Aesthetics?', 8 November 2009, http://www.shaviro.com/Blog/?p=810 (accessed 18 February 2019).

Shaviro, Steven, 'Two Lessons from Burroughs', in Judith Halberstam and Ira Livingston (eds), *Posthuman Bodies* (Bloomington: Indiana University Press, 1995), pp. 38–54.

Shaviro, Steven, *The Universe of Things: On Speculative Realism* (Minneapolis: University of Minnesota Press, 2014).

Shotwell, Alexis, *Against Purity: Living Ethically in Compromised Times* (Minneapolis: University of Minnesota Press, 2016).

Shute, Jenefer, '"So Nakedly Dressed": The Text of the Female Body in Nabokov's Novels', in Elen Pifer (ed.), *Vladimir Nabokov's Lolita: A Casebook* (Oxford: Oxford University Press, 2003), pp. 111–20.

Sjöberg, Fredik, *The Art of Flight*, trans. Peter Graves (London: Penguin, 2010).

Sjöberg, Fredrik, *The Fly Trap*, trans. Thomas Teal (London: Penguin, 2015).

Skrimshire, Stefan, 'Anthropocene Fever: Memory and the Planetary Archive', in Celia Deane-Drummond (ed.), *Religion in the Anthropocene* (Eugene, OR: Cascade, 2017), pp. 138–54.

Sleigh, Charlotte, 'Inside Out: The Unsettling Nature of Insects', in Eric C. Brown (ed.), *Insect Poetics* (Minneapolis: University of Minnesota Press, 2006), pp. 281–97.

Slote, Michael, 'Empathy as Instinct', in Neil Roughley and Thomas Schramme (eds), *Forms of Fellow Feeling: Empathy, Sympathy, Concern and Moral Agency* (Cambridge: Cambridge University Press, 2018), pp. 133–41.

Slote, Michael, *The Ethics of Care and Empathy* (London: Routledge, 2007).

Smith, Adam, *The Theory of Moral Sentiments* (1759), http://www.earlymod-erntexts.com/assets/pdfs/smith1759.pdf (accessed 18 February 2019).

Smith, Jos, *The New Nature Writing: Rethinking the Literature of Place* (London: Bloomsbury, 2017).

Solnit, Rebecca, 'Men Explain Lolita to Me', *Literary Hub*, 17 December 2015, https://lithub.com/men-explain-lolita-to-me/ (accessed 18 February 2019).

Stegner, Page, *Escape into Aesthetics: The Art of Vladimir Nabokov* (London: Eyre and Spottiswoode, 1967).

Stengers, Isabelle, *In Catastrophic Times: Revisiting the Coming Barbarism*, trans. Andrew Goffey (London: Open Humanities Press, 2015).

Stewart, Frank, *A Natural History of Nature Writing* (Washington, DC: Shearwater, 1995).

Stratton, Florence, '"Hollow at the Core": Deconstructing Yann Martel's *Life of Pi*', *Studies in Canadian Literature*, 19.2 (2004), 5–21.

Talairach-Vielmas, Laurence, and Marie Bouchet, 'Introduction', in Laurence Talairach-Vielmas and Marie Bouchet (eds), *Insects in Literature and the Arts* (Brussels: P.I.E. Peter Lang, 2014), pp. 13–20.

Tambling, Jeremy, *Allegory* (London: Routledge, 2010).

Terada, Rei, *Feeling in Theory: Emotion after the 'Death of the Subject'* (Cambridge, MA: Harvard University Press, 2001).

Tew, Philip, *Jim Crace* (Manchester: Manchester University Press, 2016).

Townsend, Chris, *Art and Death* (London: I.B. Tauris, 2008).

Tronto, Joan C., *Moral Boundaries: A Political Argument for an Ethic of Care* (London: Routledge, 1993).

Tsing, Anna Lowenhaupt, *The Mushroom at the End of the World: On the Possibility of Life in Capitalist Ruins* (Princeton: Princeton University Press, 2015).

Turner, Lynn, 'The Animal Question in Deconstruction', in Lynn Turner (ed.), *The Animal Question in Deconstruction* (Edinburgh: Edinburgh University Press, 2013), pp. 1–8.

Tyler, Tom, 'If Horses had Hands...', in Tom Tyler and Manuela Rossini (eds), *Animal Encounters* (Leiden: Brill, 2009), pp. 11–26.

Uexküll, Jakob von, *A Foray into the Worlds of Animals and Humans*, trans. Joseph D. O'Neil (Minneapolis: University of Minnesota Press, 2010 [1934]).

Van Dooren, Thom, Ursula Munster, Eben Kirksey, Deborah Bird Rose, Matthew Chrulew and Anna Tsing, 'Multispecies Studies: Cultivating Arts of Attentiveness', *Environmental Humanities*, 8.1 (2016), 1–23.

Vermeulen, Pieter, *Contemporary Literature and the End of the Novel: Creature, Affect, Form* (Basingstoke: Palgrave Macmillan, 2015).

Waldbauer, Gilbert, *How Not To Be Eaten: The Insects Fight Back* (Berkeley: University of California Press, 2012).

Waller, Sara, 'Science of the Monkey Mind: Primate Penchants and Human Pursuits', in Julie A. Smith and Robert W. Mitchell (eds), *Experiencing Animal Minds: An Anthology of Animal–Human Encounters* (New York: Columbia University Press, 2012), pp. 78–94.

Weik von Mossner, Alexa, *Affective Ecologies: Empathy, Emotion, and Environmental Narrative* (Columbus: Ohio State University Press, 2017).

Weil, Kari, 'Empathy', in Ron Broglio, Undine Sellbach and Lynn Turner (eds), *The Edinburgh Companion to Animal Studies* (Edinburgh: Edinburgh University Press, 2018), pp. 126–39.

Weil, Simone, 'Human Responsibility', in Siân Miles (ed.), *Simone Weil: An Anthology* (London: Penguin, 2005), pp. 69–98.

Westling, Louise, *The Green Breast of the New World: Landscape, Gender and American Fiction* (Athens, GA: University of Georgia Press, 1996).

Wiesel, Elie, 'Art and Culture after the Holocaust', in Eva Fleishner (ed.), *Auschwitz: Beginning of a New Era? Reflections on the Holocaust* (New York: KTAV Publishing, 1977), pp. 403–15.

Willett, Cynthia, *Interspecies Ethics* (New York: Columbia University Press, 2014).

Wolfe, Cary, *Animal Rites: American Culture, the Discourse of Species, and Posthumanist Theory* (Chicago: University of Chicago Press, 2003).

Wolfe, Cary, *Before the Law: Humans and Other Animals in a Biopolitical Frame* (Chicago: University of Chicago Press, 2013).

Wolfendale, Peter, *Object-Oriented Philosophy, the Noumenon's New Clothes* (Falmouth: Urbanomic, 2014).

Wood, James, 'Credulity', *London Review of Books*, 24.22 (14 November 2002), https://www.lrb.co.uk/v24/n22/james-wood/credulity (accessed 20 March 2019).

Woodcock, Bruce, *Male Mythologies: John Fowles and Masculinity* (Brighton: Harvester Press, 1984).

Yourcenar, Marguerite, 'Introduction', in Roger Caillois, *The Writing of*

Stones, trans. Barbara Bray (Charlottesville: University of Virginia Press, 1985), pp. xi–xix.

Zahavi, Dan, *Self and Other: Exploring Subjectivity, Empathy and Shame* (Oxford: Oxford University Press, 2014).

Zeglin Brand, Peggy, 'Disinterestedness and Political Art', in Carolyn Korsmeyer (ed.), *Aesthetics: The Big Questions* (Oxford: Blackwell, 1998), pp. 155–71.

Zupančič, Alenka, *Ethics of the Real: Kant and Lacan* (London: Verso, 2000).

Zylinska, Joanna, *Minimal Ethics for the Anthropocene* (London: Open Humanities Press, 2014).

Index

Aaltola, Elisa, 2, 11, 20, 82, 91n59,
    147
abjection, 145, 169–70, 171, 173
actants, 10, 100, 101, 103
Actor Network Theory (ANT), 10–11,
    99, 101, 103, 104
Adorno, Theodor, 46, 51–2, 56
aesthetic disinterestedness, 128, 142–3
aesthetics
    Crace, 97, 99, 112–13, 115, 117,
        118, 122
    Derrida and Kant, 161–3
    disgust, 168–74, 177n102
    empathy, 22
    ethics and, 84, 111, 141–2, 162, 164,
        167
    Hirst, 159, 161
    Martel, 42, 43, 56, 59
    Maus, 48
    Nabokov, 140, 141–7
    Sexual Selection, 163–4
    tool-being, 111–12, 117, 120–1, 122
    *We Are All Completely Beside
        Ourselves*, 87
affect, 4–8, 13, 14–15, 23, 36–7, 121
    aesthetics, 112
    anthropomorphism, 69, 74, 75–6,
        80, 81
    disgust, 170–1
    egomorphism, 84
    insects, 154–5, 167
    interruptive nature of, 99
    Lolita, 144–5, 147
    Martel, 40–1, 49, 54, 58
    Natural History series, 159, 160
    sympathy, 56
    *We Are All Completely Beside
        Ourselves*, 80, 81, 85
affective empathy, 2, 4, 15, 54, 130,
    147

Agamben, Giorgio, 15, 37–8, 39, 42
agency, 3, 10–11, 17, 99–100, 101, 182
    Fowles, 130
    nonhuman, 69, 72, 87, 96, 97–8,
        119, 163: Crace, 101, 102, 108,
        115; Martel, 39, 51, 53; natural
        history, 130, 135, 136; objects,
        104, 108, 115
Ahmed, Sara, 6, 169, 170–1
Alaimo, Stacy, 11, 15, 40–1
alienation, human: insects, 156
allegory
    Beatrice and Virgil, 45, 49, 52–4, 55,
        56, 58, 59
    Life of Pi, 42–3, 58, 59
    Nabokov, 141
    *We Are All Completely Beside
        Ourselves*, 77
allure, 111–12, 115, 117, 120, 121,
    122
Aloi, Giovanni, 155, 159, 160–1
alterity, 57, 69, 89
anima, 131
animality, 81, 87, 159, 162
    human, 42, 43, 49, 170, 171, 173
    writing, 59, 76, 77, 88
'animot', 36–7
Anthropocene, the, 66–8, 69–70, 108,
    109, 119, 166–7, 181, 182
    apocalypticism, 24, 67, 135, 164–5,
        180; *see also* anthropogenic
        destruction
    insects, 157, 160
anthropocentrism, 164–5
    anthropomorphism and, 20, 69,
        75–6, 83
    Crace, 99, 106, 113, 121
    human suffering and, 18
    humanism, 57
    insects and, 157

anthropocentrism (*cont.*)
    Life of Pi, 38–9, 42
    The Lives of Animals, 84
    move away from, 21, 72–3, 119,
        121, 165, 182: Derrida, 15, 59
    primatology, 70–1
    speciesism and, 49–50
    tool-being, 105
    *We Are All Completely Beside
        Ourselves*, 77, 83
    see also exceptionalism, human;
        Man, figure of
anthropodenial, 74–5
anthropogenic destruction, 66, 67,
        69–70, 96–7, 120, 165, 180, 181
    Latour, 10–11, 120
    Mother Earth, 134
    natural history and, 127
    see also Anthropocene, the:
        apocalypticism
anthropomorphism, 9, 36, 71, 73–6,
        77, 81–9, 96
    empathy and, 20, 68–9, 74, 80–1, 83,
        88, 173
    Life of Pi, 39, 41, 57
    Quarantine, 116
    Signals of Distress, 112
    *We Are All Completely Beside
        Ourselves*, 80–3, 89
'anthropos', 34n180, 83, 86–7, 88
anthropo-theological, the, 57–8, 165,
        182
antiracism, speciesism and, 49–50
apocalypticism, 24, 67, 135, 164–5,
        180
Armstrong, Philip, 38, 39, 43
art, 87, 161–3, 164, 167, 168, 169,
        171–2; *see also* aesthetics

'bare life', 37–8, 39, 58
Barkham, Patrick, 129, 135
Beatrice and Virgil (Martel), 35, 37,
        44–7, 49, 50–7, 58–9
beauty, 162, 168
    birds, 163
    butterflies, 131, 135, 136, 137–8,
        139, 154, 155, 161
    The Collector, 131
    The Gift of Stones, 108
    insects, 137
    Life of Pi, 40
    Lolita, 147
    Quarantine, 117
Beckett, Samuel, 46–7

being and thinking, separation of, 98
Bekoff, Marc, 74
Bellacasa, Maria Puig de la, 12–13
Benjamin, Walter, 126, 131
Bennett, Jane, 11, 13, 99, 101, 103–4,
        106, 111
Berger, John, 36
biopolitics, 6, 15, 39, 42, 58, 70, 156
Birds, The (Hitchcock), 166
Bloom, Paul, 19
Bourdieu, Pierre, 170, 177n102
Braidotti, Rosi, 6–7, 17, 172, 181,
        182
Brinkema, Eugenie, 6, 7–8, 13, 18, 23,
        121, 169, 172–3
Broglio, Ron, 159
Butler, Judith, 16–17, 18, 182
butterflies, 126, 129–42, 157, 160–1

Caillois, Roger, 96
Calarco, Matthew, 88, 89
Canetti, Elias, 155
capitalism
    alienation, 108
    anthropogenic destruction, 67
care, ethics of, 12–14, 44
'carno-phallogocentrism', 40, 45, 173,
        183
Cartesianism, 9, 14, 15, 39, 66, 71, 74
causality, 74–5, 112, 169
Chakrabarty, Dipesh, 109, 119
classification of life-forms, 70; *see also*
        taxonomies; taxonomy
Coates, Steve, 139–41, 146
Cockroach (Hage), 156
Coetzee, J. M., 21, 84, 87, 88
cognition, 14, 18, 82, 154, 155, 157
    anthropomorphism, 23, 75–6
    Derrida, 36
    empathy and, 1, 2, 35
    Harman, 110, 121
    Signals of Distress, 97
    *We Are All Completely Beside
        Ourselves*, 78, 89
cognitive empathy, 2, 4, 20, 54, 130
Cohen, Jeffrey Jerome, 108, 182–3
Cohen, Tom, 66, 67
Colebrook, Claire, 14, 22, 23, 66,
        67–8, 80, 135, 166–7
collecting, entomological, 126–42
Collector, The (Fowles), 129–33, 136
commodification: *We Are All
        Completely Beside Ourselves*, 80
compassion, 15, 19, 54, 75

conceptualisation: the Holocaust, 46
contamination from below, 162–3
Coplan, Amy, 1–2, 12, 130
correlationism, 98, 124n70
Coupland, Douglas, 133–4
Crace, Jim, 97–8, 99, 101–3, 106,
    107–9, 112–19, 120, 121–2
Crist, Eileen, 66–7, 74, 92n61
cyborg, 11, 71–2

Darwin, Charles, 139, 163–4
Davis, Karen, 49
De Boever, Arne, 37, 38, 42, 43
de Waal, Frans, 1, 9, 74, 75, 164
deconstruction, 22, 158, 161, 165, 167,
    182
  rejection of, 5, 6–7
deconstructive storytelling, 37
Dee, Tim, 138
Deleuze, Gilles, 5, 7–8
Derrida, Jacques, 10, 22–3, 25, 97
  alterity, 57, 59
  animality of writing, 76–7
  autobiography, 36, 60n13
  'carno-phallogocentrism', 40, 45,
    173, 183
  compassion, 54
  deconstruction, 167
  Deleuze supersedes, 7
  disgust, 168, 174, 177n102
  'divinanimality', 57–8
  framing in art, 161–3
  human subjectivity, 39–40
  'Man', 67–8, 87, 89
  sentience, 14–15
  singularity, 63–4n91
  supplementarity, 87
  violence, 183
  'zootobiography', 36–7, 40
Descartes, Rene, 39; *see also*
    Cartesianism
desire, 5, 131, 133, 138, 165, 182
  disgust and, 167, 171–2, 173
  nonhuman, 10, 58, 59, 138, 147,
    166, 173
Diamond, Cora, 9, 16, 38, 81
difference, cross-species: *We Are All
    Completely Beside Ourselves*, 74,
    79–80, 81–2, 86
disgust, 182–3
  insects, 154–5, 160, 167–74
dissent, disgust and, 170–1
dualism: human subjectivity/passive
    nature, 128

ecofeminism, 119, 133–9
Edelman, Lee, 165–6, 167, 170
'egomorphism', 83–4
Einfühlung, 1, 35
Eisenberg, Nancy, 2, 56
Ekel, 168, 172–3
embodiment, 15–16, 71–2
  animal rights, 9
  Beatrice and Virgil, 54
  Life of Pi, 38, 43
  literature, 23
  The Lives of Animals, 84
  Lolita, 145
  The Passion According to G.H.,
    172
emotional contagion, 2, 3, 18–19, 80
empathy, 1–23, 56, 59, 180–1
  anthropomorphism and, 68–9, 74,
    80–1, 83, 88
  The Collector, 130, 131, 132–3
  disgust and, 173, 183
  ethics and, 84, 181
  evil as failure of, 84
  insects, 20, 156, 157, 160, 172
  Life of Pi, 38, 41
  Lolita, 143, 144–5, 146, 147
  moral value of, 2, 3, 4, 19–21
  Natural History series, 159–60
  rationality and, 44, 85
  reflexive, 54
  storytelling and, 21–2, 35–6
  *We Are All Completely Beside
    Ourselves*, 77, 79, 80–1, 82, 83–4
Endgame (Beckett), 46
'Ends of Man, The' (Derrida), 67–8
entangled empathy, 12, 20, 160
entanglement, 12, 40–1
entomology, 126–42, 146, 156, 157,
    158–61
environmental ethics, 15, 17–18, 74
equipment, 104–5
eschato-teleology, 67, 68
ethics
  aesthetics and, 84, 111, 141–2, 162,
    164, 167
  empathy and, 84, 181
  environmental, 15, 17–18, 74
  exemption of insects, 20, 155, 157
  Life of Pi, 44, 45, 56, 58–9
  Lolita, 141–2
  Natural History series, 159–60
  ontology and, 12–14, 15, 16, 17–18,
    20–1
ethology: anthropomorphism, 74–6

exceptionalism, human, 15, 18, 21, 70, 74, 171
  abjection, 171
  art, 163, 164
  Crace, 121–2
  Derrida on, 57, 59, 162–3
  The Gift of Stones, 107
  language, 106–7
  Latour on, 100–1
  storytelling, 21, 107
  We Are All Completely Beside Ourselves, 86
  We Have Never Been Modern, 101
  see also anthropocentrism; Man, figure of
exposure: vulnerability, 16, 17

'Facts behind the Helsinki Roccamatios, The' (Martel), 35
females: *We Are All Completely Beside Ourselves*, 81, 85–6
fiction see storytelling
figure of Man see Man, figure of
Flaubert, Gustave, 51, 53
Flight Behaviour (Kingsolver), 157
Foucault, Michel, 126–7, 128, 139, 161
Fowler, Karen Joy, 68–9, 77–83, 84–7, 88, 89, 93n84, 146
Fowles, John, 129–33, 136
futurity, 165–6, 173

Gaard, Greta, 133
Gaia, 133, 134
gender concerns: entomology, 127–9; see also women: insects and, objectification of
Generation A (Coupland), 133–4
Gift of Stones, The (Crace), 106, 107–9, 112, 113, 114–15
God, 58, 67, 116–18
Gregg, Melissa, 5
Grosz, Elizabeth, 87, 163, 164, 165
Gruen, Lori, 3, 12, 20, 71, 132, 156
Guerrilla Metaphysics (Harman), 120

Hage, Rawi, 156
Haraway, Donna, 158
  bounded individualism, 9
  Crace and, 115
  cross-species kinship, 13, 18, 154–5
  the cyborg, 11, 71–2
  entanglement and ethics, 40–1
  Fowler and, 80, 82, 83, 87
  Martel and, 23, 43, 52

ontology, 11
primatology, 68, 69–70, 70–1, 76
prosthesis, 11, 71–2
storytelling, 21, 22, 55, 68, 72–3, 76, 87
suffering, equivalence of human and nonhuman, 48–9
Harman, Graham, 14, 96, 98–9, 100, 115–16, 120–1
  Crace and, 103–6, 109–12, 117, 118, 121–2
Harvest (Crace), 113–15
Heidegger, Martin, 21, 55, 68, 104–6
Herman, David, 22
heterosexuality, futurity and, 165–6
Hird, Myra J., 15, 22
Hirst, Damien, 158–61, 173
Hitchcock, Alfred, 166
Hodder, Ian, 110–11
Holocaust, the
  Beatrice and Virgil, 44–7, 49, 50, 52–3, 56
  magical realism, 63n81
  Maus, 47–8, 49
  meaningful response, 45–6, 63n82
homo sacer, 37–8
human, the, 18, 23, 101, 102, 121, 136
  Anthropocene, 66–7, 69, 119, 165–6, 181, 182
  anthropomorphism, 74, 75–6, 83, 89, 116
  art, 161, 162
  The Collector, 130, 131, 132
  Crace, 107, 108, 112, 114–15, 116
  The Lives of Animals, 84, 88
  Martel, 37, 38, 39–40, 45, 50, 57, 58, 59
  master-storyteller, 36, 37, 48, 57, 72, 85
  Maus, 48
  primatology, 70–1, 77, 78, 82
  Signals of Distress, 102, 112
  We Are All Completely Beside Ourselves, 78, 80, 83, 84–5, 86, 88, 89
  see also anthropocentrism; exceptionalism, human; Man, figure of
human exceptionalism see exceptionalism, human
humanism
  anthropocentrism and, 49–50, 57, 70–1, 182
  antiracism and speciesism, 49–50

Derrida, 67–8, 89, 162
  Life of Pi, 43
  sacrificial logic, 39–40, 173
  *We Are All Completely Beside
    Ourselves*, 77
humanity, fictitious universalism, 66–7;
  see also Man, figure of
Hume, David, 1
hybridity, 11, 71, 100–1, 119–20, 164,
  181

imagination, 54, 97, 156, 168, 170,
  180–1
  anthropomorphism, 73, 74, 75, 81–2
  sympathetic, 4, 21, 84–5, 88–9
imaginative perspective-taking, 2, 3,
  18–19, 35, 37, 59, 77, 131
immigrants as vermin, 156
individualism, bounded, 9, 10, 16, 17
inhuman, the, 23, 57, 59, 90n19, 166,
  167–8, 174, 182–3
  insects, 156, 167–8, 173
  Life of Pi, 42, 44, 59
insects, 126–41, 142, 145, 154–8,
  160–1, 163–4, 166, 171–3
  disgust at, 154–5, 160, 167–74
  empathy with, 20, 156, 157, 160,
    172
  exemption from ethics, 20, 155, 157
  Sexual Selection, 163, 167
  women and, objectification of,
    127–8, 129, 130–9
instrumentalisation, 40, 50, 79, 86, 87,
  158, 159
  Beatrice and Virgil, 50
  The Gift of Stones, 113
  Nabokov, 141
  *We Are All Completely Beside
    Ourselves*, 79, 86, 87, 88
interdependency, 10, 12–13, 16–17
intersubjectivity, 18, 19

John, Eileen, 144
Johnson, Kurt, 139, 140–1, 146
Josipovici, Gabriel, 141, 142, 143, 145
jouissance, 165–6

Kafka, Franz, 77, 78, 88, 156
Kakutani, Michiko, 44–5
Kant, Immanuel
  Bourdieu on, 170
  Derrida on, 161–3, 168–9
  disgust, 167, 168–9, 174
  Grosz and, 164

Harman and, 122, 124n70
Latour and, 101
noumena and phenomena, 98
taste, 168–9, 170, 174
things-in-themselves, 109–10
Kaufman, Linda, 142, 144, 145–6, 147
Keen, Suzanne, 2, 21–2, 35, 38, 55
Kim, Claire Jean, 49, 50
Kingsolver, Barbara, 157
kinship with insects, 154–5, 156, 172
Kristeva, Julia, 169, 170, 171, 173

Lacan, Jacques, 79, 165–6
Lane, Richard J., 106, 107, 109
language
  human exceptionalism and, 106–7
  natural history and, 139
  species as, 128, 137
  *We Are All Completely Beside
    Ourselves*, 76–7, 82, 85, 86, 88
Latour, Bruno, 10–11, 99–103, 104,
  108, 110, 119–20, 146–7
'Legend of St Julian the Hospitaller,
  The' (Flaubert), 51, 53
lepidoptery, 126, 129–42, 145, 160–1
Levinas, Emmanuel, 57, 111, 112
Life of Pi (Martel), 35, 37–44, 57, 58–9
linguistic turn, deconstruction and, 6–7
Lispector, Clarice, 167–8, 171–3
literature, 23, 35, 146, 181
  Beatrice and Virgil, 46–7
  Nabokov, 140
  *We Are All Completely Beside
    Ourselves*, 85, 88–9
  see also storytelling
Lives of Animals, The (Coetzee), 21,
  84, 87, 88
Lolita (Nabokov), 141–6, 147
Loo, Stephen, 20–1, 156, 157, 160

Mabey, Richard, 154
McCarthy, Michael, 135–6, 137–8
McHugh, Susan, 75
magical realism, 63n81
  Life of Pi, 42, 43
Malm, Andreas, 181–2
Man, figure of, 24, 34n180, 67–9,
  71–2, 133, 165
  alternatives to, 15, 25, 69, 87–8, 182
  The Lives of Animals, 84
  *We Are All Completely Beside
    Ourselves*, 78, 80, 85, 88, 89
  see also anthropocentrism;
    exceptionalism, human

Marren, Peter, 134–5, 136, 146
Martel, Yann, 35, 37–59, 146
mastery: natural history and
    storytelling, 146–7
materialism, vital, 11, 106
materialisms, new, 6, 7, 10, 15, 166,
    180, 181–2
  Object-Oriented Philosophy and,
    103, 104, 122
materiality
  affect theory, 5, 7
  art, 164
  creaturely ethics, 21, 41
  Life of Pi, 41
  Lolita, 146
  new materialisms and
    posthumanisms, 6–7
  Object-Oriented Philosophy, 103,
    110
  The Passion According to G.H.,
    172
  Signals of Distress, 97–8, 101
  *We Are All Completely Beside
    Ourselves*, 80
Matravers, Derek, 146
Maus (Spiegelman), 45, 47–8, 49, 141
Menninghaus, Winifred, 168, 174,
    177n102
Mensch, James, 15–16, 42, 43, 57, 85
Merchant, Carolyn, 133, 134
'Metamorphosis' (Kafka), 156
metaphor, 48
  allure and, 120
  animal as, 36, 50
  Beatrice and Virgil, 50, 52
  Lolita, 141
  Maus, 47–8, 49, 141
  nature as, 128
  perception, 97
Miller, Andrew, 73, 170, 173
Milton, Kay, 83
mirror imagery: *We Are All Completely
    Beside Ourselves*, 79–80, 81
mirror neurons, 2–3
modernity, 10–11, 38, 43–4, 57, 100–2,
    119–20, 155–6
moral value of empathy, 2, 3, 4, 19–21
Morton, Timothy, 69, 96, 119
Mother Earth, 133–4
Mother Nature, 133, 136
multispecies studies, 17–18
Mulvey, Laura, 131–2, 138
*Mushroom at the End of the World,
    The* (Tsing), 119

Nabokov, Vladimir, 128, 139, 140–7
narrative *see* storytelling
natural history, 119, 126–7, 139,
    146–7, 158–60, 161
Natural History series (Hirst), 158–61,
    173
Natural Selection, 163, 164, 167
nature, continuity of, 126–7
negative dialectics, 46
New Nature Writing, The, 134
Ngai, Sianne, 167, 169, 171–3
Nietzsche, Friedrich, 115–16
noumena/phenomena split, 98, 110
Nussbaum, Martha, 75, 171

Oates, Matthew, 136, 137
Object-Oriented Philosophy (OOP), 99,
    103–6, 109–16, 117, 121, 124n70
objectification, 10–11, 104, 113
objects
  Heidegger's theory of, 104–6
  Kant's theory of, 109–10
'On Discovering a Butterfly'
    (Nabokov), 140, 146
ontological, the, the aesthetic and,
    120–1, 122
ontology, 98, 101, 162
  affect, 5, 6
  Crace, 106, 107, 109, 118–19, 121,
    122
  ethics and, 12–14, 15, 16, 17–18,
    20–1
  modernity, 100
  Object-Oriented Philosophy, 99, 103,
    105, 110, 112, 120–1, 122
  radical alterity, 89
  vital materialism, 11
other-oriented perspective-taking, 2,
    130, 131
othering
  abjection, 170
  insects, 158, 160, 161, 173
otherness, 18–19, 59, 132, 154, 166,
    173
'Ozymandias' (Shelley), 88

pain: shared experience, 40, 54–5
panpsychism, 121
Passion According to G.H., The
    (Lispector), 167–8, 171–3
pastoralism, 134, 136
patriarchy
  The Collector, 130–2
  ecofeminism, 133–9

Generation A, 133–4
We Are All Completely Beside Ourselves, 81, 85–6
perception: nonhuman encounters, 69, 96, 97, 110, 118, 157, 159, 167
Peterson, Laura, 45, 47, 53, 58
phenomena/noumena split, 98, 110
Pick, Anat, 8, 16, 21, 23–4, 40, 41, 48, 49
post-anthropocentrism, 181, 182
posthumanism, 6–7, 10, 17, 89, 106, 166, 180, 181
poststructuralism, 7
prehension, 96, 110
Primate Visions (Haraway), 69, 71, 76–7
primatology, 69–73, 84–6, 93n84
We Are All Completely Beside Ourselves, 77–83
Prinz, Jesse, 19
progress, 46, 70, 108, 112, 119–20
prostheses, 11, 71, 72, 88, 102, 162
psychoanalysis, 5, 86, 167
Pure (Miller), 73
purism, rejection of, 41, 158–9

Quarantine (Crace), 113, 116–19
quasi-objects, 101, 102–3, 108, 120
queerness: Sexual Selection, 165

racialisation, animalisation and, 49–50
Raffles, Hugo, 126, 155, 166
Rampton, David, 142–3
rationality, 9, 14, 43–4, 91n59, 119, 133, 135, 162
reading, 7, 22, 35, 38, 181
realism: Holocaust writing, 47
Realism, Speculative, 98–9
reason *see* rationality
refugee, figure of the, 39
Regan, Tom, 8, 9, 84
relationality
    Actor Network Theory, 100, 101, 103
    cross-species storytelling, 22
    entangled empathy, 20
    The Gift of Stones, 109
    Object-Oriented Philosophy, 103, 106, 110
relations, objects and: Bennett and Harman, 103–4
'Report to an Academy, A' (Kafka), 77, 78, 88
'reworlding', 22, 24, 37, 55

rights, animal, 8–9, 12, 14, 20
romanticism: Nature, 119

sacrifice, 39–40, 45, 58
Scarry, Elaine, 54–5, 56
Schmitt, Carl, 37
Schweid, Richard, 127, 138–9, 155–6
Seigworth, Gregory J., 5
self, sense of: imaginative perspective-taking, 3
Sellbach, Undine, 20–1, 156, 157, 160
sensuality, 111, 112, 120, 135
sentience, 14–15, 16, 20, 36, 130, 135, 154, 157
Seshadri, Kalpana Rahita, 49–50
Sexual Selection, 163–4, 165, 167
shared vulnerability *see* vulnerability, shared
Shaviro, Steven, 98, 105, 110–11, 121, 155, 173
Shelley, Percy Bysshe, 88
Shotwell, Alexis, 11, 12, 41, 158–9
Shute, Jenefer, 143–4
Signals of Distress (Crace), 97–8, 101–3, 112–13, 120
Singer, Peter, 8
singularity, 19, 36, 40, 48, 63–4n91, 76, 111, 172
sinthomosexuality, 165–6, 170
'situated knowledges', 71
Sjöberg, Fredrik, 128–9, 136–7, 138
Skrimshire, Stefan, 165
Sleigh, Charlotte, 135, 156
Smith, Adam, 1
sovereignty, 11, 54, 57–8, 59, 101, 156
    Life of Pi, 37–8, 57
    We Are All Completely Beside Ourselves, 77, 89
speciesism, 8, 38–9, 40, 49–50, 107–8
specularity, 80, 83, 159
Speculative Realism, 98
Spiegelman, Art, 45, 47, 141
Spinoza, Baruch, 7–8, 101
stewardship, 36, 41–2, 53, 58, 114, 127, 148n12, 165
stone, 21, 106, 108–9, 116
storytelling, 21–3, 35–7, 55, 69, 72–3, 75
    Beatrice and Virgil, 44, 50, 51–2, 53, 56–7, 58
    Crace, 99, 107, 114, 121
    Life of Pi, 37, 39, 41–2, 43, 53, 58
    Maus, 48
    natural history, 137, 146–7

storytelling (*cont.*)
  nonhuman life, 96–7
  science and, 82
  *We Are All Completely Beside
    Ourselves*, 85, 86, 88, 89
  see also literature
Stratton, Florence, 38, 42, 43
subject/object division, 10, 71, 99, 110,
  116, 169
sublime, Kantian, 168–9
suffering
  Beatrice and Virgil, 49, 50, 52–6,
    58–9
  human and animal, 47–9, 141
  Life of Pi, 41–2, 58–9
  Maus, 48, 49, 141
supplementarity, 87
sympathy, 21, 55–6, 58, 84–5, 88–9
  distinction between empathy and,
    3–4, 56

taste: Kant's formulation, 168, 170
taxonomies, 49, 127
taxonomy, 128, 139–40, 145
technology, 102, 112, 181
  affect theory, 6
  see also cyborg; prostheses
teleology, 70, 121, 128, 159, 164–5,
  166, 167; *see also* eschato-
  teleology
Terada, Rei, 7
Tew, Philip, 102, 103, 106, 108, 112
text, 22–3
'theo-zoomorphism', 58
theory, 7; *see also specific theories*
thinking and being, separation of, 98
time, geological: Anthropocene theory,
  165
Tomkins, Silvan, 5
tool-being, 104–6, 109, 110, 111, 118
torture, 54, 58
Townsend, Chris, 158, 160
tropes, 141, 181
  Lolita, 141, 143
  natural history, 128, 135, 136
  nonhuman animals as, 35–6, 48, 55,
    97: *Maus*, 48, 55, 141; natural
    history, 128, 136, 139; *We Are All
    Completely Beside Ourselves*, 77,
    87
Tsing, Anna Lowenhaupt, 96–7, 98,
  108, 119–20
Tyler, Tom, 73, 75, 76, 82, 89, 96

Vermeulen, Pieter, 5, 6, 7, 8, 23
violence, 48, 183
  Crace, 107–8, 114
  escape from, 59
  gender, 85–6, 134
  insects, 137, 139–40, 155, 160–1,
    172–3
  Martel, 42, 49, 54, 57, 58
  Maus, 48
  Natural History series, 158, 159,
    160–1
  The Passion According to G.H.,
    172–3
  primatology, 71
  *We Are All Completely Beside
    Ourselves*, 85–6
  see also vulnerability, shared
vital materialism, 11, 106
vomit: the sublime, 168–9
vulnerability, shared, 15–17, 37,
  173
  Beatrice and Virgil, 54
  Life of Pi, 21, 38, 40–1
  Terra Amata, 156
  *We Are All Completely Beside
    Ourselves*, 88

Ways of Seeing (Berger), 131
*We Are All Completely Beside
  Ourselves* (Fowler), 68–9, 77–83,
  84–7, 88, 89, 93n84
Weil, Kari, 20
Weil, Simone, 8–9, 16
When Species Meet (Haraway), 70–1
Whitehead, A. N, 96, 110, 121
Wiesel, Elie, 45–6
Willett, Cynthia, 79
witnessing
  Beatrice and Virgil, 56–7
  *We Are All Completely Beside
    Ourselves*, 78–9, 86
Wolfendale, Peter, 106, 124n70
woman, nature as, 133–4
women
  insects and, objectification of, 127–8,
    129, 130–9
  objectification of: Nabokov, 141–7
Woodcock, Bruce, 130–2

Yourcenar, Marguerite, 96

Žižek, Slavoj, 7, 169
'zootobiography', 36, 40